records
manage

records
management

a
guide
to
corporate
record
keeping

2nd edition

jay kennedy
cherryl schauder

LONGMAN

An imprint of
Addison Wesley Longman

Addison Wesley Longman Australia Pty Limited
95 Coventry Street
South Melbourne 3205 Australia

Offices in Sydney, Brisbane and Perth, and associated companies throughout the world.

Copyright © 1998 Addison Wesley Longman Australia Pty Limited
First published 1994
Reprinted 1995 (twice), 1996
Second edition 1998

Edited by Paul Watt
Designed by Melissa Fraser
Index by Michael J. Ramsden
Set in New Baskerville 10.5/12 pt
Printed in Malaysia through Longman Malaysia, PA

National Library of Australia
Cataloguing-in-Publication data
  Kennedy, Jay (Jay Roblyn).
  Records Management : a guide to corporate recordkeeping.

  2nd ed.
  Includes index.
  ISBN 0 582 81007 8.

  1. Records – Management. 2. Records – Management – Case studies.
  3. Records – Management – Problems, exercises, etc. 4. Records – Management –
  Standards – Australia. 5. Business records – Management. 6. Information storage
  and retrieval systems – Business. I. Schauder, Cherryl. II. Title.

  651.5

Contents

List of figures   xi
Introduction to the first edition   xiii
Introduction to the second edition   xv
Acknowledgements   xvii

chapter **one** Records management—introduction and definitions   1

Overview   1
Changing perceptions of the records management function   2
A new theoretical framework   4
The Australian Records Management Standard AS 4390-1996   4
Records, documents and archives   5
    What is a record?   5
    What is a document?   7
    What are archives?   7
Records management and recordkeeping   8
    What is records management?   8
    What is recordkeeping?   9
The records life cycle model and the records continuum model   9
Records management as a field of study   12
Knowledge management and records management   13
The records management role   14
Records management personnel   15
A place for records management in the organisational structure   20
Outsourcing of records management services   23
Records management education   23
Exercise   24
Case study 1.1   24
Questions   25
Notes   25
Additional information   26
References   26

chapter **two** Assessing records management needs and
                 developing solutions   28

Overview   28
Records management program components   29
    Records management policy   29
    Records management systems and practices   29

Personnel and organisational structure   30
Budgeting and cost control   30
Facilities   30
Conducting a records management needs analysis   31
Steps in conducting a records management needs analysis   31
Exercise   39
Case study 2.1   39
Questions   44
Notes   44
Additional information   45
References   45

chapter *three* Corporate recordkeeping requirements in the
Australian environment   46

Overview   46
Recordkeeping to meet business operational needs   47
Records as evidence in the legal context   48
Statutory requirements for recordkeeping   48
Legislation affecting recordkeeping in Australia   48
Other external sources of recordkeeping requirements   55
Quality assurance standards   55
Recordkeeping professionals' standards   56
Professional and industry standards and codes of practice   56
Exercises   57
Case study 3.1   58
Questions   60
Notes   60
Additional information   60
References   61

chapter *four* Records appraisal and disposal—strategies and tools   63

Overview   63
Reviewing appraisal and disposal practices   65
Developing a business classification scheme   65
Suggested steps in classifying the business activities of an organisation
(or business unit)   66
Determining recordkeeping requirements   69
Records inventories   71
What is a records inventory?   71
Compiling a records inventory   71
Determining retention periods   77
Disposal schedules   79
Purposes of records disposal scheduling   81
Publishing the records disposal schedule   81
The role of archival agencies in authorising disposal   82
Exercise   86
Case study 4.1   86

Case study 4.2   87
Questions   89
Additional information   89
References   89

chapter *five* Creating and capturing full and accurate records   91

Overview   91
Implementing recordkeeping strategies in an age of transition   92
Characteristics of full and accurate records and strategies for
capturing them   93
    Records must be compliant   93
    Records must be adequate   98
    Records must be complete and meaningful   98
    Records must be comprehensive   107
    Records must be accurate   107
    Records must be authentic   107
    Records must be inviolate   108
Exercises   109
Case study 5.1   109
Questions   110
Notes   110
Additional information   110
References   111

chapter *six* Classification and indexing for retrieval   112

Overview   112
Classification   113
    Business classification   114
Series, files and documents   117
    Registration   117
Indexing   118
    File titling   119
    Metadata and electronic records   123
    Steps in the indexing process   123
Full text databases and networked information: indexing and
searching approaches   127
    The information technology environment   127
    Evaluating retrieval performance   128
    Indexing and searching technologies   129
    Searching approaches   130
Exercises   133
Case study 6.1   140
Case study 6.2   141
Questions   141
Notes   142
Additional information   142
References   143

chapter **seven** Constructing a thesaurus and classification scheme 145

Overview   145
The facet analysis approach   146
Using thesauri   147
Using classification schemes   147
Constructing a thesaurus   147
    Step 1 Understanding user and organisation needs   147
    Step 2 Defining the scope of the thesaurus   148
    Step 3 Collecting terms   148
    Step 4 Grouping terms into broad categories, subcategories and
        sub-subcategories   148
    Step 5 Producing the thesaurus   154
When to construct a knowledge-base classification for files/documents 158
Constructing a classification scheme   158
    Order within the classification scheme   158
    Features of coding systems   159
    Filing the assigned classification codes   160
Example of a classification scheme   160
Exercises   163
Notes   163
Questions   164
Additional information   164
References   164

chapter **eight** Managing active paper records 166

Overview   166
Centralised versus decentralised management of active records   167
Filing sequence   168
Procedures for creating and maintaining files   171
Filing equipment and supplies   174
    Equipment   175
    Supplies   183
Document and file tracking systems   184
    Manual systems   185
    Automated systems   186
    Barcoding   186
Exercises   189
Case study 8.1   190
Questions   192
Additional information   192
References   193

chapter **nine** Selecting and implementing automated records
        management systems 194

Overview   194
Records management and document management   195
Development of records management systems   196

Selecting a records management system   197
    Functional requirements of records management systems   200
    Technical requirements   206
    Reporting and statistics   207
    Help screens   207
    Support and training   207
    Costs   209
Implementing a records management system   209
    Planning   209
    User liaison   209
    Pilot phase   209
    Maintenance and support   210
    Training   210
    Manuals   210
    'System down' strategies   210
    Review   210
Exercises   211
Questions   211
Notes   212
Additional information   212
References   213

chapter *ten* Electronic document management: tools and technologies   214

Overview   214
Why electronic document management?   214
Imaging   216
    Digital imaging systems   217
    Imaging applications   222
    Microfilm imaging systems   225
COLD (Computer Output to Laser Disk)   226
Workflow systems   226
    Benefits of workflow   227
Groupware   228
Electronic document publishing   229
    Internet and intranets as document publishing systems   229
EDI (Electronic Data Interchange)   234
CALS (Continuous Acquisition and Lifecycle Support)   235
Exercises   237
Case study 10.1   237
Questions   238
Notes   238
Additional information   239
References   239

chapter *eleven* Developing a vital records protection plan   241

Overview   241
Identifying vital records   242

Methods of protection   244
    Duplication and dispersal within the organisation's offices   245
    Fireproof and secure storage cabinets or rooms within the organisation's offices 245
    Remote storage   246
Operating procedures   246
Exercises   248
Questions   249
Additional information   249
References   249

chapter **twelve** Storage of inactive records   251

Overview   251
Choosing a storage facility   253
    Major options   253
    Information to be gathered   253
    Commercial storage versus in-house storage   254
    Criteria for assessing commercial records storage services   254
    Estimating costs of operating an in-house facility   258
    Selection criteria for warehouse space   260
    In-house storage facilities: equipment and operating procedures   260
    Packing records and transferring them to storage   265
    Recording of box and file storage locations and movements   265
Secure destruction of records   265
Exercises   267
Case study 12.1   268
Questions   268
Additional information   269
References   269

Appendix A: Filing rules   271
Appendix B: Records Management Association of Australia (RMAA)   275
Appendix C: Records management and archives courses in Australia   277
Appendix D: Useful Internet sites and listservs for records management students 280
Appendix E: Forms management   284
Glossary   288
Index   304

List of figures

1.1	Elements of a comprehensive records management program	3
1.2	The records continuum model	11
1.3	Sample tasks and responsibilities of the records manager	16
1.4	Sample advertisements for Records Officer, Records Management Officer/Archivist and Records Manager	17
1.5	Sample job specifications for Records Manager and Records Officer	20
1.6	Typical local government structure showing records management located within the administration functional area	21
1.7	Organisational chart showing a records manager with both a direct and indirect staffing responsibility	22
2.1	Example of a preliminary report to management for a study focusing on an aspect of a records management program	34
2.2	Example of a simplified flowchart, in this case used to illustrate the processing of incoming mail	37
4.1	Examples of rough hierarchies produced from a functional analysis of the business of the City of XYZ	68
4.2	Illustration of a record series	70
4.3	Sample questionnaire for a records inventory	74
4.4	Sample analysis sheet for record series	75
4.5	Sample form for use with 'walk thru' method	76
4.6	Sample records retention authorisation form	78
4.7	Sample page from *Australian Records Retention Manual*	80
4.8	Sample page from the *General Disposal Schedule for Common Administrative Records* PROS 96/13	83
4.9	Sample page from *General Disposal Authority 20*, Australian Archives	84
4.10	Form for presentation of disposal recommendations	88
5.1	Sample document and data provisions in a quality manual	97
5.2	Sample topics for a document style handbook	100
5.3	Sample letter template	102
5.4	Sample job completion form	104
6.1	Examples of record series that might be managed in a firm of chartered accountants	116
6.2	Example of a file title	120
7.1	Examples of terms that might be randomly collected from files in a nutrition research organisation	149
7.2	Example of facet analysis for some nutrition terms	153
7.3	Thesaurus entries derived from facet relationships	155

7.4 Thesaurus entries for the category entitled NUTRIENTS 156
7.5 Example of an outline classification schedule on the subject of nutrition 162

8.1 Sample form for requesting that a new file be opened 172
8.2 Colour coding on files 174
8.3 Comparison of linear capacity of filing cabinets and static shelving in terms of floor space requirements 177
8.4 Filing the daily correspondence in an open shelving arrangement 178
8.5 Consulting colour coded lateral files in an open shelving arrangement 178
8.6 Consulting a file on a pull-out reference table 178
8.7 A cupboard set up for different types of record formats 179
8.8 A manually operated mobile shelving unit 180
8.9 Two sample configurations of twenty-four bays of shelving, comparing area and amount of filing space available, using static shelving and mobile shelving 181
8.10 Rotary unit with adjustable tiers to accommodate different types of records 182
8.11 Three different types of file clips 186
8.12 File movement marker—reduced from A4 size 187
8.13–8.15 Three examples of inefficient filing arrangements 191

9.1 Records management system requirements 199
9.2 Sample screens from the DOCS Open document management system 203
9.3 A sample screen from the TRIM records management system 205

10.1 Imaging system devices on a network 218
10.2 Combined microimager and scanner 223
10.3 Document imaging system—physical and process components 224
10.4 Chart showing the range of software categories from personal productivity to workflow software 229
10.5 A sample Web page—the home page for KPMG Australia 231
10.6 Transactions using EDI 235
10.7 Reasons an organisation might implement EDI 236

11.1 Examples of potentially vital records 243
11.2 Records classification 243
11.3 Vault for storage of computer media 245
11.4 Sample vital records inventory form 247

12.1 How inactive records should not be stored 252
12.2 Guidelines for the storage of permanent and long-term temporary value Commonwealth records 256
12.3 Example of racking on a large scale 261
12.4 Standard storage boxes 261
12.5 Storage box A versus box B 262
12.6 Storage boxes on long-span racking 263
12.7 Shelving layout showing fire protection features 263
12.8 Sample form for box transfer information and contents listing 266

Introduction to the first edition

This textbook sets records management in a business and government context, drawing its examples from the Australian organisational environment. It is specifically written to meet the needs of Australian students of records management in both business and information related courses at TAFE colleges and universities. It should also prove useful to practitioners and managers whose responsibilities cover the records management function.

Records management is a major and vital component of the broader field of information management, yet it is often overlooked or glossed over in textbooks in the field. With this in mind, the book should be of value to students, educators and practitioners in information management and related fields, such as business computing.

The book takes as its framework the scenario in which an organisation has appointed a records manager or records management consultant to set up a comprehensive records management program. It presents the steps involved in establishing such a program.

Because of the wide potential audience of the book, the content ranges from quite basic to more advanced treatment of records management theory and practices. Similarly, the exercises and case studies at the ends of the chapters vary in level of difficulty. Educators are encouraged to select from the text, exercises and case studies according to the needs of their students.

The book does not attempt to provide hard and fast rules to follow, or solutions for every situation. Rather, it focuses on developing the skills and knowledge that the records manager needs in order to be able to arrive at good records management practices. In this electronic age it is essential that the records manager does not 'stick by the book' too rigidly, but approaches his or her task in a manner that is flexible and forward-looking.

While the examples presented throughout the book may seem to focus on the medium to large organisation, the basic concepts presented and issues raised are relevant to all sizes of organisation. And this applies just as much to consideration of automated approaches to records management as to any of the other areas covered by the book—even the smallest of organisations should be looking to how they can utilise technology to improve control of their records and to simplify processes.

As the field of records management is developing and becoming more technologically oriented in its approach to managing information, so it is forming closer links with other fields under the information management umbrella, such as computer and communications technology, librarianship, and information science. This trend is evident in the sharing of expertise, ideas and information among the fields and also in the gradual blending of terminology. It is reflected in this book in the introduction of some terminology which is not traditional to records management but is useful in identifying concepts and practices of relevance to the field and its current direction.

The professions of records and archives management are closely related in that both are concerned with developing and maintaining systems for the proper control of records. However, while the records manager is concerned with managing active and inactive records for current operational and legal purposes, the archivist is concerned with identifying and preserving records for their continuing value. This book does not cover archival programs except in passing. There is an excellent Australian book on the topic: J. Ellis (ed.) 1993, *Keeping Archives*, 2nd edn, Thorpe in association with the Australian Society of Archivists, Sydney.

Jay Kennedy
Cherryl Schauder
October 1993

Introduction to the second edition

Since the first edition of this textbook was written, some significant trends in records management have gained momentum.

Firstly, there has been an increasing focus on the theory and practice of recordkeeping. Recordkeeping incorporates the identification and capture of records as evidence of business activity, rather than just the management of records that have already been created. Records management professionals are seen as having a major role in their organisations in identifying what records need to be captured to meet operational, legal, evidential, and quality system requirements, and in establishing necessary recordkeeping systems and practices. This changing focus has been spearheaded by the archives professionals who have a clear interest in promoting good recordkeeping practices, including those for electronic records. Their concern has arisen to a significant degree out of the rapidly growing trend to create, process, disseminate and store information electronically, and the lack of controls in electronic information systems to ensure adequate records of business activity are captured and preserved for present and future purposes. While this book is concerned with recordkeeping systems and standards to meet corporate needs, it readily acknowledges the benefits to be gained by records management and archives professionals working closely together to develop those recordkeeping systems and standards.

There has been important work done in recent years on redefining key concepts in the field, including *record, recordkeeping, records management,* and the relationship between these. These definitions, which encapsulate the responsibilities and tasks of records management within a more pro-active framework than existed in the past, are spelt out in a revised Chapter 1 but they also provide background for revisions throughout the book.

Secondly, the increasing impact on records management practices of professional and industry standards has generated a lot of attention. To assist their competitive position in the marketplace, a substantial number of businesses in Australia have sought accreditation to quality standards, namely the Australian versions of the International Organisation for Standardisation (ISO) Quality Management and Quality Assurance 9000 series. As those businesses have discovered, good documentation and document control as evidence of business practices are critical in achieving certification.

Perhaps the most important event influencing the format of this edition was the release by Standards Australia of Australian Standard AS 4390–1996: Records Management. This Standard presents guidance on records management principles and practice. It offers a conceptual framework which can assist the practitioner in selecting and implementing strategies. It includes strategies for documenting business activity; registration, indexing and classification; appraisal and disposal; storage and handling; distribution, use and accessibility. It does not attempt to cover the options for implementing those strategies in any depth; it covers the 'why' and 'what', not the 'how to'. This book, on the other hand, does take the practical approach and deals with the 'how to'. It aims to support and supplement the Standard.

Jay Kennedy
Cherryl Schauder
October 1997

Acknowledgements

The authors thank the following colleagues for their help in preparing this edition—Sue McKemmish, Barbara Reed, Don Schauder and Frank Upward from Monash University School of Information Management and Systems, and Robert Rob and Rachel U'Ren from KPMG. Barbara Reed deserves special acknowledgement for her assistance in the preparation of Chapter 9. Thanks also go to the information management departments of RMIT University and the University of New South Wales for their supportiveness.

The authors would like to express their gratitude to Standards Australia for agreeing to the reproduction throughout the book of relevant clauses from Australian Standard AS 4390–1996. This made the authors' goal of discussing records management within the framework of the Standard much easier to achieve.

chapter *one*

Records management: introduction and definitions

Overview

As business operations become more complex and the level of regulation in our society increases, so the complexity of recordkeeping requirements grows.

Records are both received and created by organisations in the course of business. They are retained as evidence of the policies and activities of the organisations and as sources of information for day-to-day management. Over half of the people employed in modern organisations are concerned in some way with the creation, use and maintenance of records.

Most organisations have a range of systems for controlling their records. In the past, developing and maintaining these systems was often seen as a low priority and was left to relatively junior staff with little systems expertise. However, in recent years, an increasing number of organisations are becoming aware of the importance of ensuring that not only are those records that are needed to support their business activities and their legal obligations created in the first place, but that they are also then managed efficiently. They are learning, sometimes from experience or the experience of others, that good records management practices are integral to good risk management.

This book takes as its framework the scenario in which an organisation has appointed a records manager or records management consultant to set up a comprehensive records management program. This approach provides a useful basis for studying the major elements of records management (see Figure 1.1). The chapters follow through the steps in setting up a program. Chapter 2 discusses the initial study that the records manager needs to undertake to establish what will be the best records management strategy for the particular organisation. Chapter 3 looks at the main factors which determine the records that organisations need to create and keep. With this essential background information, the rest of the book then looks at the types of systems and sub-programs that the organisation may implement to manage its records and recordkeeping successfully, and the tools it might use to assist in this process.

This introductory chapter is primarily concerned with defining basic records management concepts. The glossary of records management terms found at the end of the book can be referred to for definitions of further terms.

The definitions presented in this chapter are either taken direct from Australian Standard AS 4390–1996 or are in tune with the Standard's definitions. The Archives Authority of New South Wales Records Management Office (1994) has also issued a pamphlet of definitions of records and recordkeeping concepts and this has been drawn on heavily for the material in this chapter.

Changing perceptions of the records management function

The pace of change in recent years has affected records managers along with the rest of the workforce. Changes have included:

- Regulations demanding more scrupulous accounting by organisations.
- The proliferation of the PC/LAN (client–server) office environment, electronic mail, groupware, Internet and intranets, and the sharing of information across dispersed locations.
- A rapidly increasing emphasis in organisations on electronic information processing and storage. Paper records, while still prolific, are of decreasing importance compared with electronic records (Yorke 1995). The electronic record is the master copy of the record in many business applications. As noted in Chapter 3, Commonwealth evidence legislation now makes computer records admissible as evidence in court.
- An emphasis on business process re-engineering, multi-skilling and quality management for greater cost-effectiveness.
- The devolution of the records management function to the end user. Those who create records are also likely to both use and manage them (Barrett 1995).

It can be argued that there has also been a change in perception of the records management function. A number of factors have contributed to this:

- In general terms, the growing dependence of business on recorded information, and the explosion in the volume of that information, has forced a reassessment of the way it is managed and the commitment made to implementing the necessary systems and controls.
- As accountability becomes a more important issue in our society, so organisations are becoming more aware of the need to be able to produce the right records at the right time as evidence of their policies and activities. Specific legislation has also had an impact. As an example, the Freedom of Information legislation has had a substantial effect on records control in government agencies in Australia. When the legislation was introduced in the 1970s and 1980s, government organisations put a lot of effort into upgrading control of their records so they would feel reasonably confident they could meet their obligations under the legislation.

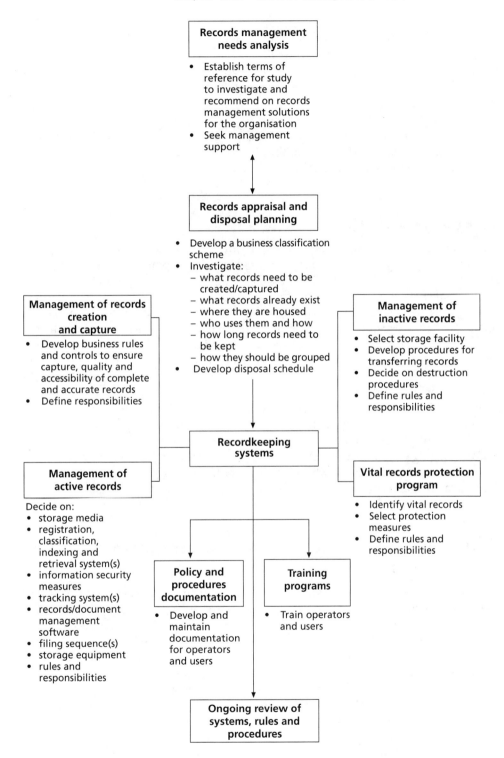

Figure 1.1   Elements of a comprehensive records management program

- The increasing trend in organisations to create, communicate and store information in electronic format put pressure on the records management and archives profession to rethink its future direction. Records managers and archivists realised that they were in danger of becoming irrelevant if they continued to concentrate so heavily on managing traditional paper-based records systems.
- The availability of technological tools to improve records control has already brought about a radical change to the way many records managers operate. The progressive records manager will continually monitor new technological developments and work with the information technology experts to further improve the control of recorded information.

A new theoretical framework

The changing environment, and particularly the issue of electronic records, spurred a number of Australians into contributing to the development of a new theoretical framework (see, for example, McKemmish (1995), and Archives Authority of New South Wales (1995)). This framework has arisen out of collaboration with, and the study of the writings of, many academics and practitioners in archives and records management overseas and locally. David Bearman of Archives and Museum Informatics in Pittsburgh has contributed much by stimulating discussion and ideas about the management of electronic records (see, for example, Bearman 1994).

This new theoretical framework incorporates a **records continuum** model of records management and archives administration which emphasises an integrated approach to managing records from the design of recordkeeping systems and the creation of records through to the preservation and use of records as archives. The disciplines of records management and archives administration are viewed as the **recordkeeping profession.** In other words, records managers and archivists are seen as recordkeeping specialists who work alongside each other in designing systems which ensure the capture of those records which have continuing value.

The Australian Records Management Standard AS 4390–1996

A major initiative of the records and archives industry in Australia (said to be a 'world first') is the development of *Australian Standard AS 4390–1996: Records Management* (Standards Australia 1996). This Standard, published in six parts (General, Responsibilities, Strategies, Control, Appraisal and Disposal, and Storage) is the result of more than two years' work by a Standards Australia technical committee (IT 21). This committee was made up of consultants and representatives from a wide range of organisations, including the professional records and archives bodies, professional bodies in related fields (e.g. the Chartered Institute of Company Secretaries in Australia), government authorities, educators, and the private sector. At the time of writing the Standard was being considered for development as an ISO (International Organisation for Standardisation) standard. Industry standards are codes which set out to define strategies and benchmarks which will encourage an organisation to achieve a high level of performance. They are reviewed and modified at intervals.

Adherence to a standard can be useful in obtaining certification under the quality assurance standards series AS/NZ ISO 9000.

The Australian Standard AS 4390–1996 incorporates the theoretical framework outlined above, and can be seen to accommodate workplace changes of the 1990s. It 'provides guidance for the implementation of records management strategies, procedures and practices …' and is 'used to measure the effectiveness of records management systems and programs' (pt. 1, p. 5). It spells out the responsibilities of organisations with respect to recordkeeping, pointing out that 'There are substantial benefits to be gained from the incorporation of records management into the strategic direction of any organisation' (pt. 1, p. 7). The Standard stresses that organisations which do not incorporate records management into their strategic directions are likely to experience accountability failures with respect to recordkeeping (pt. 1, p. 2).

An organisation may decide the extent to which it complies with every element in the Standard on the basis of its own business transactions and its assessment of risk management in relation to a given degree of compliance (pt. 4, p. 3). The authors of this text would argue further that every organisation has different sets of needs and circumstances which make it impossible to prescribe one clear and unambiguous approach with respect to records management. It must be remembered that a dynamic profession enjoys ongoing debate about concepts within its discipline, and hence definitions prepared through discussion and consensus at one point in time are subject to change in the future. However, the authors believe strongly that the current Standard provides a valuable conceptual framework or a conceptual tool kit which is indispensable to all those in an organisation who are concerned with sound records management practices.

Records, documents and archives

What is a record?

The definition of **record** in the Australian Standard AS 4390–1996 reads:

> … recorded information, in any form, including data in computer systems, created or received and maintained by an organisation or person in the transaction of business or the conduct of affairs and kept as evidence of such activity (Standards Australia 1996, pt. 1, p. 7, 4.21).

The important aspect of this definition is the reference to why records are created and why they are kept. They are created to support business activity and they are kept as evidence of that activity.

The Standard states that records should be compliant, adequate, complete, meaningful, comprehensive, accurate, authentic and inviolate (Standards Australia 1996, pt. 3, pp. 6–7, 5.3). These attributes of records are discussed in Chapter 5.

Records may be in any form. For example, they may be:

- Paper, microfilm or electronic
- Documents or files, maps, plans, drawings, photographs, etc.
- Data from business systems, word processed documents, spreadsheets, electronic mail messages, digital images
- Audio or video

- Handwritten documents
- Loosely structured records such as correspondence or highly structured records such as forms.

Records can be categorised in a number of different ways. Commonly recognised categories include:

- **Administrative records**—procedures documentation, forms and correspondence. Examples are staff manuals, rosters, logging of property maintenance jobs, travel bookings.
- **Accounting records**—reports, forms and related correspondence. Examples are invoices, bank account records, customer billing reports.
- **Project records**—correspondence, notes, product development documentation etc. related to a specific project.
- **Case files**—client records, personnel records, insurance, contracts and lawsuit files.

Records may be created or received by an organisation in any medium

Paper still represents the main medium for recorded information. However, there is no doubt that with the more widespread availability of computer and communications technology to office workers, and the decreasing cost of that technology, the amount of information stored in electronic format is increasing rapidly. It is also relevant to note that in Australia at the federal level and in some states the evidence legislation has been revised to give electronic records the same evidential weight as paper records.

What is a document?

The Australian Standard AS 4390–1996 defines **documents** as 'structured units of recorded information, published or unpublished, in hard copy or electronic form, and managed as discrete units in information systems' (Standards Australia 1996, pt. 1, p. 6, 4.12).

In the Commonwealth *Evidence Act 1995* **document** means any 'record of information', and includes:

(a) anything on which there is writing; or
(b) anything on which there are marks, figures, symbols or perforations having a meaning for persons qualified to interpret them; or
(c) anything from which sounds, images or writings can be reproduced with or without the aid of anything else; or
(d) a map, plan, drawing or photograph (Commonwealth of Australia 1995, section 47).

Not all documents created and received by organisations are *records* as defined by the Australian Standard AS 4390–1996. They do not all provide evidence of business activity. Examples are background documents which are collected in relation to a business activity but which do not form evidence of that activity. While these documents are not records, they are often stored with the records as part of the total information available on the business activity. Other examples are directories and trade literature. They do not represent evidence of a particular business activity but they are essential informational tools which support business activity.

Informational documents are often encompassed within a records management program as an important part of the corporate memory of the organisation. In this book informational documents are viewed as belonging to the knowledge-base of the organisation which assists it to achieve its goals. A university might keep files relating to job statistics or to courses offered elsewhere. A nutrition research organisation may keep extensive files on food-related illnesses. Proprietary information—information which only a few people in the organisation may have access to (e.g. recipes, product designs, chemical formulae, laboratory techniques)—may be a subset of either the knowledge-base or the records of the organisation. In practice the distinction between informational and evidential documents should not be over-emphasised. The distinction is intended to highlight the fact that records managers must give priority to documents which have evidential value, as the risk of not managing these is higher than for other informational documents.

What are archives?

Archives are 'those records which are appraised as having continuing value' (Standards Australia 1996, pt. 1, p. 6, 4.5). Records may be of continuing value for a range of reasons, including administrative, legal or historical.

In the business context, the differentiation between records and archives is useful only insofar as it acknowledges the need for special treatment for records of long-term historical value. For some organisations this may involve transferring certain records to an archives centre (e.g. a government archival agency or a university archives); for others it may involve setting up a special archival program to ensure records of historical interest are captured and preserved.

Records management and recordkeeping

What is records management?

The Australian Standard AS 4390–1996 defines **records management** as 'the discipline and organisational function of managing records to meet operational business needs, accountability requirements and community expectations' (Standards Australia 1996, pt. 1, p. 7, 4.23). It is concerned with ensuring that business activity is appropriately documented in organisations, and with designing and implementing all the associated systems, procedures and services.

Why is records management important?

- Organisations rely on efficient access to the right information. They need it: (1) to support decision making, (2) for general operational purposes, (3) as evidence of their policies and activities, and (4) for litigation support. Records management ensures that the right information can be accessed when required.

The right information presented at the right time, to the right person and at a reasonable cost

- Organisations have legal, professional and ethical responsibilities to create certain records; they are also required to retain certain categories of records for specified periods. Records management ensures these obligations can be met.
- Organisations need to control the volume of information being created and stored. This is primarily for economic reasons, as least as far as paper records are concerned—records are expensive to store and maintain—but also for operational efficiency: it is harder to find relevant information if it is buried in a lot of obsolete information. Records management includes developing controls for disposal of records and for the separation of active from inactive records.

What is recordkeeping?

Recordkeeping is 'making and maintaining complete, accurate and reliable evidence of business transactions in the form of recorded information' (Standards Australia 1996, pt. 1, p. 7, 4.19). The Standard emphasises in a number of places that record-keeping is the collective responsibility of personnel at various levels across an organisation. Organisations need to define the responsibilities of senior management and the various categories of employees who manage or perform recordkeeping processes, including business unit and functional managers, records managers, system administrators, and the individuals who create or maintain the records (Standards Australia 1996, pt. 2, p. 5–6, 5.1.3).

Recordkeeping systems

Recordkeeping systems are systems designed to capture records as evidence of business activities, to manage those records, and to make them available when required.

The Standard sees recordkeeping systems in very broad terms as including the:

- Relevant personnel (records management staff and users)
- Recordkeeping policies, procedures and practices
- Documentation presenting these policies, procedures and practices, including procedures manuals and guidelines
- Records themselves
- Specialised information and records systems used to control the records
- Software, hardware, and other equipment, and stationery (Standards Australia 1996, pt. 3, p. 9, 6.2.1).

All of these components of recordkeeping systems are discussed in this book.

The records life cycle model and the records continuum model

A popular way of viewing records management is to use a **life cycle model**. With this model, a record is said to have a life cycle, and that life cycle can be divided into five major phases—creation, distribution, use, maintenance and disposal. Within each of these phases there are various elements and activities. At the end of the initial life cycle, records may go through a second cycle—the archives life cycle. This is where the archivist identifies and appraises records of continuing value, acquires them, documents information about them, maintains them, and provides access to them.

The life cycle concept is seen as providing a useful basis for developing a records management program. However in recent years there has been support from records management and archives professionals for a different way of approaching records management called the **records continuum model**. (See Figure 1.2.)

The Australian Standard AS 3490–1996 sees the term records continuum as meaning:

> ... the whole extent of a record's existence. Refers to a consistent and coherent regime of management processes from the time of the creation of records (and before creation, in the design of recordkeeping systems), through to the preservation and use of records as archives (Standards Australia 1996, pt. 1, p. 7, 4.22).

The records continuum model focuses on the management of records as a continuous process which includes the creation of the records. It sees the need to manage records from the perspective of the activities which they document, rather than visualising it in consecutive stages, which is the emphasis of the life cycle analogy. It looks at managing records in the light of such questions as what records need to be captured to provide evidence of an activity, what systems and rules are needed to ensure those records are captured and maintained, how long the records should be kept to meet business and other requirements, how they should be stored, and who should have access to them.

The proponents of the records continuum model point out that while the records of an organisation are subject to certain processes during their lifespan which involve them being transferred from one state to another, these processes are based on particular arrangements developed for those records rather than on any 'natural' sequential stages which must occur in recordkeeping.

The continuum model encourages anticipation of the organisation's future need for evidential documentation as an integral part of both operational and strategic management.

By placing **disposal**, including the identification of records of continuing value, as the last stage in the records' life cycle, a life cycle model does not emphasise the need to design systems which ensure the capture of those records of continuing value in the first place.

This problem has become far more critical with the increasing volume of information created and stored in electronic format. Unless the controls needed to capture evidence of business activity are incorporated in the design of an organisation's business systems, the relevant information—or elements of it—may be amended or deleted to meet current requirements. For example, in a client information system, a primary requirement may be to access current information on client names and contact details for mailing purposes; however the history information on former names and contact details will form a crucial part of the evidence of earlier transactions. A way of capturing the history information and creating links between the old and new information relating to particular clients must be built into the system.

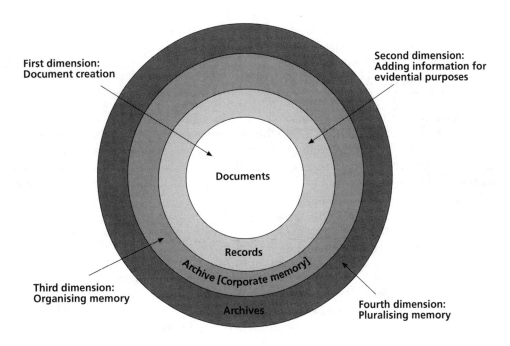

Figure 1.2 The records continuum model

Source: Based on a diagrammatic representation of the records continuum developed by Frank Upward, Monash University. For the original diagram and explanation, see Upward, F. (1997), pp. 278–81.

The records continuum model is a conceptual guide for the development of recordkeeping policies and programs. To summarise from Upward's paper (1997), the dimensions in the continuum model represent perspectives for managing documents which must be taken into consideration by records managers and archivists. Across the continuum records may be accessed physically (e.g. in local paper files), or virtually (through the mediation of digital technology), and located at individual, group, organisational or inter-organisational/society-wide levels. The four dimensions are explained below.

- **First dimension**—records of business activities (as defined in the Australian Standard AS 4390–1996) are created as part of business communication processes within the organisation, e.g. through e-mail, document management software, or other software applications.

- **Second dimension**—records which have been created or received in an organisation are tagged with information (metadata) about them, including how they link to other records.
- **Third dimension**—records become part of a formal system of storage and retrieval which constitutes the corporate memory of the organisation.
- **Fourth dimension**—certain records which are required for purposes of societal accountability (e.g. by corporate law) or other forms of collective memory become part of wider archival systems which comprise records from a range of organisations.

In contrast to the life cycle analogy, because of developments in information technology, practical operations within the dimensions may take place simultaneously (see Figure 1.2). Metadata (data about data) may be added automatically, or by human input. The metadata tagging needed for a document to serve various requirements can be included at the point of creation, or at any subsequent point (within given cost and technological constraints).

Upward supplied the following example to the authors to illustrate the applicability of the records continuum model:

A pharmaceutical company has to register its products with a variety of international and national bodies. To do this it must manage its documents from the time product research begins. It has to link documents created by work groups, organise the records at a corporate level, and submit them to a variety of bodies which regulate the product registration processes in different countries. Control over recordkeeping needs to be incorporated into document creation processes from the outset. There is also a continuing need for the company and/or other organisations involved in the process to add metadata which link together accountability documentation of all critical stages in the development, marketing and use of the product, e.g. clinical trials and product approvals.

Records management as a field of study

Records management and archives administration are both recordkeeping disciplines. They share a distinct body of knowledge relating to recordkeeping. The barriers that have traditionally existed in Australia between the two areas are gradually breaking down as the common goals and tasks are acknowledged and the lines separating functions become more blurred. It is in the purposes and outcomes of the recordkeeping activities that the differences may emerge. This is because traditionally records managers have operated in the corporate context and view records for their role in supporting the business activities of the organisation and in protecting the organisation in case of challenge, whereas archivists have a broader collective perspective on the role of records in society; they are concerned with the cultural and social value of records as well as their business and legal value.

The blurring of the lines between the records management and archives disciplines is reflected in the trend for educational programs to bring the study of the two areas together. It is also reflected in the increasing references in the literature and at conferences to records managers and archivists as belonging to the same profession but with different specialisations.

In addition to their own distinct body of knowledge, the records management and archives disciplines draw on the knowledge and skills of related fields, such as management, information science, librarianship, legal studies, systems analysis and information technology, and history.

Records management may also be viewed in the context of the broader field of information management. One writer puts it this way:

> Information managers are concerned primarily with the management and retrieval of information (including its generation, storage and disposal). The information may be the content of a record, a database, a journal, or something else. In this context and with a business process focus, all information management professionals have a vital role:
>
> - Records managers have a role as managers of the business rules that surround an organisation's records (evidence of business), their generation, management and disposal
> - IT professionals have a role as providers of solutions to facilitate the routine conduct of business which is enabled by technology
> - Corporate librarians have a role as classifiers and retrievers of information from sources within the public arena.
>
> These roles will blur or merge (Ellis 1996).

Knowledge management and records management[1]

In contemporary organisations and their wider social environments, records management forms a major part of developments described by terms such as *groupware, intranet, extranet* and *knowledge management.* The intranet movement uses the technical protocols (TCP/IP) of the Internet to provide a platform for communication within organisations no matter how large or physically dispersed they may be. Groupware is software which facilitates collaboration among members of an organisation in the development of documents and is increasingly becoming compatible with such intranets. *Extranets*—which also conform to Internet standards— allow the selective sharing of communication between organisations and selected clients, suppliers, or other external collaborators, for mutual benefit. Commonly intranets/extranets also link to information resources on the wider Internet, where these resources are relevant to the knowledge-base in the organisation.

Knowledge management aims to create a *learning organisation* (Boisot 1995). It is a concept which identifies the **tacit** knowledge of members of an organisation as among its most important assets. Through appropriate human resource policies and practices, it seeks to achieve a translation from tacit to **explicit** knowledge which can be shared among members of the organisation (Nonaka & Horotaka 1995). Such explicit knowledge, appropriately disseminated, stored and retrieved, can contribute significantly to the avoidance of risk and the realisation of opportunities by organisations.

Databases of evidential records are likely to be among the information assets to which an intranet would typically provide access. Like other categories of information on an intranet, such access might be restricted to defined categories of users.

However, these databases of evidential records would not necessarily constitute the whole of the content of an intranet, or even a major part of it. Intranets comprise operational and strategic communication of all kinds—much of which may never be captured in documents or organisation-level databases. Of that which is captured and organised, some would be evidential records and some would be other knowledge-base documents.

All information practitioners, including recordkeeping professionals, would today be expected to understand and contribute to the development of organisational intranets and knowledge management strategies. Records managers need not only to understand in depth their own special roles within this context, but also to acquire sufficient skills and insight to contribute overall. The intranet/knowledge management arena is a focus of rapid convergence among information roles, where multi-skilling and versatility are greatly valued.

The records management role

In the past, records management was most commonly perceived as maintaining a central registry of policy and correspondence files. The emphasis was on centralised control so that anyone in the organisation could gain access to files when needed, anyone could find out what files existed, and duplication could be avoided. There could be several physical locations for the files but the system was still based on centralised control of the files. Business unit files remained the domain of the business units which created them. And the management of electronic records was the domain of the computer staff. This is still the situation in many organisations but the last decade has seen a gradual change in thinking within the records management profession on the role of records management within organisations. While centralised physical control of some categories of records may still be seen as important, it is now generally acknowledged that records management should be concerned with the management of recorded information across the organisation, regardless of format (paper, microform, electronic, etc.), originator or location. And that records management is not just concerned with managing records that have already been created, but with establishing programs and systems to ensure that the information necessary to record the business activities of an organisation is effectively captured in the first place.

Records managers must be pro-active in working with other information professionals in their organisations, as well as the managers responsible for the different business functions, to achieve the following:

- Define the recordkeeping needs relating to the business activities of the business units—define records should be created and how long they should be kept
- Develop business rules and standards to support the creation and capture of complete and accurate records
- Develop systems and controls to ensure the capture of complete and accurate records
- Develop systems and services which will provide efficient and appropriate access to records
- Set up processes to monitor compliance with external and internal recordkeeping requirements
- Ensure the organisation is appropriately prepared for audits of records by external regulatory bodies, such as the Australian Taxation Office and the Australian Securities Commission.

Records managers must demonstrate to management the cost and efficiency benefits that can be achieved from good records management practices. In fact, some large organisations have made this a fundamental requirement by structuring records management so that it is provided on a 'user-pays' basis; business units must be convinced of the need for records management systems and services and be prepared to budget for them.

Records managers may also need to demonstrate to management the dangers of not having adequate recordkeeping systems. They can readily draw, if it is useful to do so, on well-publicised cases to demonstrate the potential difficulties faced by organisations unable to produce sufficient documentation of business activity.[2]

Records management personnel

Depending on the size of the organisation and the size and complexity of the records management program, there may be three categories of records management personnel:

* Professional staff
* Para-professional staff
* Clerical staff.

Records managers have a major coordinating role; being responsible for the development of policy, systems and procedures and for working with the units within their organisations on their records management needs. They may have direct responsibility for all records management activities and records management staff in the organisation, or may have an advisory role, or a mixture of the two. An example of a mixed role would be where a records manager has total responsibility for certain records management functions, for example, the management of inactive records, but provides a 'user-pays' consultancy service to the business units for the development of recordkeeping systems and other records management practices relating to current records.[3]

The para-professional staff are responsible for the day-to-day running of records management services and activities such as correspondence filing systems, electronic document management systems, secondary storage, filing equipment review and maintenance. The para-professional staff may include analysts working under the direction of the records manager in analysing records management needs and setting up systems. The clerical staff undertake tasks such as filing, retrieving, and processing records for storage.

Needless to say, in small to medium organisations, the roles will often be filled as part of the duties of the office manager and selected clerical and secretarial staff.

In addition to records management staff, many other staff in an organisation have recordkeeping responsibilities. These responsibilities should be clearly documented in the practice manuals relevant to the particular functional areas, and where appropriate, included in job descriptions.

Figure 1.3 lists the types of responsibilities that may be attached to a records manager's position. Figures 1.4 and 1.5 present some sample advertisements and job specifications for records management positions. It should be borne in mind that these advertisements and job specifications represent a view of how particular organisations perceive the records management role, not necessarily how the records management profession perceives it.

Management
- Overseeing the entire records management program
- Recruiting, supervising and training staff
- Managing budget and equipment
- Liaising with relevant personnel at all levels
- Developing and documenting recordkeeping and records management procedures

Systems
- Developing, maintaining and reviewing systems
- Selecting and implementing commercially available systems
- Monitoring new technology
- Advising on controls, standards and systems for electronic recordkeeping

Classification and indexing
- Classifying and indexing records
- Maintaining and reviewing indexing and file numbering systems
- Maintaining and developing in-house thesauri

Enquiries
- Satisfying enquiries from the user departments
- Satisfying enquiries under freedom of information legislation

Records appraisal and disposal
- Establishing recordkeeping requirements and monitoring compliance
- Establishing approved disposal schedules
- Determining records disposal action
- Implementing records storage procedures, including organising of secondary and archival storage.

Figure 1.3   Sample tasks and responsibilities of the records manager

ABC Company

Records Officer

[Salary and benefits]

An experienced Records Officer is required to assist with the Records Management function of ABC Company.

The Records Management function involves itself with a variety of project and consultancy tasks, including:
- Application of workflow and imaging technologies
- Creation and implementation of document standards
- Establishment of disaster recovery plans and vital records programs
- Participation in working groups, project teams and management committees
- Planning of facilities and site inspections
- Development of an electronic work management architecture
- Management of existing and proposed contracts with external suppliers of various records management products and services.

Records Management is well supported by senior management and offers an innovative, diverse and challenging records and strategic information working environment for a records professional. Most work will be conducted in the ZZZ Office, but interstate travel will be required from time to time. Records Management works with various areas of ABC Company to offer an integrated records management architecture for all aspects of Company operation.

The successful applicant will have a tertiary qualification in records management or a related field and at least three years experience in the industry. Applicants who have completed a substantial part of their tertiary course will also be considered. IT skills or qualifications would also be an advantage.

Applications close [date and time] and should be forwarded to: [Position, address, phone, fax]

Further information can be obtained from [contact details] on the above telephone number.

Records Management Officer/Archivist

This newly created position reports to the Library and Information Manager. The successful applicant will be responsible for assisting to establish an integrated Records Management Program for the Company aimed at ensuring that all records are managed efficiently and that archival records are identified, preserved and protected.

Specific responsibilities will include:

- The development of appropriate storage and retrieval systems
- Operation of the Company's archives and non-current records repository
- The development of a records retention and disposal schedule
- Provision of advice and training on records management procedures.

Experience is essential; a professional qualification in records/archives management is desirable, also familiarity with online storage and retrieval systems.

Salary would be negotiable, depending on qualifications and experience. Further information may be obtained by contacting [name and phone details]. Suitably qualified persons should apply in writing by [date and time], to [name, address, fax].

Records Manager

The City of XYZ seeks applicants for the position of Records Manager to establish and implement a modern records management system.

The Records Manager would be required to develop and implement systems and procedures; establish a thesaurus of indexing terms; plan and commence the conversion of the existing records; develop user training procedures.

The successful applicant should have extensive experience in the establishment and operation of modern records management and information retrieval systems at both manual and automated level; have appropriate academic qualifications and a proven record in records management; be prepared to work cooperatively in transferring records management skills.

Salary would be in the range of [range specified] and normal local government conditions of employment apply.

For a job specification please ring [contact details]. Closing date for applications is [date]. Written applications should be addressed to [name, address].

Figure 1.4 Sample advertisements for Records Officer, Records Management Officer/ Archivist and Records Manager

KPMG

Records Manager

Function

To develop and manage an organisation-wide records management program designed to ensure that records practices are effectively meeting the organisation's records management needs.

Duties and Responsibilities

- Establish procedures and direct the implementation of the records management program
- Cooperate with management to define and monitor functional recordkeeping requirements
- Establish systems and processes to enable those requirements to be met
- Monitor compliance with legislative and other recordkeeping requirements
- Develop recordkeeping and records management standards and rules, including those for electronic recordkeeping
- Provide technical support and coordination of personnel resources necessary for the successful operation of the program
- Provide technical training to business unit records personnel as required to achieve desired results
- Responsible for addressing and resolving problems within the records management areas
- Responsible to the Information Technology General Manager for the records management budget and cost control and provision of advice to business units with respect to business unit records management budgets
- Provide expertise and guidance to users in cost controls associated with records storage and retrieval
- Provide advice on systems and procedures to meet special business unit records and document management needs
- Establish procedures for the evaluation, implementation and review of manual and automated records systems
- Design and implement effective records disposal schemes
- Advise on and implement effective strategies for storage of active records (electronic and paper)
- Manage an offsite storage program for inactive records
- Prepare periodic reports for the Information Technology General Manager with respect to the records management operations.

Qualifications and experience

- Tertiary qualifications in records management are essential
- The incumbent should have at least five years records management experience, ideally in a supervisory role
- Experience in implementing and maintaining a computer-based records system is highly desirable.

City of Whitehorse
Records Officer

Position objective
Assistance in the provision of an efficient records management system and mail processing system to service the whole of Council's operations.

Accountabilities
The Records Officer is accountable for:
- Accurate recording of file data and movement of files throughout the organisation
- Availability of files on demand
- Collection and distribution of outwards mail
- Processing of inwards mail
- Establishing files as directed
- Identifying property based data and establishment of property files.

Judgement and decision making
- Needs to have sound knowledge of Council and departmental operations
- Needs to make judgement and decisions on property correspondence and data
- Needs to nominate and select correspondence for action officers when required.

Key responsibilities and duties
System development
- Establish and maintain the property series files under the direction of the Records Coordinator.

File maintenance support
- Assist with the sorting, opening and recording of all inwards mail
- Data entry of inwards mail; classification of same as required
- Assist with the maintenance of current file records; responsible for property files
- Circulate files to officers in accordance with established procedures
- Follow up unanswered correspondence
- Assist in file tracking and control systems
- Assist with archival culling and ordering of files
- Provide assistance and information on status of files
- Operate the re-submit system.

General duties
- Assist with coordination of copier maintenance
- Assist with files courier services as required
- Assist with collection and processing of all outwards mail as required.

Organisational relationships
Reports to: Records Coordinator and in his/her absence, Senior Archives
                     and Records Officer
Internal liaisons: All departments and management level
External liaisons: Suppliers.

Specialist skills and knowledge
- Needs records management experience
- Needs computer/PC/keyboard skills
- Broad knowledge of activities and operations of local government
- Experience with land management systems and property based records
- General understanding of Public Records Act and PRO schedules.

Management skills
- Ability to work within specified timelines to achieve set objectives.

Interpersonal skills
- Ability to liaise with staff at all levels and assist them in records and research functions professionally
- Needs to write, read and reason in English
- Needs to have good comprehension skills and be able to speed read and precis
- Essential to work in team environment to achieve a team objective.

Qualifications and experience
- Year 11 minimum
- Progress towards records management certificate
- Computer experience or formal qualifications in EDP field (certificate)
- Keyboard skills
- Physically fit, able to climb step ladders, carry reasonable weights
- Able to drive a vehicle.

Figure 1.5   Sample job specifications for Records Manager and Records Officer

Source: Reproduced with permission of KPMG, Melbourne, and City of Whitehorse, Victoria

A place for records management in the organisational structure

Most commonly, records management is placed within the business services area of the organisation. In some cases it is established as an independent unit reporting directly to the head of the business services area; in some cases it may be part of an information services unit which includes other information functions such as a library service; in other cases still it comes under the information technology umbrella and functions alongside the computer systems and services area. Whatever the vertical relationships are, it is essential that the records management staff work as a team with the staff of other units concerned with information and office systems. It is particularly important that a good working relationship is established between the computer systems manager and the records manager because the two areas need to cooperate closely in making the best use of technology to promote effective records management and recordkeeping in the organisation, and also in managing electronic records. It is also important that the records manager works jointly with the managers responsible for the various business functions of the organisation to establish the recordkeeping requirements related to those functions—some formal lines of communication may need to be set up to ensure this cooperation occurs.

Figures 1.6 and 1.7 present two examples of the placement of records management in Australian organisations.

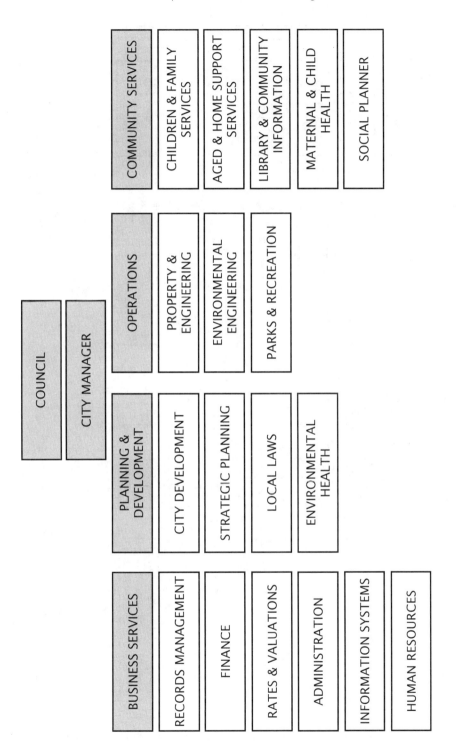

Figure 1.6 Typical local government structure showing records management located within the administration functional area

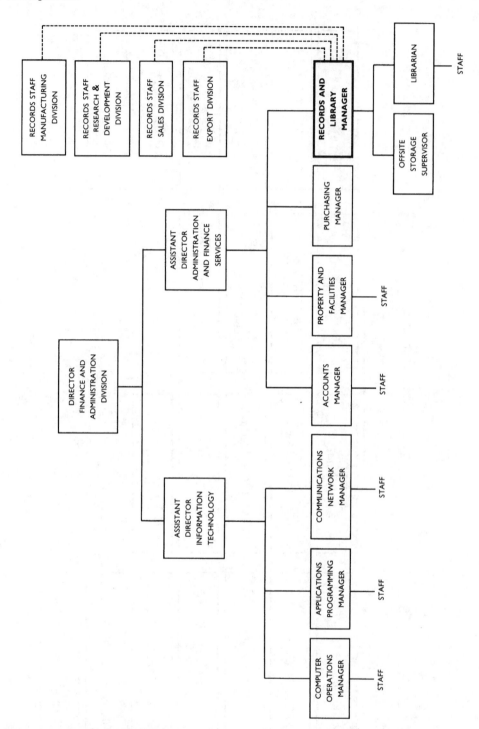

Figure 1.7 Organisational chart showing a records manager with both a direct and indirect staffing responsibility

Note: The records staff in each division of the company report to their divisional administration managers. The records manager is responsible for defining their tasks and procedures and for advising them on their day-to-day work.

Outsourcing of records management services

Outsourcing means to contract out services and functions. It is a strategy which enables organisations to concentrate their resources on their core business, leaving service delivery in selected areas to businesses which have proven expertise and can deliver at a cost-effective price.

Records and information management businesses in Australia are increasing in number and are marketing their products and services more aggressively than in the past. A growing number of government and private sector organisations, in turn, are investigating the benefits of outsourcing records management services. This is particularly the case with technology-based services such as document and image management but also with traditional paper-based systems and services, such as paper files management.

Whereas in the past outsourcing tended to be limited to managing resources that could be processed and/or stored away from the client's workplace, an increasing trend is for contractors to provide services on site, including the staffing of those services (e.g. mailroom services).

Records management education

The changing role of records management professionals is reflected in the changing nature of education for records management in Australia and the sort of qualifications employers are seeking. Initially, training courses were mainly confined to the technical/TAFE (Technical and Further Education) area but over recent years more and more tertiary institutions are offering records management courses. These vary from full undergraduate and postgraduate courses in records management, often combined with archives administration, to single units within business, information technology, and information services/librarianship courses.

Education for records management staff at the para-professional level is currently undergoing considerable change with the development of a comprehensive National Curriculum. This National Curriculum consists of a series of core modules to be taught at TAFE level. Individual institutions select from the range of modules to create a course leading to the award of certificate, advanced certificate, associate diploma or diploma.[4]

Records management and archives courses offered in Australia are listed in Appendix C. In addition to these courses, short courses in records management and archives are offered by the professional associations, including the Records Management Association of Australia, universities, state records and archives bodies, and consultants.

In Australia, only a small percentage of records management personnel have qualifications in records management. Many come up through the ranks starting as filing or records clerks; some come into the profession from related information areas such as librarianship. Employers vary in the qualifications they seek, depending on how they view the position and on their expectations. Some ask for records management or archives qualifications, or qualifications in a related field such as librarianship; some specify information systems experience; some ask for undergraduate qualifications, some for postgraduate qualifications; some do not specify any qualifications at all.

The forthcoming publication of National Records and Archives Competency Standards by the Finance and Administration Industry Training Advisory Body for records management and archives personnel in Australia should provide a useful recruitment tool for organisations to help them clarify what level and type of personnel they need for particular roles.

Once published and implemented, the competency standards should have a major impact on future developments in records management education and training and certification. The standards define the skills, knowledge and standard of performance required at all levels in order to meet industry needs, and the education and training system must provide the appropriate courses to impart those skills and knowledge.[5]

Exercise

Choose any organisation (20+ staff) known to you and arrange an interview with the staff member responsible for records management within that organisation. The aim of the interview is for you to gain an overview of the records management systems and practices of the organisation.

Start with an explanation of what you mean by records management and recordkeeping. Ask questions on the following topics:

- What are the positions of the staff with records management responsibilities? Is their records management role full-time or part-time? What are their records management duties?
- What is the role of the records management staff in assessing the recordkeeping requirements of the organisation and in designing recordkeeping systems?
- What are the main categories of records, including non-paper records, held by the organisation?
- What type of recordkeeping systems exist? How are records stored?
- Are there any procedures for separating active from semi-active and inactive records? When and how are records destroyed?
- Are records management procedures documented?

Summarise the results of your interview.

Case study 1.1

The Head Office of the Oil and Gas Mining Company in Perth, Western Australia wishes to appoint a records manager.

The company has been involved in expensive litigation on two occasions because it was unable to produce adequate evidence that it had carried out the appropriate actions in particular situations. It recognises the importance of getting its recordkeeping and records management procedures in order.

There are 450 staff in Head Office. They are all housed in the one building.

There are approximately 30 000 file folders containing information on all topics of concern to the company. There is also an increasing amount of information being stored in electronic format.

There are at least seven different file locations in the building. Secretarial staff, who are responsible to the business unit heads, are expected to maintain files for their business units in addition to their other duties. There is a central registry of policy and correspondence files run by a records clerk and three assistants. There is little formal communication between the registry staff and the secretarial staff and practically no communication between the registry staff and the computer staff who are responsible for maintaining control systems for electronic records.

Storage facilities for many of the records are inadequate. No files have been destroyed for the past ten years. There is no uniform language for naming files, and no common retrieval system. Each file location has its own system for file retrieval, some of which are numerical, others are alphabetical and others depend on the memories of the secretarial staff. Files are often missing or difficult to find. There is no standard charge-out system for files.

Most staff members store their electronic documents on their PC hard drives. There is a central server with a directory structure but there are no controls to ensure this server is used for storing particular categories of documents.

No automated control systems have been applied to the company's records.

Your task

On the understanding that the company is prepared to pay whatever is necessary to attract a competent records manager, prepare a job advertisement for the position.

To complete this task you may find it useful to scan the newspapers over a two to three month period for sample advertisements in records management and related information fields; there are also some sample advertisements reproduced in this chapter (see Figure 1.4). Studying these advertisements will help you to ascertain appropriate terminology and layout.

Questions

1 List some of the business activities in organisations which require a significant expenditure of time and resources on recordkeeping. What type and level of staff are likely to be involved in the recordkeeping?
2 Are there certain types of organisations which are particularly vulnerable to legal action if they do not keep accurate and complete records of their business activities? If so, which and why?
3 The definition of *document* in the Commonwealth *Evidence Act 1995* is quite detailed. What is it trying to achieve?
4 Look up some dictionary definitions of *record* and compare them with the definition in the Australian Standard AS 4390–1996. Are there differences? Do they present different perspectives?
5 List some records management functions and activities which might be candidates for outsourcing. What are the advantages and disadvantages that would need to be considered by an organisation in deciding whether to outsource these functions and activities?

Notes

1 This section was paraphrased from personal lecture notes supplied to the authors by Don Schauder, Monash University.
2 For some Australian examples from the 1990s see Roberts (1994).
3 See Smart (1994) for a case study of an internal records management consultancy service.

4 The National Records Management Modules were published by ACTRAC (Australian Committee for Training Curriculum) in 1995. The Project Coordinator was Peter Smith, TAFE NSW.

5 The National Records and Archives Competency Standards Project is being coordinated by FAITAB (Finance and Administration Industry Training Advisory Body) and has representation from a range of records and archives bodies including the Records Management Association of Australia and the Australian Society of Archivists.

Additional information

The standard texts in records management such as Ricks & Gow (1988, Chapter 1), Penn, Pennix & Coulson (1994, Chapters 1 & 2), Gill (1993) and Skupsky (1989) all provide overviews of records management principles and practices; they can be used for reference in studying the topics throughout this book.

For records management students and practitioners in Australia, the Australian Standard AS 4390–1996 (Standards Australia 1996) is compulsory reading; if it is published as an international standard (it was being considered by the International Organisation for Standardisation at the time of writing), it will be an important source of information and guidance for records management students and practitioners throughout the world.

It is also useful to read papers which challenge the traditional approach to records management and encourage records professionals to question their current direction and thinking. Two good examples are papers presented by Sue McKemmish (1995) and Kerry Gordon (1995) at the Records Management Association of Australia 12th National Convention.

References

Archives Authority of New South Wales 1995, *For the Record: Managing Records in the New South Wales Public Sector*, no. 6, May, pt. 1, p.4.

—— Records Management Office 1994, *Records and recordkeeping: introducing new concepts*, Sydney.

Barrett, M. 1995, 'The "operation successful patient died" problem', Records Management Association of Australia, 12th National Convention, Melbourne, September 1995, *Redefining Records Management: Conference Papers*, RMAA, Melbourne, pp. 16–19.

Bearman, D. 1994, *Electronic Evidence: Strategies for Managing Records in Contemporary Organizations*, Archives & Museum Informatics, Pittsburgh.

Boisot, M. H. 1995, *Information Space: A Framework for Learning in Organizations, Institutions and Culture*, Routledge, London.

Commonwealth of Australia 1995, *Evidence Act 1995*.

Croft, A. 1995, 'Is records management a candidate for outsourcing?', *Informaa Quarterly*, vol. 11, no. 1, pp. 5–7.

Ellis, J. 1996, 'Managing organisational culture: how to achieve success', in Document and Records Management Conference, Sydney, 25–26 June.

Emmerson, P. (ed.) 1989, *How to Manage Your Records: A Guide to Effective Practice*, ISCA Publishing, Cambridge, Chapter 1.

Gill, S. L. 1993, *File management and information retrieval systems: a manual for managers and technicians*, 3rd edn, Libraries Unlimited, Englewood Cliffs, Colo.

Gordon, K. 1995, 'Diversification of records management in the modern environment', in Records Management Association of Australia, 12th National Convention, Melbourne, 18–21 September 1995, *Redefining Records Management: Conference Papers*, RMAA, Melbourne, pp. 38–48.

Holswich, R. 1995, 'The three "Ws" of competency standards', *Informaa Quarterly*, vol. 11, no. 3, pp. 20–22.

Jose, M. L. 1996, 'Implications of outsourcing record keeping and the effect on government accountability', *Informaa Quarterly*, vol. 12, no. 4, pp. 23.

McKemmish, S. 1995, 'Educating recordkeeping professionals for the 21st century—issues and challenges', in Records Management Association of Australia, 12th National Convention, Melbourne, 18–21 September 1995, *Redefining Records Management: Conference Papers*, RMAA, Melbourne, pp. 85–102.

Nonaka, I. & Horotaka, T. 1995, *The Knowledge Creating Company: How Japanese Companies Create the Dynamics of Innovation*, Oxford University Press, New York.

Penn, I. A., Pennix, G. B & Coulson, J. 1994, *Records Management Handbook*, 2nd edn, Gower Publishing Co., Aldershot, Hants, Chapters 1 & 2.

Ricks, B. R. & Gow, K. F. 1988, *Information Resource Management: A Records Systems Approach*, 2nd edn, South-Western Publishing Co., Cincinnati, OH, Chapter 1.

Roberts, D. 1994, ' "Sports rorts": recordkeeping and accountability', *Informaa Quarterly*, vol. 10, no. 3, pp. 11–14.

Skupsky, D. S. 1989, *Recordkeeping Requirements: The First Practical Guide to Help You Control Your Records*, 2nd edn, Information Requirements Clearinghouse, Denver, Colo.

Smart, K. 1994, 'Development of an internal records management consultancy service at BP Australia', *Informaa Quarterly*, vol. 10, no. 2, pp. 5–9.

Southwood, G. 1995, 'Outsourcing your information resources', *Records Management Journal*, vol. 5, no. 2, pp. 101–13.

Standards Australia 1996, *Australian Standard AS 4390–1996, Records Management*, Homebush, NSW. Part 1: General; Part 2: Responsibilities; Part 3: Strategies; Part 4: Control; Part 5: Appraisal and Disposal; Part 6: Storage.

Upward, F. 1990, 'Records resource management', *Informaa Quarterly*, vol. 6, no. 1, pp. 48–52.

—— 1997, 'Structuring the records continuum part one: post-custodial principles and properties', *Archives and Manuscripts*, vol. 24, no. 2, pp. 268–85.

Wilson, V. 1995, 'Sources of expertise: education and training for tomorrow's records and information manager', *Informaa Quarterly*, vol. 11, no. 2, pp. 7–20.

Yorke, S. 1995, 'The role of the records manager—threats and opportunities', Records Management Association of Australia, 12th National Convention, Melbourne, September 1995, *Redefining Records Management: Conference Papers*, RMAA, Melbourne, pp. 115–32.

chapter two

Assessing records management needs and developing solutions

Overview

In Australia, there is a growing acknowledgement of the need to bring a systematic and integrated approach to the task of managing corporate records and recordkeeping processes. In many cases this reassessment has been forced on those organisations with medium to large collections of records by the realisation that their records are critically out of control. They are running out of space for records, are constantly frustrated and embarrassed by missing files, are spending unacceptable amounts of time tracking down files, and are concerned that they may not be able to produce the necessary records in the case of legal or other challenges. They realise that they need efficient records systems but that the existing filing staff (often departmental secretaries and filing clerks) lack the necessary skills to develop such systems. If they are really concerned to tackle the problems, they will probably do so in one of the following ways:

- Appoint a records manager to their staff to develop, implement and coordinate a records management program
- Appoint an information or records management consultant to develop a program which can then be maintained by the existing administrative or clerical staff
- Utilise the skills of existing staff, often from related areas such as the library, to develop and coordinate the maintenance of a program.

Clearly the choice of approach will depend partly on the size both of the organisation and of the records management function, and partly on management perceptions of the importance of the function.

The first task in setting up a comprehensive records management program for an organisation is to carry out a needs analysis to review what the recordkeeping and records management needs of that organisation are, and to identify the most appropriate solutions. This initial study is likely to focus on:

- Establishing records management policy for the organisation
- Analysing the organisation's recordkeeping requirements
- Investigating the best strategies for meeting those requirements.

The initial study may be followed at a later stage by smaller studies looking at specific records management needs and processes.

Any records management needs analysis should take into account a number of components which all essential to a records management program. This chapter briefly discusses each of these components and then goes on to set out the steps involved in carrying out a records management needs analysis.

Records management program components

The initial detailed records management needs analysis should identify and define the essential components of the records management program in terms specific to the needs of the particular organisation. Once these components have been defined, later studies can use them as a framework for further development. In summary, these components are:

- A records management policy for the organisation
- Records management systems and practices appropriate to the organisation
- Personnel and organisational structure
- Budgeting and cost control
- Facilities.

Each of these components is discussed in turn.

Records management policy

The records management policy of an organisation is the official charter for performing all records management functions and should be written in terms as broad as possible. It should refer to a total records management program for the organisation and include a clear statement outlining the role of records management and how it relates to the organisation's recordkeeping requirements. It should also spell out the objectives of the program and the need for staff at all levels of the organisation to accept their share of responsibility for efficient recordkeeping.

It is useful to include in the policy definitions of the major concepts, such as **records** and **documents, recordkeeping, records management, recordkeeping systems** and **records management systems**, so that records management and other staff have a common understanding of the concepts and terminology.

The records management policy should be endorsed by senior management and be made readily available to staff at all levels of the organisation. It should sit alongside policy on other matters where best practice is critical to the achievement of the organisation's goals.

Records management systems and practices

The records management systems and practices identified as appropriate for the organisation should be concerned with managing all of the processes involved in capturing and maintaining adequate records of the business activities of the organisation. They should incorporate responsibility for procedures, standards and controls related to all types of records.

Systems and practices should be designed to support the following sorts of activities:

- Recordkeeping in the different functional areas of the organisation
- Storage of both physical (paper, microform, etc.) and electronic records in their active, semi-active and inactive stages
- Providing an enquiry and records retrieval service to the staff of the organisation
- Providing advice and assistance on any records management matters
- Preparing and disseminating records management standards and procedures
- Running training programs on records management matters
- Designing and maintaining special programs to manage different types of records (e.g. vital records, forms, reports, regulatory and procedural documentation, quality records)
- Maintaining current information on legislative and regulatory requirements and any external or internal standards relevant to recordkeeping in the organisation
- Monitoring compliance with such requirements and standards
- Developing and implementing performance measurement strategies.

The review and further development of records management systems and practices is an ongoing process within the records management program.

Personnel and organisational structure

The staffing needs of the records management program will be determined by the size of the organisation and the complexity of the records management functions and activities. The various options for staffing, the nature of records management positions, and the issue of where records management may be placed in the organisational structure are discussed in Chapter 1.

Budgeting and cost control

A commitment by management to support the records management program should also mean a commitment to finance the program on an ongoing basis. This may not be difficult to obtain if the initial study can clearly demonstrate firstly, long-term cost savings in areas such as equipment and supplies, secondly, substantial gains in document searching and retrieval efficiency, and thirdly, the potential legal consequences to the organisation of inadequate recordkeeping and records control.

It is desirable for the records manager to control the records management budget so that priorities can be established and expenditure on such items as equipment and supplies can be readily monitored and controlled. Alternatively business units may control their own records management budgets but should do so in consultation with the records manager.

Facilities

Facilities are those physical assets and support services (chiefly equipment, furniture, accommodation, and services such as mail and reprographics) which are necessary to carry out records management functions and activities.

Conducting a records management needs analysis

The size and complexity of records management needs analyses vary greatly. The administration manager of a small company may second a staff member to spend, say, two months investigating and implementing a simple but efficient system which streamlines its recordkeeping processes. Or at the other extreme, a large company with offices in each state may employ a consultant for two years to develop a company-wide electronic document management system utilising the best of the computer and communications technology available. Not only will the duration of the latter project be much longer than the former, but the data collection and analysis techniques applied are likely to be more sophisticated. However, the basic steps are the same at both ends of the spectrum and it is these steps which form the focus of the rest of this chapter. It is beyond the scope of this book to present detailed guidance on management analysis techniques; this information is readily available in the management literature as well as in some records management textbooks.[1]

Steps in conducting a records management needs analysis

1 Seek management support

Initial meetings with senior management should be held to:

- Discuss the purpose of the study and to gather information on perceived problems to be addressed
- Obtain relevant documentation such as organisational charts and any previous records management reports
- Gain the active support of management in seeking the cooperation and participation of staff in the study.

2 Establish the detailed terms of reference of the needs analysis

A **preliminary review** of the existing systems, problems and user requirements needs to be carried out before the detailed terms of reference can be established. Out of this preliminary review should come a report to management presenting the proposed **objectives**, **scope**, **personnel**, **timeframe** and **costings** of the study.

The **objectives** must clearly reflect the advantages to be achieved from the study as perceived by both senior management and the records manager. They must be presented in the context of the organisation's recordkeeping responsibilities and needs, and its overall information management strategy.

Broadly, the objectives of a comprehensive records management needs analysis will be to present recommendations for improved recordkeeping and records control. However, specific objectives should be listed in order of priority and should reflect desired outcomes in terms of such factors as improved productivity, workflow, access to information for operational purposes, and ability to produce evidence of business activity when required.

The **scope** of the study should define what the study will cover and not cover, under what constraints (e.g. time) it is being conducted, and who will be affected by it. It will specify whether the whole organisation is to be studied, one business unit only or simply a pilot group.

Personnel required for the study should be defined. This may involve existing records management staff or outside consultancy staff; it is certainly likely to involve some time commitment from managers and other administrative and professional staff within the organisation. To arrive at a realistic assessment of personnel requirements, the following steps are necessary:

- Develop a list of tasks to be performed (including types of data to be collected and methods)
- Allocate tasks to personnel
- Estimate how long tasks will take to complete, and
- Calculate personnel costs, if required, on the basis of salaries plus overheads (superannuation, etc.) or consultancy costs.

The calculation of the **timeframe** of the study and the **costings** can also be based on the information gathered above; in addition, the estimate of costings should include other resources needed during the study such as equipment, materials and travel.

ZZ Smith and Co.

Preliminary study

Office filing systems: Overview and space requirements

Background
The company is moving into new premises sometime during the next two years and plans are being currently finalised for office accommodation.

Introduction
ABC Consulting Pty Ltd are office filing system consultants specialising in active file storage and retrieval systems.

The purpose of this document is to outline a study on the office space needed to operate an efficient company-wide filing, storage and retrieval program for ZZ Smith and Co. with particular emphasis on:
1 Floor space requirements for centralised filing systems
2 A brief overview of the current systems to determine:
   ▪ The filing space requirements for each department of the company
   ▪ Any obvious inadequacies and/or duplications.

Objectives
1 To ensure that the plans currently being finalised will provide facilities for an adequate space and cost-efficient filing program, which allows for 40 per cent expansion
2 To overview current systems, identifying strengths and weaknesses
3 To provide a report which:
   ▪ Details information in 1 and 2 above
   ▪ Highlights areas for further consideration, and
   ▪ Contains preliminary information and considerations to form the basis for development of a total records management program for the company.
ABC Consulting Pty Ltd proposes this study as stage one; later stages will be necessary to formulate the basis for specific storage and retrieval system options.

The project

An initial Filing Systems Study concentrating on active, hardcopy file documentation to include:

1 An overview of current systems in nominated departments to identify:
- Filing procedures
- Indexing methods
- Rate of activity to information
- Strengths and weaknesses existing in the present approach.

2 A study to establish that the allocated floor space is sufficient to:
- Accommodate the necessary hardware components for a cost and space-efficient company-wide storage and retrieval program
- Allow for a 40 per cent expansion in active file storage.

Methodology

1 Overview of current systems

- To be carried out at ZZ Smith and Co.'s premises
- Each department will be studied in isolation to establish any unique and/or specific requirements.

ZZ Smith and Co. is requested to provide:
- A list of departments, in order of priority to ensure that the most important departments are studied in the first instance
- A contact in each department with a letter of introduction to ensure that total cooperation is attained
- A plan of where the departments will be located in the new building and a brief résumé of any specific interaction between the individual departments in relation to sharing of files, etc.
- An available authority to liaise with in relation to access to information and personnel.

2 Floor space/office plan

A desk evaluation to be carried out at the office of ABC Consulting Pty Ltd.
- The completion of the overview will allow the calculation of floor space requirements for both the systems as they are currently and as they would be if modified and improved; in both cases providing for 40 per cent expansion.
- In this stage, as far as time permits, a general overview report will be compiled together with a report on any inadequacies of the current systems.
- During the study, areas will be identified which may be suitable for alternative processes and storage media. This will form the basis for a specific study which will have to be carried out by department/area at a later date.

Timing

1 Overview Stage

- To be carried out on site at ZZ Smith and Co.   (One week)

2 Desk study and reports

- To be carried out off-site however with liaison from time to time with ZZ Smith and Co.   (One week)

As time is of the essence in this particular study we request approval to proceed by close of business on Friday, 2 April, 1993.

> We would require a letter of appointment accepting project parameters, fees and terms prior to commencement.
>
> **Financial**
>
> *1 Fees*
>
> - A fee of $200.00 per hour will be levied plus any specific outgoings directly related to the project
> - Outgoing expenses of any significance will require approval prior to being incurred.
>
> *2 Terms*
>
> - $5000.00 payable with letter of appointment
> - Balance on presentation of Report.

Figure 2.1   Example of a preliminary report to management for a study focusing on one aspect of a records management program, i.e. storage requirements for physical records

3 Gather information

Fundamental to an analysis of records management needs for an organisation is a thorough understanding of the business activities of that organisation. Australian Standard AS 4390–1996 talks about the need for organisations to develop a business classification scheme which maps in detail their functions, activities and transactions (Standards Australia 1996, pt. 4, pp. 5–7). This business classification will underpin many of the processes in managing records. For example, it will be used to determine which records of business activity must be captured to ensure the organisation's business needs are met and its interests protected. It will also assist in creating links between related records, ensuring consistent naming approaches, retrieval of records relevant to an activity, determining retention periods, allocating user permissions, distributing incoming correspondence for action. (More detailed information on the process of devising a business classification is provided in Chapter 4.)

So the first requirement is to gather information on the business activities of the organisation and to map them into a classification scheme.

The second requirement is to use that classification as the basis for establishing what records of business activity need to be created.

Other information to be gathered includes:

- Any legislative and other external requirements determining the creation and retention of records relevant to the business activities of the organisation
- Information on who needs to access the records of business activity and for what purposes
- Staff (including records management staff) perceptions of requirements, problems and solutions
- The nature and type of existing records, recordkeeping systems and records management practices, and any gaps in recordkeeping
- Facts about the work to be done, as far as can be ascertained from existing systems—its nature, volume and purpose
- Costs of existing systems and operations—personnel costs, equipment and material costs, service costs such as bureau fees, and overhead costs such as telephone.

Methods of gathering information

The records manager or consultant carrying out the study should consider the following methods of gathering information:

- **Read existing documentation** including previous records management reports, statements of organisational goals, functions, and activities, practice manuals and internal regulatory information applying to the various functional areas of the organisation, job descriptions.

Become immersed in the situation where the problem(s) exist

- **Study published information** relevant to the organisation's recordkeeping practices, including legislation, and standards and codes of practice developed by industry and professional bodies.
- **Interview managers** on the business activities in their functional areas and their understanding of recordkeeping requirements.
- **Become immersed in the situations where problems exist**. Work with the staff responsible for managing records (paper and electronic) for several days; discuss their jobs with them and how they think systems could be improved; do their work and become thoroughly familiar with existing systems and procedures.

- **Interview selected staff**, including those with large personal filing systems. Establish what records they create and receive; establish what records they use, why, when and how they use them; gather their views on likely growth patterns in records and changes in usage rates; find out their perceptions of the strengths and weaknesses of existing systems and procedures. Gather views from all levels within the organisation or business unit. Use structured group interviews as a supplementary technique to gain a level of consensus on problems.
- **Use activity logs**—ask business units to maintain logs over a set period of time to record information on movement of records, and activities of users and operators.
- **Conduct a survey** of existing record series and recordkeeping systems to gather information on the volume, scope, usage, and location of the record series within the organisation. (Whether an initial overview of record series or a detailed inventory is required at this stage will depend on the objectives of the study. In most cases an overview will be adequate for the purposes of arriving at recommendations for future action. Records inventories are discussed in more detail in Chapter 4.)
- **Gather information** from managers in other service areas of the organisation such as Computer Systems, Purchasing, Library, Personnel. Become familiar with existing resources, services and administrative procedures within the organisation.
- **Gather information** on records management options and solutions. Talk to other records management professionals about how they have tackled similar problems, read the information and records management literature, attend seminars and trade exhibitions.
- **Make contact with suppliers** and study their products and literature. They can be useful in suggesting solutions and in organising demonstrations of equipment, supplies and systems.

4 Analyse the information and develop alternative solutions

In this step the information gathered is summarised, analysed and used as a basis for developing and evaluating alternative solutions for meeting the recordkeeping requirements of the organisation. It may involve techniques ranging from simple flowcharting[2] (see Figure 2.2) to sophisticated modelling, depending on the size and complexity of the study.

It is the most important and most demanding step of the study. It means taking a totally fresh and objective approach to the recordkeeping requirements under review. It means focusing on the best way to achieve those requirements, rather than just asking how the existing systems can be improved. It means taking into account all of the aspects related to capturing and managing the records, including their purpose and usage, storage, classification and indexing, retrieval, tracking, and security. It also means taking into account the following issues and constraints:

- The availability of funding to initiate and maintain the proposed system(s)
- Any additional staffing requirements
- The time it will take to convert the existing system(s) and for benefits to become apparent
- Requirements for additional equipment and other facilities
- Reliance on support from other parts of the organisation
- The availability of suitable technology
- Existing office layout and available space.

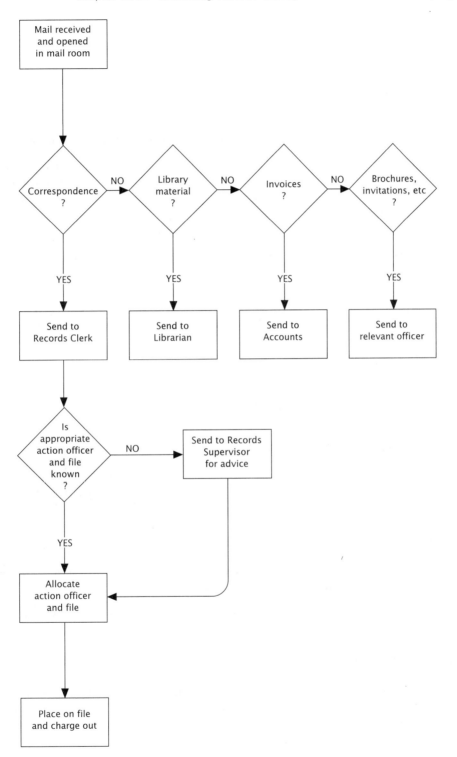

Figure 2.2   Example of a simplified flowchart, in this case used to illustrate the processing of incoming mail

5 Carry out a cost-benefit analysis

Depending on management attitudes it may be necessary or at least desirable to carry out a cost–benefit analysis of the system alternatives. It may be important in terms of the credibility of the study in the eyes of senior management.

In a cost–benefit study the costs of the alternative systems are charted along with the benefits of the systems, and compared with the costs and benefits of the current system.

Costs are presented in the two categories of **development** and **operational**:

- Development costs include salaries, equipment and any other expenditure associated with the setting up of a new system and conversion from an old one.
- Operational costs include ongoing supplies, space and rental, salaries, services and overheads.

Benefits are generally divided into direct financial benefits and service benefits, sometimes referred to as **tangible** and **intangible** benefits.

- Examples of direct financial benefits are savings in rental from reduction in space used, and lower costs for supplies (such as file covers) from bulk ordering. If improved productivity of records management staff and users and/or increased revenue for the organisation through improved records management practices can be demonstrated in dollar terms, these benefits are also well worth including.
- Examples of service benefits are better client relationships and improved staff morale from more efficient systems and procedures. Service benefits cannot be easily quantified and are therefore more difficult to present.[3]

6 Prepare and present the study report

The report presents the results of the study to management. It covers:

- Background information on the study—the terms of reference and timeframe.
- The methodology—how the information was gathered and analysed and who was involved.
- A summary of the findings.
- Recommendations—an outline of alternative solutions and cost benefits and a proposed course of action. The proposed course of action should be supported with information on its economic, technical and operational feasibility.

It may also include a draft implementation plan to demonstrate to management the steps that would need to be taken.

The report should include a one-page executive summary. *This may be the only part management will read*; they may rely on a verbal presentation for the rest of the information.

The importance of the study report cannot be over-estimated. Once the recommendations are endorsed by management, the report can then be used as a tool to guide the implementation of the program, and to seek the ongoing support and commitment needed for its success.

Exercise

Prepare a flowchart of the following file creation procedures.

In ABC Carpets Pty Ltd the most common way for a file to be initiated is for a staff member to ask the records management staff to create a new file. The records management staff then ask this staff member to complete a form giving details of suggested file name and title, and any other relevant information.

Alternatively, the records management staff may decide a new file is needed. If a file is thick, they may decide to open a new part. Or if they receive a piece of correspondence for which there is no file, they will open one. In the latter case, they will consult with the relevant staff member if they are unsure of the type or title of file to be created.

Once the file is ready to be opened, the file request form is passed to the records clerk to allocate a file number. It is then directed to the records supervisor to check the details and to authorise the creation of the file. The form is then handed to another records clerk who registers the file on the automated records management system, produces a label for the file, and attaches it to the file cover. The file is then handed back to the first records clerk who sticks the colour code labels for the file number down the tab of the file cover and places any correspondence on the file. The file is then either placed in the trolley ready for filing on the shelves or it is charged out to a staff member and sent off via the internal mail.

Case study 2.1

There are two tasks attached to the case study presented here. *The first task may be completed after studying this chapter*. It is designed to test your grasp of the basic steps in carrying out a records management needs analysis. The *second task* requires a more detailed knowledge of records management functions and *should be attempted after most, if not all, of the topics in the book have been studied*. It is suggested that at this stage you note what is required to complete the task and gather your information as you progress with your study of records management.

Background information

You have been appointed as records manager to the Sydney office of a large partnership of chartered accountants, V. G. Summs and Legers.

The firm has grown rapidly over the past ten years through a series of significant mergers. It currently has 190 partners and 1500 staff. At times the growth has been so rapid that there has not been time to properly integrate the systems of the merging firms before the next merger has taken place. As a consequence, the firm has a lot of major clients but its systems efficiency leaves a great deal to be desired. You are part of a general move to bring in experts to recommend and implement better systems.

The firm has six major divisions—Tax, Audit, Insolvency, Business Services, Management Consultancy, and Finance and Administration. Historically, each division is like a separate business—its partners make the decisions about how the division will function and how it will spend its money. In the past, firm-wide policy on matters such as records management has been rare. However, there are now some senior people, particularly in the Finance and Administration area, beginning to express views about the economies and efficiencies to be achieved through firm-wide approaches to operational matters. For example, the Director of the Information Technology

Section has been promoting the need for standardisation of desktop software, in order to achieve economies in processing and sharing of information.

The firm is actually quite rich in technology. There are approximately 900 networked PCs, mostly used by the accountants for client work; also a number of file servers for the divisions to store their documents. Many of the staff have laptops and they can access the network remotely if required. In addition there is a practice management system which is used on a firm-wide basis for controlling client, employee and financial information. The firm has its own intranet for facilitating access to information.

Currently the firm is spread across four buildings, three in the city and one in the outer suburbs. However, in twelve months time the firm will be brought together into one city building. Each division will be located on one floor. Planning is currently going ahead for the fitout of the new building.

Each division will have its own central file room, with space allocated within those rooms for staff and filing equipment. Management plans to relocate any existing equipment that is in reasonable condition to the new building.

Security to the building, and within the building, will be controlled by a computerised card access system; this will also apply to the file rooms after hours.

Types of records held by the firm

1 Administrative records (personnel, finance, administration).
2 Client records. These make up the bulk of records. There are about 100 000 paper client files in total held in the four office buildings; many of the documents are also held on the divisional file servers or on individual staff members' PCs. These electronic copies are retained for two reasons—firstly, in case the paper copies are mislaid, and secondly, to use as the basis for similar documents on future occasions.

The major categories of files are:

- **Tax**—(company income tax, individual income tax, sales tax, fringe benefits tax). These files are sent to secondary storage when they become too thick. They may cover several years.
- **Audit**—New files are opened for each audit; the previous year's files are also needed for reference. Audit files vary greatly in size from one thin file to over 100 physical parts.
- **Accounting**—New files are opened for every accounting period (usually quarterly or annual); the previous year's files are required for reference.
- **Insolvency**—These are both the files that belonged to the insolvent companies, and the files about the companies.
- **Management consultancy**—There are client files for the various areas in which the firm provides consultancy (e.g. financial management, tourism, executive selection, marketing). Categories of management consultancy files are project files, proposals and reports, correspondence files.

In divisions where the work for clients is ongoing (such as tax, audit and accounting jobs), there are several sub-categories of files—working paper files, files of permanent or master documents, correspondence files, fees files, and files of general ledgers in the form of A4 sized computer printouts. There are also files of documents kept in secure fireproof rooms—these are mainly documents belonging to clients, such as trust deeds and wills. And there is an increasing trend to store working papers and data in machine-readable format only, mostly on floppy disks. In most cases these are simply held by the individual staff member who has done the work.

Summary of records procedures and associated problems

Currently, each division maintains its own records, both paper and electronic. There is no corporate policy on records management, although there is a requirement for copies of all documents to be stored in paper form on the relevant files. There are few written procedures, certainly no firm-wide procedures. Staff use the divisional filing 'systems' as they think suitable, rather than according to agreed standards and procedures.

Although there are practice manuals which set out for the client staff what documents need to be created for particular types of jobs and how long they need to be kept, these tend to be largely ignored and decisions on documentation are made on a job-by-job basis. Some of the partners and senior staff are beginning to realise that from a risk management perspective, such ad hoc practices are dangerous.

Most of the divisions have at least one filing clerk. These filing clerks are untrained in records management principles and practices, and are generally appointed at a fairly junior level. They have a reactive role—they work under direction from the client and administrative staff in setting up files, filing, chasing missing files, sending files to secondary storage, etc. They each report to a partner in their respective divisions. They have no authority to develop and enforce procedures such as the completing of file movement forms and the inclusion of file references on documents sent for filing. They have no responsibility for managing electronic records.

The only common records procedure across the divisions is that the paper files are in alphabetical sequence, in most cases by client name.

In each division there are two or more large filing areas located in reasonable proximity to the group of staff using the files; there are also numerous smaller collections of files scattered around the work areas. Because the firm is located mainly in very expensive city office buildings, available space is very limited; consequently, as the firm has grown and the number of files has grown, further filing equipment has had to be fitted in wherever space can be found.

Records are housed in a variety of storage equipment, namely:

- A lot of mobile shelving units of various sizes and makes
- Open static shelving; most divisions have some open static shelving—in only two is it predominant
- A lot of two- and four-drawer filing cabinets, used for central filing, personal filing, and for partners' confidential filing, and
- A range of cupboards of various sizes and makes.

Some of the equipment is lockable, some is not.

The files are housed either directly on the shelves, in boxes on the shelves, or hung in one of three different types of suspension systems. Most divisions have a mixture of shelf and suspension filing. The files held in the different suspension systems are not readily interchangeable because different sorts of rails or shelves are required for each system. This incompatibility of equipment creates great problems when groups of staff are relocated to different areas. Either the filing equipment has to go with them, or the existing equipment in their new area has to be adapted. Either option is expensive.

In many of the filing areas, space utilisation is very poor, both in shelf layout and in the filing techniques. Filing staff frequently have to redistribute banks of files to fit new ones into the alphabetical sequence.

There is also a great variety of filing supplies used across the firm:

- Every division utilises suspension filing and therefore uses hanging pockets (different types for different systems).
- Most divisions have some shelf filing in storage boxes (11 cm wide x 38 cm deep x 18 cm high)—one or more boxes per client. For a major client there may be over 100 boxes for a single year's job such as an audit; for small clients there may be only one or two files in a box.
- Divisions choose their own file covers so there is a considerable range across the firm. Some use coloured file covers to distinguish different file series, some use plain buff; some use two-ring binders for working paper files, others use sturdy soft-covered folders. As mergers have taken place over the past few years, the merged firms have tended to keep their own file covers, so even within a file series there are variations.

There is no agreed structure for file titles, resulting in confusion as to what information should be placed on what files.

Most of the divisions have no listing of what files exist—they rely on the tags on the pockets or the labelling on the storage boxes to tell them if a file exists for a particular client. The lack of indexes, and in particular a central index, means there is no corporate knowledge of files. This can be a considerable disadvantage because it is common for more than one division to do work for a particular client.

Some partners and staff members have a habit of creating client files themselves and holding them within their personal office systems without ever informing the filing staff of their existence. There are no suspension pockets or boxes for these files so it is assumed by everyone except the individuals concerned that there are no files for the particular clients. Because of a lack of faith in the filing procedures and also critical space shortages in some filing areas, staff tend to hold large numbers of files at their workstations. This creates all sorts of problems in file control but it also means a lot of areas look extremely untidy and cluttered.

Two of the divisions have a simple sort of file movement system—they rely on the honesty and cooperation of staff to fill out a form when a file is taken. Because the files for each of these divisions are spread over several locations, it is impossible for the filing staff to exercise the necessary controls over file movements.

A great deal of time is wasted by both the client staff and the filing staff in searching for missing files. It is recognised as a major problem and causes a lot of frustration and embarrassment, particularly when clients discover their files are missing.

There is also an unacceptably high level of misfiling of documents. This is largely due to inadequate directions from the client staff to the filing staff. In addition, there is duplication of files and problems with retrieval because there are no established rules on citation and filing order of client names. A file for B. H. Tallboy and Co. may be found under B or it may be under Tallboy. A file for the Arthur Pottle Family Trust may be under Arthur or it may be under Pottle.

In most of the divisions processing of semi-active and inactive files for secondary storage is undertaken in a haphazard sort of way. There are no set times or procedures for sending files to secondary storage and many of the filing areas hold a great deal of non-current information. The process happens when a particular staff member decides a file is too thick; or maybe when the firm no longer handles the work of a particular client; or when there is no space left in a filing area. Some staff members are not confident that information will be successfully retrieved from secondary storage, so there is a reluctance to send files there.

A number of the divisions have never put a destruction date on a file, so the number of files in secondary storage is fast growing to unmanageable proportions and it is costing the firm a great deal of money.

Currently, the files are stored in boxes in three different warehouses. Two of these warehouses, and their contents, have been inherited from mergers and are no longer being added to. They are both full. One is located in the inner suburbs and one in the outer suburbs, one hour's drive from Head Office. In one of these two warehouses the files are stored in tea-chests, and in the other the boxes are simply piled up on top of each other in very rough order. It is very hard to locate and access a file in either warehouse, not just because of the poor physical arrangement of the boxes but because the listings of the contents of the boxes are extremely inadequate and incomplete. For one of the warehouses, which houses approximately 40 000 files, the files are listed in nine different registers covering different periods and they appear in random order under each letter of the alphabet. Heaven help the poor filing staff if they are asked to retrieve a file of an unknown date!

The files in the third warehouse (located in an inner suburb twenty minutes drive from Head Office) are far more efficiently stored. Yet the method of recording the files is totally manual and very cumbersome, with all records having to be written in two separate places; but at least it is fairly easy to locate a file. The files are boxed according to destruction dates—the dates are established according to statutory requirements, with a few years added on as a safety measure. The firm employs a storeperson to manage the files in the warehouse and retrieve them as required.

Two of the divisions also use a commercial storage company to store their files.

In terms of managing electronic documents, the divisions have established their own procedures and rules, including directory and document naming standards, retention periods by document and job type, procedures for transferring documents to offline storage, and procedures for retrieving offline documents. There is no standardisation and it is predicted that this will cause problems in the future as the extent of cross-divisional work increases and the volume of electronic information and communication grows.

Your tasks

You have been appointed by the firm to assess its present records practices and initially to advise on what steps should be taken to overcome the substantial problems currently being experienced in the area of records control.

Management perceives the problems in the following way:

- A lot of time is wasted looking for missing files and documents
- It is often difficult to establish whether a file exists for a particular client or not
- There is a constant demand for more space for files; this is very expensive, and in some areas the space is simply not available
- The existing filing areas are poorly organised and overcrowded, so staff resort to poking files into any little corner they can find or to holding files at their desks—this does not promote good work practices and it is certainly not an environment for clients to see
- The filing staff complain of spending a lot of time redistributing banks of files in order to fit in new ones
- The filing staff also complain that they are often given no direction as to what file to place a document on
- There is a high turnover of filing staff—morale seems to be low.

Task 1—(To be attempted now)
Prepare a concise report to management presenting your proposed terms of reference for the study. This should include the objectives and scope of the study, an outline of how you will carry out the study (e.g. how you will gather your data), personnel requirements and a broad timeframe.

Task 2—(To be attempted later—see note on p. 39)
Explain the need for the development of an appropriate records management program for the firm's client records, and discuss the standards, systems and activities that will need to be incorporated in such a program. Your answer should include consideration of electronic as well as paper records management, and of how technology might be used to improve records control within the firm. (Note. Do not discuss the filing equipment for housing the documents if you have already done, or are going to do, the filing equipment case study at the end of Chapter 8.)

Questions

1 What purpose does a written records management policy for an organisation serve? What matters should it cover?

2 Is it preferable for records management costs (including staffing) to be budgeted for within the business units of an organisation or to be managed centrally by a records manager? What are the advantages and disadvantages of the two ways of operating?

3 To gather the background information necessary to complete a successful records management needs analysis, the records manager or consultant must not just collect facts but also understand the culture of the organisation. What does *culture* mean in this context? How can the records manager or consultant develop an insight into how it affects the work practices of the organisation?

4 Implementing a records management program in an organisation may mean introducing significant changes to work practices (e.g. the way staff borrow files, the way they name and store their electronic documents). What strategies might be appropriate for introducing such changes?

5 An organisation planning to implement a records management program will probably either employ a consultant to do an initial needs analysis, or appoint a full-time records manager to the staff. What factors will management need to take into account in making this decision?

Notes

1 A good example is Penn, Pennix & Coulson (1994), Chapters 6 & 7.

2 Flowcharting is a valuable tool for the records manager in analysing information and document flow. Two brief but useful references are Linton (1990), pp. 128–33, and Penn, Pennix & Coulson (1994), pp. 70–74.

3 The techniques for preparing and presenting a cost–benefit analysis are not dealt with in this chapter. For those readers who wish to pursue this topic further, an example of one approach is included in Dymet (1991).

Additional information

The references in this chapter represent a range of approaches to planning a records management program. Most of the textbooks listed cover in some detail the two questions of what makes up a records management program and how to arrive at the most appropriate records management solutions for a particular organisation.

The Australian Standard AS 4390–1996 includes a Model Implementation Plan (Standards Australia 1996, pt. 3, pp. 18–23) which is a valuable guide. It presents a detailed generic structure for developing a records management implementation plan starting with the initial preparation phase, through information collection, analysis, systems design, and implementation. Many of the matters listed in the plan are covered in other chapters of this book.

References

Carlisle, D. 1987, 'Gaining credibility', *Records Management Quarterly*, vol. 21, no. 1, pp. 29–31.

Doukas, M. E. 1987, 'A perspective for IRM-related cost–benefit studies', *Records Management Quarterly*, vol. 21, no. 3, pp. 15–17.

Dymet, B. 1991, 'Cost justification of records management systems', *Informaa*, official newsletter of the Victorian Branch of the RMAA, vol. 24, no. 4, pp. 6–3.

Gordon, K. 1995, 'Diversification of records management in the modern environment', in Records Management Association of Australia, 12th National Convention, Melbourne, 18–21 September 1995, *Redefining Records Management: Conference Papers*, RMAA, pp. 38–48.

Hayes, K. V. 1987, 'Are you too small for records management?', *Records Management Quarterly*, vol. 21, no. 1, pp. 22–28, 44.

Linton, J. E. 1990, *Organising the Office Memory: The Theory and Practice of Records Management*, University of Technology, Sydney, Kuring-gai Campus, Centre for Information Studies Publications, Chapter 3 & pp. 128–33.

Parker, E. A. 1989, 'Developing the program', in P. Emmerson, (ed.) *How to Manage Your Records: A Guide to Effective Practice*, ICSA Publishing, Cambridge.

Penn, I. A., Pennix, G. B. & Coulson, J. 1994, *Records Management Handbook*, 2nd edn, Gower Publishing Co., Aldershot, Hants, Chapters 4–7.

Ricks, B. R. & Gow, K. F. 1988, *Information Resource Management: A Records Systems Approach*, 2nd edn, South-Western Publishing Co., Cincinnati, OH, Chapter 2.

Smith, M. 1986, *Information and Records Management: A Decision Maker's Guide to Systems Planning and Implementation*, Quorum Books, New York, Chapters 8 & 10.

Standards Australia 1996, *Australian Standard AS 4390–1996, Part 3: Strategies*, Homebush, NSW, pp. 18–23.

Wolchak, W. H. 1986, 'Conducting a systems analysis', *Records Management Quarterly*, vol. 20, no. 3, pp. 16–19.

chapter *three*

Corporate recordkeeping requirements in the Australian environment

Overview

The recordkeeping requirements of an organisation are determined largely by business and legal considerations and the regulatory environment in which it operates. An organisation maintains records of its business activities:

- To provide it with the body of information necessary to continue or further develop or revise those activities
- To protect itself in case of legal or other challenges, that is, to enable it to produce evidence to show that it has acted appropriately on a matter and has met its obligations
- To meet the accountability requirements imposed on it by the regulatory environment in which it operates.

The Australian Standard AS 4390–1996 includes a useful definition of accountability in the records management context:

> Accountability—the principle that individuals, organisations and the community are required to account to others for their actions. Organisations and their employees must be able to account to appropriate regulatory authorities, to shareholders or members, and to the public to meet statutory obligations, audit requirements, relevant standards and codes of practice, and community expectations (Standards Australia 1996, pt. 1, p. 6, 4.1).

The Standard places a lot of emphasis on the importance of organisations identifying the accountability requirements to which they are subject and putting into place recordkeeping systems which will ensure those requirements are met.

It is widely acknowledged that the regulatory requirements with which businesses in our society must comply are becoming ever more complex and voluminous. In many cases the steps that must be taken by organisations to ensure they comply with the law involve the setting up of efficient recordkeeping and reporting systems.

The Australian Standard AS 4390–1996 spells out four categories of recordkeeping requirements emanating from external sources; those which are:

(a) Stated explicitly in the legislation, formal directives and other instruments to which an organisation may be subject.

(b) Stated in guidelines by authorities for which an organisation must have due regard; for example, in the reports of Ombudsmen, audit authorities or investigative bodies.

(c) Identified by examining relevant industry standards and best practice, which depend on the nature of the organisation's business.

(d) Identified by finding and analysing less explicit accountability requirements that logically require adequate recordkeeping to meet them. Often this will involve an assessment of the risks associated with not having adequate evidence and by that failing to meet the requirements (Standards Australia 1996, pt. 3, p. 8, 5.6).

This chapter presents an overview of the main categories of recordkeeping requirements relevant to organisations. It focuses particularly on the types of legislation, standards and codes of practice which affect corporate recordkeeping in Australia. Chapter 4 looks at the tools and processes for establishing and documenting the specific recordkeeping requirements of an organisation.

Recordkeeping to meet business operational needs

Organisations create and retain those records which enable them to operate their business.

Management and employees create records to communicate information and to document how they have acted on a matter; they document policy and procedures to facilitate action and ensure consistency in the way matters are handled; they retain records as sources of background information to assist with future planning; they also retain records to use as precedents or models for subsequent action.

The records manager needs to work closely with management in the various business units and functional areas of the organisation to establish the business needs for records—what records need to be created and how long they need to be kept.

The active life of most records for business purposes is very short. For example, records which are created for an activity which takes place on an annual or other regular basis are active at the time they are created, may then be required for reference for the following year's work, and thereafter may be required for occasional reference or not at all.

It has been estimated that approximately 35 per cent of records in organisations could be disposed of immediately after use and 20 per cent need only be retained for the current period of the business activity to which the records relate.[1] In other words, 55 per cent do not need to be retained for a lengthy period for business or in fact any other reasons.

Records as evidence in the legal context

Organisations need to determine what records should be captured and retained as evidence in case of legal and other challenges. That is, they need to identify the records that could be required as evidence of how the organisation conducts its business, the records that could be useful in defending the organisation or in prosecuting claims on the organisation's behalf, the records which document the legal bases of the organisation's operations.

Some records can readily be classified as 'legal' documents, including contracts and agreements, leases, deeds, statutory declarations, signed copies of company accounts and audit reports. Many of these documents are classified as vital records. However it is also important that organisations identify the areas of potential liability and then establish recordkeeping systems to ensure the appropriate records are captured and retained. One area of potential liability that has received a great deal of prominence in recent years is occupational health and safety, and organisations have become very conscious of the need to keep accurate and full records in this area. Another area is the environment, where organisations may need to produce evidence to show that they have acted responsibly in assessing the impact of a project on the environment, and in meeting the requirements of the environmental legislation. Yet another significant area is where professionals such as accountants carry out work on behalf of clients; the risk of being sued by aggrieved clients is quite high and it is essential that they keep detailed records to demonstrate that they have carried out their work properly and according to the standards laid down by the relevant professional body and the requirements specified by the client.

Statutory requirements for recordkeeping

There are several types of legislation of concern to records managers in Australia:

- Legislation which specifies or implies the requirement to create and retain certain records
- Legislation which specifies how long records should be retained
- Legislation which governs the format in which records may be stored if they are to be admissible as evidence in a court of law
- Legislation which affects access to records, including the privacy and freedom of information legislation
- Public records and archives acts which cover disposal of government records.

Legislation affecting recordkeeping in Australia

In Australia there is a whole range of legislation which includes clauses on the creation and retention of records. In many cases the requirements are laid down in vague terms and do not specify exact retention periods. A further complicating factor for the records manager is that where one piece of legislation may specify a particular retention period for a group of records, another piece may specify a different period for the same group of records. In addition, legislation on the same topic may vary in its clauses on records retention and use from state to state, and between federal and state; this creates particular problems for organisations located across more than one state.

For all of these reasons, while the records manager must do the initial investigation of legislative requirements for records creation and retention, he or she should seek advice from other sources in deciding on retention periods. For example, the managers of the human resources, finance and other business units within the organisation may provide useful information; as may the professional and industry associations relevant to the organisation's functions. In situations where legislative requirements are still not clear-cut, is also advisable to seek legal opinion before final decisions are made.

The Australian legislation dealing with records retention is too detailed to be covered in depth here. A valuable reference source in the area is the *Australian Records Retention Manual*. This lists hundreds of records series and retention periods and details the legislation on retention requirements.

The following is a selection of the major legislation affecting recordkeeping in Australia. This legislation is of general applicability to organisations regardless of functional area, although some categories apply to government agencies only. There are also acts and regulations which spell out recordkeeping requirements in specific industry areas, for example, mining, health and transportation.

Statutes of limitations

Two examples are the New South Wales *Limitation Act 1969* and the *Limitation of Actions Act 1958* (Vic).

This legislation sets the period within which litigation can be initiated by an aggrieved party. Litigation can take place six years after cause of action accrues so records need to be kept for long enough to cover the possibility of such litigation. This is the basis of the seven year statutory retention period which applies to a lot of records, but even this retention period will not provide total protection because in some situations the cause of action could still occur after the seven year period is finished.

Tax legislation

The tax legislation is specific in its statement of retention periods. At the time of writing the following retention periods applied. They are spelt out in detail to illustrate how retention periods vary from act to act even within the same general category.

Capital gains tax records (Section 160ZZU, *Income Tax Assessment Act*)	5 years after date of disposal of relevant asset (Exceptions Section 160ZZU(3))
Fringe benefits tax records (employers) Statutory evidentiary documents (Section 123, *Fringe Benefits Tax Assessment Act*)	5 years from assessment date for relevant year to date thereafter of final determination of objection or appeal
Other records that record and explain relevant transactions/acts (Section 132, *Fringe Benefits Tax Assessment Act*)	5 years after completion of the relevant transactions/acts to which they relate

Substantiation records (employees, self-employed) (Section 82KZA, *Income Tax Assessment Act*)	
Car and travel expenses	7 years from the lodgement date of the return for the relevant year to date thereafter of final determination of objection or appeal
Other	3 years 6 months ... (as above)
Taxation records generally, kept for purposes of the *Income Tax Assessment Act* (Section 262A(4), *Income Tax Assessment Act*)	5 years after the date on which the record was prepared or obtained, or the completion of the transactions or acts to which the record relates, whichever is the later, or the date of any extended assessment period (Exceptions Section 262A(5))
Sales tax records (Section 127(1), *Sales Tax Assessment Act* (no. 2))	5 years after completion of the transactions to which they relate
Payroll tax records (Section44(1), *Payroll Tax Act*)	5 years after completion of the transactions to which they relate

The Australian Taxation Office has issued a series of useful booklets covering records retention requirements in various business spheres, and also a booklet specifically devoted to information stored in electronic format.

Corporations legislation

Under the *Corporations Law 1989* (S289(2); Chapter 7, Section 1116), accounting records must be kept for seven years.

Financial institutions legislation

The *Financial Institutions Duty Act 1982* (Vic) requires retention of records for five years after completion of the transaction to which they relate.

As noted previously, it is important to remember that two different pieces of legislation may specify different retention periods for the same group of records. An example of such an occurrence is highlighted in Smith (1990, p. 60). She points out that while the *Financial Institutions Duty Act* requires retention of records for five years, if the organisation were part of a financial institution subject to the *Proceeds of Crimes Act 1987*, it would be necessary to determine whether any of the documents required by the *Financial Institutions Duty Act* are regarded as 'essential customer generated financial transaction documents' (Section 76–77); in which case the *Proceeds of Crimes Act* requires them to be retained in their original format for seven years.

Trade practices legislation

In July 1992 a new Part VA 'Liability of manufacturers and importers for defective goods' was added to the *Trade Practices Act 1974*. Part VA provides that if a corporation supplies a product manufactured by it which has a defect, and as a result of the defect an individual suffers injury, loss or damage, the corporation is liable. In terms of records, the effect of this amendment is that manufacturers, importers and distributors need to keep for eleven years (the period in which action can be initiated) detailed documentation relating to the products they have manufactured and/or sold.[2]

Health legislation

An example of recordkeeping requirements in the health area is the *Health Services (Private Hospitals and Day Procedures Centres) Regulations 1991* (Victoria), made under the *Health Act 1958* and the *Health Services Act 1988*. These regulations, which private hospitals must comply with in order to be registered, set out information on what records must be created and how long they must be retained. They include details of what registers are to be maintained and what types of information are to be contained in a patient record.

Evidence legislation

Evidence legislation exists at both federal and state levels in Australia. Many problems are caused by the variations in the legislation; what is admissible as evidence in a court of law in one state may not be admissible in another. These problems are currently being addressed by moves to implement uniform legislation across Australia.

The evidence legislation has a significant impact on records management in a number of ways, including by defining the format in which documents are admissible as evidence and their manner of production. In common law the *Original Document Rule* states that if a litigant wishes to prove the contents of a document, the original document must be produced (not a copy of it, or a secondary document derived from it, or oral evidence of it). There are in fact many exceptions made to this rule and the courts of law frequently accept copies of documents on the basis that they are the best available evidence. In some states, including Queensland, Victoria and Western Australia, there have been legislative provisions for some years modifying the *Original Document Rule* and allowing for the replacement of paper records with microfilm records. The records must be microfilmed on cameras approved by the relevant government ministers. For example, in Victoria, Section 53Q of the *Evidence Act* deals with the use of microfilm copies in lieu of original documents. It states that if a document is required for longer than three years a negative will suffice for evidential purposes provided it has been filmed with an approved camera as defined within the Act (Section 53C). This means that records managers may choose to retain documents after three years in microfilm format only, provided there is no other legislation which requires that those documents be kept for longer as paper copy. It should be noted that the provisions covering approval of cameras have not kept pace with the technological advances in the area and are not always adhered to.

The admissibility of computer-generated information has been a problem area for many years. With the phenomenal increase in recent years in the volume of information produced electronically, it has become even more important that the issues be tackled comprehensively in Australia.

Evidence legislation in Queensland and Victoria deals specifically with the admissibility of computer-generated information. For example, in Queensland Section (1) 95 and in Victoria Section 55B allow a computer-generated document to be tendered in court, providing that the computer could be shown to have regularly stored and processed information over the period in question; that it was regularly used in the ordinary course of business; that over the period in question it was operating properly and that any problems that arose did not affect the production of the document or its accuracy; and that information in the document was derived from information entered during the normal course of business. However, it is still far from clear cut that a particular computer-generated document will be accepted as evidence. Arguments tend to centre on the validity and accuracy of the information in the document—it may be difficult to prove that a document has not been added to or amended since it was created.

At the time of writing there were significant steps in place to introduce uniform evidence legislation at the federal and state level in a way that recognises the increasing importance of not just records created electronically (e.g. word processed documents) but also records stored electronically (e.g. digital images). South Australia, in its *Evidence Amendment Act 1990*, took a major initiative by allowing a document to be admissible in a court provided it 'accurately reproduces' the contents of the original. The Act allows for an approved process, such as imaging, to be prescribed in the regulations. The Attorney-General's Department in South Australia issued a set of *Image System Compliance Criteria*, 1991; these provide for an approved authority to certify the status of existing image systems at regular intervals.

Most significantly, at the federal level, the Commonwealth *Evidence Act 1995* allows a document to include any paper, material or article on which information is stored, and any copy or duplicate.[3] It will permit a document to be taken to be a copy of another document, even if it is not an exact copy of the document, provided it is identical in all relevant aspects. It abolishes the *Original Document Rule* and sets out the ways in which the contents of a document can be proved. This includes tendering a document where:

> ... the document in question is an article or thing on or in which information is stored in such a way that it cannot be used by the court unless a device is used to retrieve, produce or collate it—tendering a document that was or purports to have been produced by use of the device.[4]

The *Explanatory Memorandum* to the Bill gives the example of computer output or a document produced by an optical laser disk reader.

In addition, the Act allows for such a document to be used in evidence without someone having to attest that the device or process was working correctly when the document was produced and that no mistake was made in its production.

The New South Wales Government worked closely with the Commonwealth Government on the revisions to the evidence legislation and its *Evidence Act 1995* embodies the substance of the revised Commonwealth Act. It is also planned that other states will use the legislation as a model. These changes to the evidence legislation will have a significant impact on records management practices in the long term. They will mean that organisations will be far more confident about choosing to store records in optical or magnetic format only.

In the meantime some legal experts still caution organisations against the practice of destroying the original paper copies of documents which have been transferred to electronic media. They claim there will still be cases where only an original document can demonstrate to a court whether changes have been made to the document. Concerns have been expressed about the stability of information stored on optical disk and the ability to prove the information has not been altered.[5] While it is important to note these cautionary warnings, it is clear that the legislation incorporates the intent to enable organisations to take advantage of the new storage technologies. The Explanatory Memorandum to the Commonwealth evidence legislation includes as its financial impact statement:

> The Bill will permit significant savings in Commonwealth storage costs. Departments and statutory authorities will be able to abandon storage of original documents, after their microfilming or transfer to other modern storage media (for example, optical laser disk), now necessary because of the 'best evidence' rule and diverse state and territory laws relating to documentary evidence (Commonwealth of Australia 1991, p. 3).

Privacy and freedom of information legislation

Neither the Commonwealth *Privacy Act 1988* nor the freedom of information legislation relating to access to government records specify retention periods for records. For example, contrary to the belief of some people, they do not say that records relating to individuals have to be kept indefinitely; the retention of such records is governed by relevant legislation such as long service leave acts and workers' compensation acts.

However, both the privacy and the freedom of information legislation are concerned with the proper management of records so that they can be accessed according to the intent of the legislation.

The *Privacy Act* is chiefly concerned with controlling the way Commonwealth government agencies use information entrusted to them by members of the public. In addition it restricts the use made of information supplied to tax file number recipients and credit reporting agencies and credit providers. There are two main areas of protection under the Act. The first relates to the use of information by Commonwealth agencies and the requirements are set out in the *Information Privacy Principles*, under Section 14 of the Act. These Principles include the requirement that the 'record keepers' ensure that proper safeguards are put into place to protect against loss and unauthorised access and use (Principle 4). They also require that systems be developed which will enable people to establish what information exists about themselves and why it is kept. They include details of the type of information that must be maintained—information about the records, their purpose, how long they are kept, who is entitled to access to the information in them, and how access is to be provided (Principle 5).

The second relates to the use of tax file number information and Section 17 of the Act provides for *Tax File Number Guidelines* to be issued by the Privacy Commissioner. These Guidelines spell out requirements related to the collection, storage, use and security of tax file numbers. They are important not only to organisations which handle tax and related matters on behalf of clients but to all organisations with staff records which include tax file numbers.

Both the privacy and the freedom of information legislation are concerned with the proper management of records so that they can be accessed according to the intent of the legislation

Some states have considered privacy legislation but the only concrete development at the time of writing was the *Privacy and Protection of Data Bill 1994* (NSW). Private enterprise, including those organisations with incentive to intrude on privacy, is not subject to the controls spelt out in the Information Privacy Principles; there are, however, proposals to extend the legislation to cover the private sector in 1997 or 1998. Both the continuing privatisation of government functions and services which handle large volumes of personal information, and the drive to employ more and more sophisticated technologies to process business information, are significantly increasing the risk of intrusions into personal privacy. Advances in cheap computer storage media, smart cards, data matching techniques, visual surveillance equipment, and the integration of computers and communications technology, have all had a major impact on the extent to which personal information can be readily captured. It has become relatively easy for private sector organisations to develop databases of information on individuals (in many cases without the knowledge of those individuals) which can then be used for providing customer lists and online services.

The *Australian Privacy Charter*, launched in 1996, is an acknowledgement that the legislation lags well behind community expectations, and that organisations should be encouraged to develop effective policies and practices on privacy issues. It is discussed further on p. 57.

Freedom of information legislation exists at the Commonwealth level and in each state. It was introduced to extend the right of Australians to obtain access to information in the possession of government. Like the privacy legislation and Privacy Charter, it incorporates the right of people to access information about themselves and the right to obtain corrections of that information if it is misleading or untrue. It also requires governments to make information available about their structure, decision-making processes and records held. Although governments have gradually eroded the ability of people to obtain information under the freedom of information legislation by increasing fees and adding categories of exempt documents, the legislation has still been useful as a tool to promote government accountability.

In the context of people's right to personal privacy and freedom of information, records managers have a significant role in both encouraging their organisations to accept responsibility for developing policies and best practice, and in ensuring the necessary recordkeeping systems and controls are in place to meet the intent of the legislation and the principles.

Legislation governing the disposal of public records

This body of legislation is designed to ensure that public records of continuing value are not destroyed and to provide for the authorised and timely destruction of records of temporary value. The Commonwealth *Archives Act 1983* and its state equivalents regulate the disposal of records in government agencies and spell out the role of Australian Archives and the state bodies in this regard. For example, under Section 55 of Queensland's *Libraries and Archives Act 1988*, state and local government agencies must obtain written permission from the State Archivist before destroying records. Similarly, Victorian state and local government agencies are obliged to obtain disposal authorisation from the Keeper of Public Records in line with procedures established in standards issued under Section 12 of the *Public Records Act 1973*. Some of the archival agencies support this function by:

• Publishing general disposal schedules for certain categories of records
• . Assisting agencies to develop agency specific schedules
• Authorising the destruction of certain identified records on an ad hoc basis, and
• Identifying categories of records which may be destroyed without the need to obtain authorisation.

Other external sources of recordkeeping requirements

In addition to legislation, there are other external sources of authority which determine or influence recordkeeping requirements. These include standards (international and national), codes of practice, and rules and directives. These may be general in applicability or industry-specific. The following section includes some examples of these sources of recordkeeping requirements.

Quality assurance standards

ISO 9000 is a series of international quality assurance standards issued by the International Organisation for Standardisation.[6] They have been adopted by many countries around the world, including Australia (Standards Australia AS 3900 series). These standards provide a framework for businesses in the manufacturing and service industries to develop a quality management system which will ensure they operate with maximum efficiency in meeting their customers' requirements. The system must cover all of the business functions from the original design of the product or service through to the ultimate dispatch. A business can gain certification as a 'Quality Endorsed Company' and can advertise itself as such to promote its competitive position in the market.

To gain certification a business must comply with stringent rules in relation to product quality assurance and the ongoing administration of the quality management system. Adherence to these rules is monitored by independent quality assurance auditors.

Efficient recordkeeping plays a critical role in a quality management system. Firstly, the quality management system must be fully documented in a quality manual, including policies, procedures, organisational charts, and position specifications of those involved in the quality program.

And secondly, there are strict requirements for the control of all information relating to the quality assurance process. Records must be created which demonstrate that the quality management system is operating effectively. The quality manual, or an associated index, must show what records are kept and for how long, where they are stored, and who is responsible for them. The recordkeeping requirements incorporated in the quality assurance standards are discussed further in Chapter 5. An example of how the document and data control provisions might appear in a quality manual is given in Figure 5.1 (see pp. 94–97).

Recordkeeping professionals' standards

The Australian Standard AS 4390–1996 referred to frequently throughout this book, is itself an example of a standard which impacts on the recordkeeping requirements of organisations which adopt its recommendations. It provides guidance to organisations on how to identify and meet their recordkeeping responsibilities. It also provides references to other international and national standards which have an impact on recordkeeping and records management practices.

A good example of a state initiative is in New South Wales where at the time of writing, new state records legislation was being drafted. This legislation will require New South Wales public agencies to manage their records management programs in accordance with standards issued by a newly established State Records Authority. It is intended that these standards will act as benchmarks to assess the adequacy of recordkeeping and records management in agencies.[7]

Professional and industry standards and codes of practice

Professional and industry associations and other similar bodies play a major role in regulating and guiding practice in their respective professions and industries. One of the main ways they do this is through issuing codes of practice and technical and ethical standards.

For example, the Australian Society of Certified Practising Accountants and the Institute of Chartered Accountants in Australia issue a large number of Accounting and Auditing standards. In order to practice in Australia, accountants must belong to one of these bodies. Both bodies have a mandatory code of conduct for members which includes compliance with the Accounting and Auditing Standards.

The Standards include directions on recordkeeping. For example, Auditing Standard AUS 208 sets out specific information on how auditors should document matters which are important in providing evidence to support an audit opinion and to show that an audit was carried out in accordance with the Australian Auditing Standards. Recordkeeping is also explicit or implicit in the requirements on ethical and quality control issues throughout the Standards.

By complying with the Standards when working with their clients' financial information and reporting practices, accountants are bringing to bear professional best practice in recordkeeping not just to their own work but the operations of their clients' businesses as well.

Voluntary codes of practice of general applicability

The *Australian Privacy Charter* is an example of a published code of practice which influences recordkeeping requirements.

The Charter, launched in 1996, has been developed to assist governments and private enterprise to implement best practice principles for protecting privacy.

The Charter includes a range of principles of direct relevance to records managers, including the:

- Need to limit the collection and retention of personal information to the minimum amount and period required for the purpose specified
- Individual's right to know what information is held about them
- Individual's right of access to information about them
- Individual's right to obtain corrections to information about them in cases of error
- Need for security of personal information.

Exercises

1 Locate a piece of Australian legislation in each of the following categories:
   a An Act which specifies a records retention period.
   b An Act which presents the evidence law of an Australian state.
   c An Act which sets out the functions of a particular government archival agency.
      Summarise the main clauses in each of these acts which would affect the development and maintenance of a records retention and disposal plan for any organisation to which the legislation applies.
2 Pick any type of business (e.g. a bank, a medical clinic, a firm of accountants, a car manufacturing company). Investigate and document the main external sources of recordkeeping requirements for that type of business in Australia.

For this exercise it would be helpful to interview relevant personnel working in the business area you have chosen. Managers and professionals, including records managers and archivists, should have an understanding of the role of external sources in determining what records need to be kept by their organisations.

Case study 3.1

The following case study was prepared by Tim Dixon, Director, Australian Privacy Foundation, for presentation at an Information Privacy Best Practice Seminar, 1995. It is based on the Principles set out in the Australian Privacy Charter, and lists under each Principle the questions that need to be addressed when a visual surveillance system is to be installed in a workplace.

Applying the Australian Privacy Charter—visual surveillance in the workplace

The purpose of this case study is not to focus on the issue of visual surveillance, but on how the Privacy Charter might guide an organisation in developing its policies on issues with significant privacy implications.

- Principle 1: Justifications and acceptance
  - Is there adequate justification for installing video cameras in this workplace?
  - What is the problem that we are trying to address?
  - Have alternatives to CCTV (closed circuit television) been considered?
- Principle 2: Consent
  - Will the people affected by the use of this equipment have any choice concerning whether or not CCTV equipment is installed?
  - Will they be able to contribute to determining the locations and operating times of CCTV?
- Principle 3: Accountability
  - Who in this organisation will be responsible and accountable for ensuring that the organisation complies with its policy on the use of this equipment?
  - How will we assess the effectiveness of the visual surveillance equipment?
  - Will cameras be removed after the problem they are intended to address is resolved?
- Principle 4: Observance
  - How will we ensure that the operation of the surveillance system is in accordance with best practice for protecting privacy?
  - How will we deal with breaches of the policy?
- Principle 5: Openness
  - How and when will people be informed about the intentions of the organisation to install a CCTV system?
  - Will they be informed fully about:
    - Why it is being installed
    - What purposes it will be used for
    - When and where it will operate
    - Who will have access to the recordings
    - How the recordings are intended to be used
    - Its effectiveness after an initial test period?
  - Will there be signs indicating the areas which are under surveillance?
- Principle 6: Freedom from surveillance
  - Does this use of CCTV take into account the basic individual right to be free from surveillance?

- — Will the use of CCTV result in the systematic observation and recording of the behaviour and personal communications of employees?
- — Is the surveillance intended to be accessible live or only on tape after an incident has occurred?
- — Are there other less intrusive means of dealing with the same problem?
- — Are there ways in which the use of CCTV can be limited in order to respect privacy?
- Principle 7: Privacy of communications
  - — Is there a danger that the use of this equipment will unintentionally record private conversations?
  - — Are there ways in which this might be avoided?
- Principles 8 and 9: Private space, private communications
  - — Are rights to private space and physical privacy compromised by the use of this equipment?
  - — Are there areas in which cameras should not be placed because of the right to private space?
- Principle 11: Collection limitation
  - — Will CCTV operation be limited only to the specific places in which it is necessary to collect information?
  - — How will CCTV make recordings:
    - – Only when activated
    - – Recording with a 'buffer' (e.g. 1 minute) which is constantly erased
    - – Constant recordings, e.g. time-lapse 24 hour tapes?

  Are there any times of the day in which it will not be necessary to operate the equipment?
- Principle 13: Access and correction
  - — If an accusation about the conduct of an employee arises from the use of the visual surveillance equipment, will individuals have a right to view that recording?
- Principle 14: Security
  - — What measures will be taken to make sure that access to the video recordings is restricted?
  - — What actions will be taken against unauthorised access to video recordings?
- Principle 15: Use and disclosure limitations
  - — Under what circumstances (if any) would this information be disclosed to any outsiders?
  - — How will we respond to requests for the information from third parties who might wish to access the recordings?
- Principle 16: Retention limitation
  - — How quickly will tape recordings be erased?
  - — If the information needs to be stored, for what period of time will it be stored before its erasure?
  - — What practices will ensure its secure storage?
  - — What practices will ensure secure erasure?

Your task

Write a short essay (about 500 words) on what role the records manager should/can play in dealing with the sorts of questions raised in this case study, and how the records manager's responsibilities relate to those of other personnel in the organisation in implementing best information privacy practice.

Questions

1 Occupational health and safety, the environment, and accountancy are identified in the chapter as three areas where the risk of litigation is high and therefore meticulous recordkeeping is essential. What other high-risk areas have received prominence in recent years and what have been the main recordkeeping issues raised?

2 What steps can a records manager in private enterprise take to establish the statutory recordkeeping requirements applying in the industry in which the particular organisation operates?

3 What impact is technology having on the rights of individuals to have information about themselves protected? From your reading of the press and other relevant literature, what do you believe are the trends in personal data collection, data matching and information privacy protection, and what are your predictions for the future?

4 In some organisations the records manager is also the freedom of information officer, that is, the person who processes requests for information made under the freedom of information legislation and manages the procedures and documentation. What are the benefits of combining these two roles?

5 External authorities such as professional and industry associations, often have standards and codes of practice which imply rather than spell out for their members the need to create and retain certain records. What are some examples of how this might occur?

Notes

1 H. L. Lugwia III & M. McDonnell, 1990, quoted in P. W. McDonald, 1994, 'Private enterprise records retention', *Informaa Quarterly*, vol. 10, no. 1, p. 10.

2 For more detailed information, see the *Australian Records Retention Manual* 1995, vol. 2, pp. 21–24.

3 Commonwealth of Australia Parliament, House of Representatives 1991, *Evidence Bill 1991, Explanatory memorandum*, p. 5.

4 Commonwealth of Australia Parliament 1995 *Evidence Act 1995*, Section 48(1)(d).

5 For a summary of some issues of concern expressed by legal experts, see the *Australian Records Retention Manual* 1995, vol. 2, pp. 11–14.

6 ISO 9001 *Quality systems—Model for Quality Assurance in Design, Development, Production, Installation and Servicing;* ISO 9002 *Quality systems—Model for Quality Assurance in Production, Installation, and Servicing;* ISO 9003 *Quality systems—Model for Quality Assurance in Final Inspection and Test;* ISO 9004 *Quality Management and Quality System Elements;* ISO 9004–1 *Part 1: Guidelines.*

7 Further details of this project can be found in 'Records management standards and codes of best practice', 1995, *Informaa Quarterly*, vol. 11, no. 2, p. 39.

Additional information

For those who wish to pursue information on legal requirements relating to the retention and use of records, the main sources of information are of course the acts and regulations themselves. However, references for background information are Howe (1992), *Australian Records Retention Manual*, vol. 2, Roder (1991) and Smith (1990).

The various state archives authorities issue publications setting out the obligations of agencies under the relevant archives legislation; many of these publications are readily available and in some cases can be accessed on the Internet. See Appendix D for some examples of Internet addresses for archives authorities.

There is a wealth of literature on information privacy and freedom of information, including the impact on recordkeeping requirements. The paper by Haines (1994) is an excellent exploration of the impact of technology on privacy, and quotes many interesting examples. Tucker (1992) provides valuable background on information privacy law.

The trend for organisations to seek endorsement under the ISO 9000 quality assurance standards has had a major impact on recordkeeping. There have been a number of books and papers written specifically to help records managers operating in a quality management environment, for example, Brumm (1995) and Weise & Stamoolis (1993).

Other important sources of information on recordkeeping requirements are publications issued by professional and industry bodies which have a role in regulating and guiding practice, including setting and monitoring standards, issuing guidelines and directives, developing statements of best practice, and putting pressure on organisations to be accountable for their actions. Such publications include members' handbooks, also separately published standards, rules and regulations, codes of ethics and professional practice, and annual reports.

References

Australian Records Retention Manual, Records Management R & D, Glen Waverley, Victoria. vol. 1: The Record Retention Programme (reissued periodically); vol. 2: Record Retention Law (reissued annually); vol. 3: Guide to Procedures (including Retention Schedules) (reissued periodically).

Brumm, E. K. 1995, *Managing Records for ISO 9000 Compliance*, ASQC Quality Press, Milwaukee.

Commonwealth of Australia 1991, *Evidence Bill, 1991 Explanatory Memorandum*, p. 3.

Ellis, J. (ed.) 1993, *Keeping Archives*, 2nd edn, Thorpe in association with the Australian Society of Archivists, Sydney.

Haines, J. 1994, 'Invasion of privacy in an age of high technology', in Records Management Association of Australia, 11th National Convention, Adelaide, 11–14 September 1994, *Conference Papers: Secrets and Sources—Records Uses and Abuses in the 1990s*, RMAA, Adelaide, pp. 1–14.

Howe, T. 1992, 'Law and its effects in information management', in Records Management Association of Australia, Victorian Branch, State Seminar, Lorne, *Papers Presented*, 11p (unpaged).

Lang, A. 1994, 'Law & records management: preliminary issues', in *Informaa Quarterly*, vol. 10, no. 4, pp. 15–17.

Pratt, G. 1995, 'Emerging technology—evidentiary issues—the South Australian approach', *Informaa Quarterly*, vol. 11, no. 1, pp. 8–13.

Reynolds, P. 1992, 'The legal risks of inadequate records management', *Informaa Quarterly*, vol. 8, no. 4, pp. 15–18.

Roder, M. 1991, 'Document management and the law', *Informaa Quarterly*, vol. 7, no. 1, pp. 22–28.

Skupsky, D. 1992, 'Destruction of records ... your legal obligations', *Records Management Quarterly*, vol. 26, no. 4, pp. 30, 32, 34, 56.

Smith, H. 1990, 'Legal obligations and liabilities for record keepers', *Informaa Quarterly*, vol. 6, no. 1, pp. 58–63.

Standards Australia. 1996, *Australian Standard AS 4390–1996, Records Management*, Homebush, NSW. Part 1: General, Part 2: Responsibilities, and Part 3: Strategies, all contain information relevant to this Chapter.

Tucker, G. 1992, *Information Privacy Law in Australia*, Longman Professional, Melbourne.

Weise, C. E. & Stamoolis, P. G. 1993, 'ISO 9000: an opportunity for records management professionals', *Records Management Quarterly*, vol. 27, no. 4, pp. 3–8, 10–12.

Wilkinson, V. & Looker, P. 1995, 'Information collection, data matching and privacy—Part 1', *Informaa Quarterly*, vol. 11, no. 2, pp. 26–28.

chapter four

Records appraisal and disposal—strategies and tools

Overview

The need to bring some organisation and method into the disposal of records is often the main incentive, rightly or wrongly, for an organisation to appoint a records manager. The costs and inconvenience of storing ever-increasing quantities of inactive records affect both management and users and eventually reach the point where remedial action is imperative. There is also the fear that if records are cleared out and destroyed on an ad hoc basis whenever space runs out, there may be some that are destroyed inappropriately. Records that are required in the future for operational or legal reasons may be destroyed because a staff member makes an uninformed decision that the organisation can manage without them. Litigation may arise; the organisation may lose a court case and suffer high costs because of lack of supporting evidence. Accountability is becoming an increasingly important issue in our society; organisations must protect themselves against the consequences of inappropriate records destruction.

This chapter uses the definitions of *appraisal* and *disposal* presented in the Australian Standard AS 4390–1996 as the basis for considering these critically important records management functions.

> Appraisal—the process of evaluating business activities to determine which records need to be captured and how long the records need to be kept, to meet business needs, the requirements of organisational accountability and community expectations …

> Disposal—a range of processes associated with implementing appraisal decisions. These include the retention, deletion or destruction of records in or from recordkeeping systems. They may also include the migration or transmission of records between recordkeeping systems, and the transfer of custody or ownership of records (Standards Australia 1996, pt. 1 p. 6).

Records may be destroyed inappropriately

Chapter 3 presents an overview of the type of recordkeeping requirements that may apply to organisations in the Australian environment. This chapter looks at strategies and tools for establishing and documenting the specific recordkeeping requirements of an organisation. It discusses how to determine what records need to be captured into recordkeeping systems as evidence of business activities, how to survey existing records, how to determine retention periods for records, and how to document this information in a disposal schedule.

The increasing trend in organisations to create, use and store information in electronic format has triggered a great deal of debate within the archives and records management profession and reassessment of the traditional approach to appraisal and disposal planning. Some of the existing practices which assume that appraisal and disposal decisions can be made at the end of a record's active life, are no longer considered appropriate. This is because with electronically created, processed and stored information, the appropriate records of business activity may not be created at all if the necessary controls are not built into the electronic systems (both document-based and data-based) in the first place. The types of controls and standards that are needed to ensure electronic records are captured, managed and disposed of in a way that meets business and legal requirements are raised in a number of chapters throughout the book, in particular, Chapters 5, 9 and 10, as well as this chapter.

Reviewing appraisal and disposal practices

Developing effective and well-documented appraisal and disposal practices for its records should be a priority for any organisation. However they are often developed in a piecemeal and ad hoc manner in response to immediate problems such as lack of space to store records or embarrassing litigation where the organisation is unable to produce evidence of particular business transactions.

In reviewing the appraisal and disposal practices of an organisation, the records manager must investigate a number of key issues.

- What records should the organisation be capturing as evidence of its business activities?
- How long do the records need to be retained?
- Where should they be located (in physical and/or electronic format)?
- How well do the existing records and recordkeeping systems fit these requirements and are changes necessary?

The process of investigating and arriving at decisions on each of these issues requires strong senior management support and close cooperation between the records manager and managers in the functional areas concerned. As an example, in developing appraisal and disposal practices for personnel records, the records manager needs to work closely with the personnel manager. In addition the project team may include representatives from other areas of the organisation as users of the personnel records. If the organisation has a legal department, a legal officer may also be on the team to provide advice on legislative requirements and on the potential liability of the organisation if appropriate records are not retained.

Developing a business classification scheme

The first major project for the records manager in reviewing the appraisal and disposal practices of an organisation is to analyse and document the business functions of that organisation in the form of a business classification scheme (if such a scheme does not already exist), and to then use that classification scheme as a framework for identifying, and documenting recordkeeping requirements. It is essential to gain senior management support for the project. This is particularly important in view of the fact that records managers are traditionally seen as custodians of existing records and not as having a role in deciding what records need to be captured in the first place. Records managers need to demonstrate to senior management the relevance and value of their skills in establishing recordkeeping requirements and systems.

The Australian Standard AS 4390–1996 stresses the need to develop a business classification scheme (Standards Australia 1996, pt. 5, p. 5, 6.2.2).

As mentioned in Chapter 2, this business classification scheme is seen to underpin all of the key components of a records management program, including:

- (a) providing linkages between individual records which cumulate to provide a continuous record of activity;
- (b) ensuring records are named in a consistent manner over time;
- (c) assisting in the retrieval of all records relating to a particular activity;
- (d) determining appropriate retention periods for records;
- (e) determining security protection appropriate for sets of records;

(f) allocating user permissions for access to or action on particular groups of records;

(g) distributing responsibility for management of particular sets of records; and

(h) distributing records for action (Standards Australia 1996, pt. 4, pp. 5–6, 7.1).

Suggested steps in classifying the business activities of an organisation (or business unit)

Step 1 Gather sources of information

Assuming that senior management support has been obtained for this project, begin gathering information on the objectives and functions of the organisation and on the terminology commonly used to describe them. This involves reading relevant documentation, for example, mission statements, organisational charts, strategic plans, review documents, annual reports, staff directories, position advertisements, descriptions and specifications. A functional chart may be available to save much work! Interview personnel in the functional areas under review, including both the managers and the staff performing the business activities.

Step 2 Obtain an understanding of the overall mission or objectives of the organisation

The organisation may be able to provide a clear statement of its objectives that is quite adequate for the purpose. If not, derive a set of statements from the documentation which sums up the overall objectives of the organisation, and check these with suitable personnel. The broad mission of a city council might be to run the city efficiently in the interests of all ratepayers and residents. The broad mission of a telephone equipment company might be to manufacture and sell quality products to the benefit of both company shareholders and customers. The broad mission of an adult education college might be to provide education for adults of all ages which will enable them to obtain qualifications and operate in their lives through new insights and a widened understanding of the world.

Step 3 Derive the functions of the organisation by means of which the objectives of the organisation are achieved

From studying the sources and information obtained, derive a set of functions or activities at the broadest possible corporate-wide level by which the organisation's overall mission or objectives are achieved. The functions of the city council might be to undertake city planning and management, provide human services, administer parks, gardens and pools, undertake engineering works, etc. The functions of a telephone equipment company might be the manufacture, wholesaling and repair of products. The functions of a university might be the teaching, assessment and graduation of students across a range of courses and qualifications. In addition to these primary functions of the organisation there are also support functions which are common to the running of all organisations to a greater or lesser extent—examples are maintenance of the organisation's infrastructure—buildings, vehicles, equipment, information technology, etc; human resource management; procurement of supplies for the daily operations of the organisation. These functions should be mutually exclusive of each other.

Step 4   Examine and note the activities at different levels which support each function

Now study the functions in greater detail. What kinds of *activities* support the functions which have been identified? Examine the individual tasks of groups and individuals at this point to obtain a view of activities, sub-activities and sub-sub-activities. These activities should be unique to the functions which they support. Each function may have a large number of different activities at different levels in a hierarchy which support the given function.

Step 5   Examine and note the kinds of transactions undertaken as part of each activity

For some functions it may be appropriate to document activity down to the level of tasks undertaken by each staffing position. Transactions are specific actions which operationalise an activity and usually involve creating an individual record relating to its broader activity—for example, recording an order, or preparing a receipt.

Step 6   Identify processes

While analysing activities and their sub-activities, it is inevitable that many activities will be found which are common across more than one function. Hammer & Stanton (1995) define a process as an activity which cuts across functions, is results oriented, has inputs and outputs, goals and ends, and relates to clients and their needs. Handling complaints, establishing policies, setting up committees, holding meetings, appointing consultants might all be termed 'processes', though this will vary from context to context.

Step 7   Produce a map of functions, activities, processes and transactions

Document the information gathered in a format which maps and describes the functions, processes, activities and transactions—in other words, develop the classification scheme. The degree of detail recorded for each functional area will be largely determined by how critical the particular function is to achieving the goals of the organisation, and how important the recordkeeping is to protecting the organisation in the case of legal or other challenges.

Below, as a rough example, is a small extract from a functional analysis undertaken by the records manager for the City of XYZ.

City of XYZ

Broad mission

To run the city efficiently in the interests of all ratepayers and residents with particular emphasis on quality residents' services, both physical and human; the protection and enhancement of the city's built and natural environments; and the facilitation of sustainable economic development.

Functions

Primary functions

- **Residents' services**—human services; library services; recreation and leisure; arts and cultural activities; the provision and administration of local laws with respect particularly to traffic supervision, animal control and health issues.
- **Built and natural environments**—coastal reserves; parks and gardens; waste management and recycling; drainage; road networks.
- **Economic development**—industry development; planning approvals; commercial centres; regulatory functions; transport strategies; landscape and urban design strategies.

Support functions

- Corporate services—civic facilities and infrastructure; administration; human resource management.

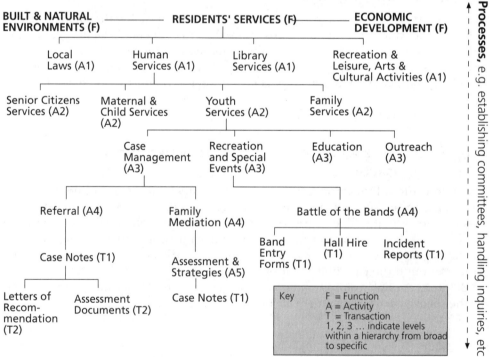

Figure 4.1 Examples of rough hierarchies produced from a functional analysis of the business of the City of XYZ

Advantages and disadvantages of the functional analysis approach

This task of creating a function-based classification aligns the records manager closely with the essential strategic activities of the organisation, and the accountabilities and risk management relating to recordkeeping for evidential purposes; moreover functions are perceived to be more stable over time than the organisational and staffing structures set up to achieve given outcomes. A mapping of organisational structures against these functionally based hierarchies will be helpful in revealing clearly who is responsible for record generation and recordkeeping in relation to each function. It could be argued that a problem with functional analysis is the time it would take in a large and complex organisation to adequately map every function down to its transactional level. Priority may have to be given to certain functions in the short term, with additions to the classification being made on an ongoing basis.

Determining recordkeeping requirements

Having produced the business classification, the determination of recordkeeping requirements may now proceed as follows.

1 Using the information in the business classification as a framework for analysing and documenting recordkeeping requirements:
   a Work closely with the specialists in the various functional areas to identify the information that must be captured to ensure business transactions are adequately documented, including transactions processed by business systems such as financial systems and human resource systems.
   b Investigate the statutory requirements for recordkeeping to which the organisation is subject, and seek legal advice where appropriate.
   c Identify any other external sources of recordkeeping requirements which may impact the organisation, for example, industry and professional codes of practice and standards.
   d Look at the areas of potential liability of the organisation and assess the business risks if particular records are not captured and retained.
   e List the existing **record series** of the organisation (see Figure 4.2 and definition, p. 71). Depending on need, this exercise may be anything from a brief overview to the compilation of a full inventory of the records.
   f Review the adequacy with which existing records meet recordkeeping requirements.
2 Develop systems and procedures to ensure the recordkeeping requirements are met and any gaps in existing recordkeeping practices are filled. (Systems and procedures are discussed in various chapters throughout the book, including Chapters 5, 8 and 9.)
3 Determine how long each record series should be retained.
4 Develop disposal procedures and controls, including a disposal schedule for the organisation's records.

The rest of this chapter looks in more detail at three important processes in records appraisal and disposal mentioned so far—compiling records inventories, determining retention periods, and disposal scheduling. In the context of disposal scheduling, it also looks at the role of the government archival agencies.

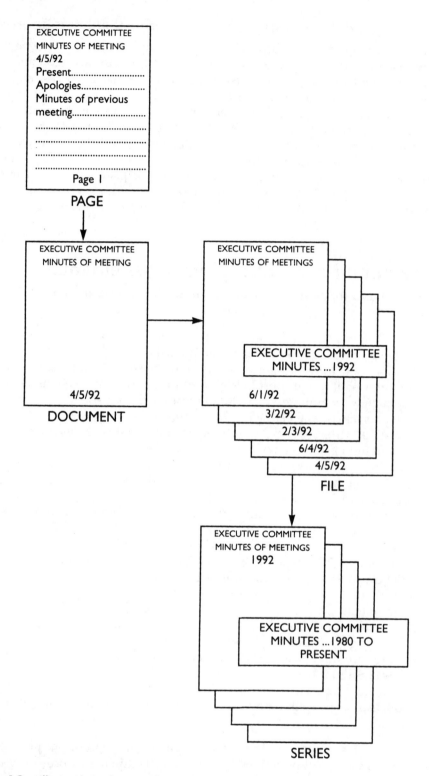

Figure 4.2 Illustration of a record series

Records inventories

In reviewing appraisal and disposal practices, the records manager's primary concern is to pull together information on what records of business activities need to be captured into recordkeeping systems, how long they need to be kept, and where they should be located. In this context, information also needs to be gathered on existing record series to assess how adequately they are already meeting the recordkeeping requirements of the organisation, and to provide background information for developing recordkeeping systems and controls for capturing future records. The level of detail gathered into a records inventory will depend on the use to which the organisation wants to put the information and on the time and resources available.

What is a records inventory?

A records inventory is a summary of records held by an organisation or part of an organisation. It includes all categories of records regardless of whether they are held in central records systems or in individual offices, in paper, microfilm or electronic format. Records inventories are most commonly compiled as part of the planning process for developing records appraisal and disposal practices, but they are also valuable for records management planning in general.

It would be, of course, out of the question to list every individual record held by an organisation or business unit. That is why records are normally listed by series. A record series can be defined as 'a group of identical or related records that are normally used and filed as a unit …' (Robek, Brown & Stephens 1996, p. 585; see Figure 4.2). A record series may consist of one record or thousands or even millions of records.

Records inventories are compiled to pull together information on:

- The purpose and functions of record series
- Where record series are currently stored
- The types of equipment and supplies currently used for storing records
- The age and frequency of access to individual record series
- Current retrieval systems for record series
- The amount of space taken by records
- Current disposal practices.

This information can assist not just with assessing how well the records are meeting the recordkeeping requirements of the organisation, but also with planning a range of records management activities including disposal scheduling and procedures, secondary storage services, vital records protection, and rationalisation of the storage and management of active records.

Compiling a records inventory

The process of gathering information on the records of an organisation is commonly called a records survey. Before a records survey is commenced, decisions have to be made on what information is to be collected and how.

Deciding on information to be collected

Decisions on what information is to be collected must be driven by the purpose or objectives of the survey, namely, why the information is to be collected and what it will be used for. This may seem obvious but experience shows that sometimes organisations spend a great deal of time and resources on collecting information which is never used. This is usually because the objectives are not properly defined and documented in the first place.

The decision to collect detailed information on each record series can certainly only be justified if a good business case can be made to demonstrate that the information is really needed.

When the purpose of the survey has been clearly defined, then the next step is to develop an inventory form which lists the data to be collected for each record series. For example:

- Title of series
- Purpose (why and how created and by whom)
- Format (paper, microfilm, computer files, etc.)
- Description of contents
- Date range
- Quantity (linear feet, number of computer tapes used, etc.)
- Location (e.g. central records section, another organisational unit, a staff member's office, a secondary storage area, a mainframe computer or networked server)
- Description and condition of the storage equipment and supplies
- Frequency of use and usage patterns
- Access restrictions (e.g. for personnel records)
- Description of filing system and any indexes maintained
- Charge-out or tracking systems, if applicable
- Whether current/active or not
- When the records become semi-active and then inactive
- Legal requirements for retention of the records
- Any duplication of the records or information elsewhere in the organisation
- Linkages to other record series
- Whether other records from the same series are stored elsewhere
- Whether the records are vital

For records in electronic business systems there may be additional information to be collected about the context and structure of the records which will make them meaningful and complete as evidence of business activity. (With paper records, such as correspondence, the context and structure can be readily ascertained by studying the documents themselves and other documents on the same and related files.) This additional information may include:

- What system(s) and computer program(s) are used to create the records
- How the records relate to other records in the system(s); which are the primary records of the transactions, which are the security records (e.g. audit trails and backup files), which are the facilitative records (e.g. indexes and statistics)
- The type of information about the records captured by the system(s) (e.g. author/ data entry operator, authoriser of the transaction, receiver, dates and times)
- How the records are accessed and used

- The format in which the records are stored
- What reports are produced and how often
- What back-up copies are made and where stored
- Whether original versions of records are kept or only updated versions.

These are the most common types of data to be collected in a records survey. There may be other information which is specifically required for a particular project. For instance, information on the physical condition of paper records may be sought for a project on the costs of transferring such records to optical disk.

Deciding on methodology
There are only two workable methods for collecting the data.

Questionnaire
Each unit of the organisation is given the task of completing questionnaires covering all the information required for each record series. This method can be successful if there is a high level of commitment to the project, and effective training and ongoing contact between the surveyor and the staff completing the questionnaires. But it has substantial limitations:

- Staff will tend to give priority to their regular and more interesting duties and defer completing the questionnaires. Result—they may never complete them at all or do them in a rushed and inadequate way.
- It is hard to be sure that staff fully understand the terminology. If they don't, they may not give the right answers.
- It does not give the surveyor a real 'feel' for the records and the problems. There is nothing like getting the hands dirty to gain a real understanding.

Sanders (1987) presents a good case study of the use of the questionnaire method. Figure 4.3 is a sample questionnaire form for a records inventory. It includes many of the questions that would be relevant to any records survey; other questions could be added to meet local requirements.

Physical or 'walk thru' inventory
The person conducting the survey 'walks thru' every office, storage area and computer system (including documentation), and gathers all the required information by querying, looking, and measuring, as the questions on the inventory form require. This is a very time consuming method of collecting the data but will certainly get the best possible results.

Figures 4.4 and 4.5 are reproductions of forms developed by W. D. Osburn, a records management consultant, for use with the 'walk thru' method of collecting data. Osburn uses the 'walk thru sheet' for gathering the initial data on each record series; he then uses the 'record volume analysis sheet' (one per record series) to summarise information on volume, location, whether it is vital, whether it has a security rating, how long it is active, semi-active, inactive, whether it has any statutory retention requirements, whether it has any long-term value, and when it can be destroyed. Osburn uses the information he has gathered to analyse the value of the records to the organisation and to prepare a records disposal schedule.

RECORD INVENTORY SHEET

DEPARTMENT
CONTACT NAME   TELEPHONE
DATE

GENERAL DESCRIPTION OF RECORDS
Name of record series (e.g. executive committee meeting minutes) _____

For what purpose are the records created? _____

What information do the records contain? _____

In what format are the records stored? (e.g. A4 paper, cards, computer tape or disk, microfilm) _____

What is the date range of the records? _____

FILING, INDEXING AND USAGE
How are the records filed? (e.g. alphabetic by name, numeric by account no.) _____

Describe the system used to control the records (e.g. register, index) _____

Who refers to the records and how often? (per day, week, month, etc.) _____

STATUS OF RECORDS
Is record series
☐ official record copy   ☐ duplicate   ☐ vital

Is there information in other records which duplicates or summarises information contained in these records?
☐ yes   ☐ no
If yes, describe

Do the records provide evidence of the origins, structure, functions and policies of the organisation?
☐ yes   ☐ no
If yes, explain _____

Do the records have significant value for researchers?
☐ yes   ☐ no
If yes, explain _____

VOLUME AND STORAGE
What is the volume of existing records in linear centimetres?
– active records (i.e. in current use) _____
– inactive records (i.e. not in use) _____
Expected growth rate per month? _____
Where are the records stored? _____

What type of storage is used? (e.g. 4 drawer filing cabinet, mobile shelving) _____

What condition is the storage equipment in?
☐ poor   ☐ fair   ☐ good
What type of filing supplies are used? (e.g. lever arch files, manila folders, diskette boxes) _____

RETENTION INFORMATION
After what period do the records become inactive? _____
After what period are they no longer required for reference? _____
Is the retention of the records affected by any legislation or regulations?
☐ yes   ☐ no
If yes, name the legislation and give the required retention period _____

Are the records needed for external or internal audit purposes?
☐ yes   ☐ no

Figure 4.3   Sample questionnaire for a records inventory

Source: Based on Public Record Office Victoria Form 11B which was developed by the Public Record Office, Victoria for use by agencies when they are seeking approval to have records destroyed

Figure 4.4 Sample analysis sheet for record series

Source: Reproduced with permission of the Records Management Association of Australia, WA Branch

W D OSBURN & ASSOCIATES Consultants in Records Management Microfilm and Archive Systems					
WALK THRU SHEET				Date	
				Sheet No.	
Floor	Div/Dept	Section	Contact		
Equipment Type	Record Description			Volume	

Figure 4.5   Sample form for use with 'walk thru' method

Source: Reproduced with permission of the Records Management Association of Australia, WA Branch

Determining retention periods

Deciding how long records should be retained is an integral part of deciding what records of business activities need to be captured, and of assessing the value of existing records.

Some specific questions that may be asked to determine the retention period for a record series include the following:

- Are the records likely to be needed by the organisation in its current and future operations, and if so, for how long?
- Do the records relate to functions or activities of the organisation which are essential to the mission of that organisation or are even vital to its survival? Or do they relate to support functions or activities which are beneficial to the organisation but not essential?
- Are the records used to support processes or decision making in other parts of the organisation?
- Do they relate to functions or activities which are unique to that organisation? Or to functions or activities which are common across organisations operating in the same area of business?
- Do the records have evidential value in the legal context? Can they serve as evidence of how the organisation conducts its business? What is the likelihood that they could be used in defending the organisation or in prosecuting claims on the organisation's behalf?
- Do the records document the legal bases of the organisation's operations?
- Do they record information which may serve to protect the legal, civic or other rights of the organisation's clients or public?
- Is the information in the records readily available elsewhere?
- Are there audit requirements for the retention of the records?
- Are there statutory requirements for the retention of the records?
- Do the records contain information of ongoing significance for the organisation? For example, are they records which provide information on the origin, functions and policies of the organisation (such as board minutes and policy files)? Will they provide precedents or other background information for the organisation to assist with future planning?
- Do the records have historical significance for researchers? Are they records which document political, social or economic history (e.g. case files of historically significant groups)?

The primary purpose of a record series will be the main determinant of its value, but any secondary purposes also need to be taken into account. The purpose of a record may change from one period of its lifespan to the next. For example, it may be created to support a particular activity of the organisation but then may be retained as a precedent for how to organise that activity in the future. It may be developed for an operational purpose but be kept for its ongoing historical significance. In addition, a record may depend for its access and interpretation on the existence of another record (for example, a record may be part of a chain of records which document a particular business process; or a record series may act as an index or key to another record series). So in determining value, records need to be seen in relation to other records, as part of a system.

For most organisations the main factors in determining retention periods will be the business and legal value of the records and any statutory requirements for retention of the records. The records manager must work closely with other staff in the organisation, and with legal experts looking after the interests of the organisation, to ensure the best decisions are made. In some cases an assessment of business risks may suggest that records should be kept for longer than the statutory retention period. Bearing in mind that usually only a very small percentage of records kept will be used in the future, the risk of not having the information needs to be weighed against the costs of storing it. On the other hand, in some cases an organisation may consider that there is a business risk in actually retaining particular information. It will weigh up the potential losses to which the organisation would be liable if particular records were destroyed against the potential risks and costs of keeping them.

There may be quite lengthy negotiation between the records manager and other staff before agreement is reached on retention periods. There are always people who want to retain records for longer periods 'just in case', and sometimes people who want to get rid of them sooner than is advisable.

When decisions on retention periods have been reached, the records manager should ensure the relevant business unit or functional manager signs off against each record series. This process may be formalised through a **records retention authorisation form** (see Figure 4.6).

RECORDS RETENTION AUTHORISATION			
RECORD TITLE/SERIES			
ORIGINATING DEPARTMENT	CONTACT		PHONE
RETENTION PERIOD			
OFFICE	STORAGE	DESTROY	EFFECTIVE DATE

APPROVALS	SCHEDULE REF	FIRST ENTRY IN SCHEDULE
DEPARTMENTAL MANAGER		YES ☐ NO ☐
FINANCE MANAGER	VITAL RECORD	
CORPORATE	YES ☐	NO ☐

SPECIAL INSTRUCTIONS (including review processes and reasons for revisions)

RECORDS MANAGER SIGNATURE	DATE

Figure 4.6 Sample records retention authorisation form

This form is used for additions and revisions to the master records disposal schedule. It contains the information about the record series gathered during the records survey, the agreed retention period, who approved it, and any review processes.

There are always people who want to retain records for longer periods 'just in case', and sometimes people who want to get rid of them sooner than is advisable

Disposal schedules

A disposal schedule (alternatively called a records retention schedule or disposal authority) is a list of the record series of an organisation with directions for how the records are to be disposed of after their creation and initial use. The schedule spells out how long the records are to be retained, including any that are to be retained indefinitely; it may also include instructions on when records are to be transferred to secondary storage or archives.

There are two main types of schedules; those that are developed by individual organisations specifically for their records and those that are developed and published for use across a particular group of organisations. The latter type chiefly applies to general disposal schedules developed by government archival agencies with a legislative responsibility to ensure the preservation of public records of permanent value. The role of these agencies in retention scheduling is discussed later in this chapter. In addition to published schedules, there are also published guidelines to retention periods; these can be useful so long as any legislative changes that have occurred since the compilation of the guidelines are taken into account. An example of such guidelines covering Australian business records is the *Australian Records Retention Manual* (see Figure 4.7).

RECORD RETENTION SCHEDULES

Record Series No	Record Description	Suggested Retention in Office	Suggested Total Retention (if different)	
FGA.05	GENERAL ACCOUNTING & COSTING REPORTS REQUIRED FOR AUDIT TRAIL AND NOT COVERED BY OTHER SCHEDULES			
FGA.05.1	* Official copy of nominated reports required for 7 years in responsible office.	F+1	F+7	
FGA.05.2	* Official copy of nominated reports required for 10 years in responsible office	F+1	F+10RA	Subject to review and archival selection before destroying
FGA.05.3	* Official copy of nominated permanent reports in responsible office	F+1	F+10P	
FGA.05.9	* Other copies	As long as useful		
FGA.06	GENERAL ACCOUNTING, COSTING & PROFITABILITY REPORTS NOT REQUIRED FOR AUDIT TRAIL	As long as useful		
FGA.07	GENERAL RECONCILIATION RECORDS JOURNALS, LEDGERS & TRAIL BALANCES (not covered by FGL or other schedules.)	F+1	F+7	Number of years
FGA.08	EXPORT ACCOUNTING FILES (if separate from FAR & MAR series)	F+1	F+7	
FGA.09	IMPORT ACCOUNTING FILES (if separate from FAP & PUR files)	F+1	F+7	Fiscal year
FGA.10	INSURANCE RECORDS (see SRG.21)			
FGA.10.1	* Insurance Policy Register	CF+7V	P	Permanent
FGA.10.2	* Insurance Policy Documents (public liability, workers compensation)	T(policy)+7	P	Store in vault conditions
FGA10.3	* Insurance Policy Documents (other than those of FGA.10.2)	T(policy)+7	–	When termination occurs
FGA10.4	* Insurance Claims Register	CF+7	P	Completion of file
FGA10.5	* Insurance Claims Records (public liability, workers compensation)	CP+7	P	Completion of project
FGA10.6	* Insurance Claims Records (other than those of FGA.10.5)	CP+7	–	

Figure 4.7 Sample page from *Australian Records Retention Manual*

Source: *Australian Records Retention Manual*, 1994; Reproduced with permission of Records Management R & D, Glen Waverley, Victoria

Schedules may include three categories of records based on retention period:

- Those with specific retention periods—many transactional record series (such as accounting records) fall into this category.
- Those which are to be kept permanently, including vital records such as board minutes, annual reports, leases, computer system specifications.
- Those which need to be reviewed at a later date. It is important that this category is not used as an excuse for keeping everything; at the same time it is not always possible to predict the ongoing importance of records for an organisation. The subject correspondence files of an organisation often fall into this category.

Purposes of records disposal scheduling

A disposal schedule is the basis of an organisation's records disposal program. It is the tool by which the organisation can achieve the following objectives with efficiency and economy:

- Destroy records which are no longer useful to the organisation or which in fact may be a commercial burden for the organisation to retain.
- Ensure that records that may be required by the organisation for operational or legal purposes are retained for the appropriate period of time.
- Ensure that statutory requirements for the retention of records are met.
- Identify and preserve records which may be of social or historical importance.
- Legitimise destruction of records. This can become particularly important if litigation arises. The disposal schedule can be used to show that the records concerned have been destroyed under an approved policy, rather than being no longer available for reasons no-one can explain.
- Support the maintenance of a vital records protection program.

A disposal schedule also assists the organisation to achieve the following objectives related to space planning, workflow, and the effective use of equipment. It:

- Removes inactive records from expensive office accommodation, and to store them in less costly storage facilities.
- Improves storage and retrieval of active records—current information is easier and quicker to access when it is not mixed up with a lot of outdated information.
- Frees up computer storage media for re-use.
- Plans effectively for present and future growth.
- Plans how to group records in the most appropriate way to facilitate the disposal process—grouping by the date the records are to be transferred to secondary storage, or by probable destruction date can save a lot of time in the long term.

Publishing the records disposal schedule

The schedule is commonly produced in two formats:

- A separate schedule for each business unit of the organisation, covering the records of that business unit
- A master schedule covering all record series.

Record series are commonly listed on the schedule in alphabetical order within the relevant section of the business classification scheme for the organisation. The schedules may list record series title by title, or they may group record series together with a scope note giving guidelines on how to determine retention periods for each record series within the group. The former type of schedule is clearly easier for staff to use but it also involves more work in constant updating.

Even though individual business unit or functional managers have signed off the retention periods for record series, it is still important to ensure the schedule is issued with the authority of the organisation's senior management. The records manager is then protected in the event of any dispute over the destruction of records, provided he or she has abided by the schedule.

In some organisations a retention committee is established consisting of the records manager, business unit or functional representatives, and possibly a legal officer. The role of this committee is not only to reach agreement on retention periods for the initial schedule, but also to ensure that retention periods are reviewed on a periodic basis and that new business functions and activities and their record series are added to the schedule.

The role of archival agencies in authorising disposal

The archival agencies in Australia have a responsibility to ensure that public records of permanent value are identified and preserved. Thus all public records are assessed against broader considerations in addition to their immediate use to the creating or controlling office. Such considerations may include:

- Statutory requirements (e.g. records retention periods)
- Legal, financial and administrative requirements
- Historical significance and value.

Disposal schedules

Scheduling is one of the techniques these archival agencies use to manage the disposal of public records. The schedules are used to:

- Identify permanent records and to indicate when they should be transferred to the relevant archival agency
- Identify temporary records and indicate when they can be destroyed
- Specify custody arrangements to apply to the records pending transfer or destruction, and
- Provide continuing authorisation for destruction of the records.

There are two types of schedules produced:

- General disposal schedules
- Schedules specific to the records of a particular office.

General disposal schedules

These cover records common to a number of public offices (e.g. central government accounting, buildings and services, stores and transport, and personnel records; school records; hospital records; categories of municipal records).

Some examples of general disposal schedules include the following:

- The Queensland State Archives, the Archives Authority of New South Wales, the Public Record Office Victoria, the State Archives of Western Australia have all developed local government schedules.

Finance and Accounting

10 October 1996

Public Record Office Victoria: General Disposal Schedule

Function	Process Description	Disposal Action	Examples of Records
	Note: Finance & Accounting is the process of systematically evaluating an agency's financial transactions.		The following is a list of common examples, it is not an exhaustive list
FINANCE & ACCOUNTING CORPORATE, STRATEGY, PLANNING & REPORTING	**4.1.0** The management of finance & accounting in departments & agencies that operate autonomously, to identify current status & determine future strategy		
	4.1.1 The process that consolidates financial transactions on an annual basis for Corporate reporting purposes	Permanent Transfer to PRO after administrative use is concluded	• Consolidated Annual Reports • Consolidated Financial Statements • Statement of Financial Position • General Ledger
	4.1.2 The process that supports & consolidates financial transactions on a periodic basis (less than annual) superseding those from the previous period. Does not include journals and subsidiary ledgers and cash books (see 4.2.2)	Destroy when administrative use is concluded	• Consolidated Monthly & Quarterly Reports • Consolidated Monthly & Quarterly Financial Statements • Working papers for the preparation of the above • Monthy Accrual Statements

- Normal Administrative Practice should be used with duplicate records, reference copies, print-outs, external publications, circulars.
- This authority covers all records including paper & electronic formats.
- The above schedule is designed around the functions of the Finance and Accounting activity.
- Individual records are noted in the examples of records, however these are examples only, representative of the types of records used to document the function & process.
- Disposal action for all classes is minimum time allowed.

Figure 4.8 Sample page from the *General Disposal Schedule for Common Administrative Records*, Public Record Office Standard (PROS) 96/13, Public Record Office Victoria, October 1996; Reproduced with the permission of the Keeper of Public Records, Victoria

GENERAL DISPOSAL AUTHORITY 20

Records Common to Third Level Agencies: Offices Controlled by State or Regional Offices

Entry	Description of Records	Disposal Action
	SCOPE NOTE	
	GDA 20 generally replaces GDA 12, 12A, 13, 14, 15, 16, and 17 for agencies at the 'third' level of regional structures (see Introduction for further information). However, if any function (for example personnel administration) is carried out autonomously, without reference to a higher level regional or national office, you may need to use a GDA other than GDA 20. Please contact the office to which you are responsible or the Australian Archives for advice.	
1	**ADMINISTRATION**	
	See also Entry 4 — Correspondence and Entry 7 — Records Management	
1.1	Records which document events or information of potential historical and/or research interest including:	**Retain Permanently**
	• records relating to the construction, use, repair or maintenance of historical properties occupied by the office.	
	• unique information relating to the history of the office (e.g. when and why it was established and any significant events concerning the office or its staff)	
	Note: Only records relating to buildings or events of considerable significance should be kept under this entry. Most offices will not have any records in this category. Examples of the types or records which might be covered are: • records relating to the history, construction, maintenance of heritage listed buildings • records relating to a visit to your office by a head of state or similar VIP • records documenting damage or injury caused by a major natural disaster or bombing.	
1.2	Records relating to administrative matters within the office, which *do not* involve liaison with your state or equivalent office	Destroy 5 years after action completed

Figure 4.9 Sample page from *General Disposal Authority 20*, Australian Archives; Reproduced with the permission of Australian Archives

- The Public Record Office in Victoria has issued a *General Disposal Schedule for Common Administrative Records*, May 1987 (re-issued in 1996 with extensive revisions and an new approach which emphasises records sentencing by business function; see Figure 4.8), plus a number of schedules covering specialised areas, such as *General Disposal Schedule for Examination Records*, May 1989. The Archives Authority of New South Wales has also issued a functionally based *General Records Disposal Schedule—Administrative Records*, 1996.
- For Commonwealth records, Australian Archives maintains a set of regularly updated General Disposal Authorities (GDAs), and in addition each agency has a specific authority. The general authorities cover:
  — Finance and accounting records
  — Accommodation, property and works records
  — General administrative records
  — Tender and contract records
  — Asbestos related records
  — Staff and establishment records
  — Records of short-term value that have been copied
  — Records relating to the intelligence function in any Commonwealth agency
  — Also authorities covering records common to state/regional and other offices and overseas posts.

Figures 4.8 and 4.9 show sample pages from general disposal schedules.

Schedules specific to the records of a particular office

The archival agencies work with the public offices concerned to develop schedules which cover the operational records peculiar to those offices. At the Commonwealth level, there are well over 1000 current agency specific authorities.

Ad hoc disposal authorisation

Ad hoc disposal authorisation may be sought for public records not covered by a disposal schedule. Government agencies find this option useful when clearing out backlogs of records and for records in series which are no longer produced and therefore do not warrant inclusion in a schedule. Authorisation may be sought to destroy records, or to transfer them to the archival agency if they have permanent value.

Disposal without authorisation

The destruction of some public records is permitted without authorisation under normal administrative practice (NAP). This includes such items as drafts, spare copies and rough notes. Agencies considering destroying records under this provision would need to check with the relevant archival agency which categories of records are covered.

Electronic records

Some of the archival agencies have a retention policy on electronic records. For example, Australian Archives requires agencies to transfer to it on a regular basis a preservation copy of electronic records of permanent value. It also requires agencies which hold electronic records of permanent value to ensure that the records remain accessible and are migrated with each system upgrade; also that the supporting documentation and software are maintained.

Standards and guidelines

In most cases archival agencies issue, in addition to the schedules, other standards and guidelines on the assessment and disposal of records.

It should be noted that while the legislative authority exercised by the archival agencies may impose restrictions on public offices which may frustrate records managers at times, it should also make it easier to ensure that statutory requirements for records retention are met. Records managers in private enterprise do not have this sort of support. They may find they can obtain advice from professional bodies relevant to their organisation. They should certainly ensure they are familiar with all the relevant legislation affecting the records in their organisation and should seek legal assistance where necessary.

Exercise

Choose four record series from within an organisation with which you are familiar, or from your personal or family records. Using each of the categories of information listed on pp. (72–73), summarise the relevant information on each of the record series.

Case study 4.1

You have just been appointed records manager to a state government agency. The agency has recently come under attack from the Ombudsman for being unable to identify whether requested records exist or not. The Executive Committee decided that practices in the agency should be overhauled.

The agency has approximately 400 staff. Its current areas of business are Children's Services, Women's Services and Mental Health Services. The agency has been in existence since 1950 and has been in the same building since that time.

As a government agency, it has been affected by government reorganisation on several occasions. Originally in 1949, the agency was established to service the needs of children of servicemen killed in action in the Second World War. This function ceased in 1964. The agency then broadened its role to include services for all children in the state. Due to the close link between maternal and child health issues, the agency unofficially found itself dealing with 'Women's Services'. In 1980, it officially took on Women's Services. Due to changes in portfolios, it also briefly had responsibility for Veteran Health Services, however after eight months this was transferred to another agency.

In 1982, due to the abolition of the Mental Health Board, the agency took on the responsibility for Mental Health Services. Since 1988, there have been no further changes.

In your preliminary investigation of the records in the agency, you are made aware of the chronic shortage of space for active records. On inspection of the basement you find two large electrical mobile shelving units occupying almost an entire floor. Boxes of files are stacked on the shelving and along the walls of the basement. The compactus aisles are littered with rubbish, overturned boxes and spilt files. There is broken shelving and other equipment tossed against the walls. None of the boxes are labelled.

A quick look at the contents of several of the boxes has provided the following analysis:

- Case files dating 1959–1963, 500 boxes
- Complaints correspondence to the Minister dating 1950–1968, 40 boxes
- Executive meetings, minutes and background papers, 1950–1988, 80 boxes
- Personnel records, 1970–1979, 50 boxes
- Documents relating to the transfer of Veteran Health Services to the agency, 1980, 2 boxes
- Invoices for equipment and supplies for 1950–1990, 200 boxes.

You establish from discussions with the records staff that there is no agency-specific records disposal schedule.

Your task

Prepare an action plan in the following format for the Director of Administration for the proper disposal of these records.

1 List the steps that will be necessary to ensure that the best retention and disposal decisions are made.
2 Make a copy of Figure 4.10 and use it to present recommendations for the disposal of the records.

Case study 4.2

You are a records management consultant who has been hired by a medium-sized motor accessories manufacturing company to carry out a feasibility study on developing an electronic system for managing the company's extensive technical documentation. On a recent overseas trip the Managing Director visited another motor accessories company and was shown such a system and now feels this is probably the way to go. You are asked to investigate the relative advantages and disadvantages of continuing to distribute the documentation in paper format, or converting across to a fully electronic system, or a combination of the two.

Currently, the company's technical information (technical manuals and reports, specifications, laboratory notes, drawings, product sheets, working papers, etc.) is all held in paper format by the staff who work with it the most. These staff have all devised their own ways of storing, registering and retrieving the documentation. In many cases out-of-date information is held along with the current information. Only the staff who have prepared the documentation have access to it in electronic format.

After initial discussions with senior management and with each business unit head, you decide that a crucial step in the study is to carry out a survey of the company's technical documentation. You plan to use a questionnaire to gather your data.

Your tasks

1 Prepare a memo for senior management to send to all staff who will be affected by the survey, seeking their cooperation. Explain to them the reason for the survey, briefly what they will be expected to do, and an overall timeframe.
2 Design a questionnaire for the survey including all the categories of information you wish to gather.

| DISPOSAL EXERCISE | | | DISPOSAL ACTION | |
DESCRIPTION OF RECORDS	PERIOD COVERED	Status of records (e.g. inactive)	Retention and disposal recommendations	Basis of recommendations

Figure 4.10 Form for presentation of disposal recommendations

1 A records manager in a manufacturing company needs to establish and document the recordkeeping requirements for the company sales function. How will he/she set about establishing those requirements? What steps should be taken?

2 What criteria should be taken into account in deciding whether a record series is of sufficient value to justify the cost of retaining it?

3 What information should be gathered in order to determine how long a record series needs to be kept to meet business operational requirements?

4 What strategies might be adopted to ensure the disposal schedule of an organisation is kept up-to-date?

5 Why is assessing the value of electronic records more complex than paper records?

Additional information

Records appraisal and disposal is dealt with extensively in the literature of both records and archives management, and it is a topic which is receiving increasing attention as the problems associated with the management of electronic records are becoming more widely recognised.

The references listed for this chapter fall into fairly distinct categories. Firstly, there are those which present an overview of the topic, such as Linton (1990, Chapter 11), Osburn (1989), Parker & Emmerson (1989, Chapter 4), Penn, Pennix & Coulson (1994, Chapters 8 & 9) and Ricks & Gow (1988, Chapter 3). Some of these sources, in particular Parker & Emmerson, and Penn, Pennix & Coulson, give more attention to appraising records for their archival value than do the others and are useful to readers who wish to follow up this aspect. Australian sources which present the topic from the archivist's perspective are Ellis (1993, Chapter 6), Iacovino (1993) and also various articles in the journal *Archives and Manuscripts*.

There is a growing body of literature on the management of electronic records; references of particular relevance to this chapter include Hedstrom (1993), O'Shea (1994), Parer & Terry (1993), Picot (1995), Reed & Roberts (1991), and Theodore (1991).

Readers needing further information on the roles and operations of the archival agencies in relation to records retention and use should contact the relevant agency. They all publish information on their statutory obligations and issue standards and guidelines on various aspects of records retention and disposal.

Further information on the benefits of records inventories and the processes involved in compiling them can be found in most of the standard textbooks on records management, such as Robek, Brown & Stephens (1996, Chapters 2 & 3). There are also a number of useful case studies in the journal literature, such as Sanders (1987).

References

Archives Authority of New South Wales 1993, *Records Scheduling and Disposal Handbook: Guidelines on How to Write and Implement a Disposal Schedule*, Sydney (Standards and Guidelines no. 2).

Australian Records Retention Manual, Records Management R & D, Glen Waverley, Victoria. Vol. 1: *The Record Retention Programme* (reissued periodically); vol. 2: *Record Retention Law* (reissued annually); vol. 3: *Guide to Procedures* (including Retention Schedules) (reissued periodically).

Diers, F. V. 1992, 'The bankruptcy of records retention schedules', *Records Management Quarterly*, vol. 26, no. 2, pp. 3–4, 6–8, 10.

Ellis, J. (ed.) 1993, *Keeping Archives*, 2nd edn, Thorpe in association with the Australian Society of Archivists, Sydney, Chapter 6.

Ellis, S. & Stuckey, S. 1994, 'Australian Archives' approach to preserving long-term access to the Commonwealth's electronic records', in *Playing for Keeps: the Proceedings of an Electronic Records Management Conference*, Canberra, 8–10 November 1994, the Authors and the Commonwealth of Australia, pp. 113–32.

Gannon, A. 1992, 'Know your merchandise: the records management inventory', *Records Management Quarterly*, vol. 26, no. 2, pp. 12–19.

Hammer, M. & Stanton, S. A. 1995, *The Engineering Evolution—a Handbook*, Harper Business, Sydney.

Hedstrom, M. (ed.) 1993, *Electronic Records Management Program Strategies*, Archives & Museum Informatics, Pittsburgh (Technical Report no. 18). Particularly papers by D. Parer, pp. 30–37, and D. Bearman & M. Hedstrom, pp. 82–98.

Iacovino, L. 1993, 'Accountability for the disposal of Commonwealth records and the preservation of its archival resources', in S. McKemmish & F. Upward (eds), *Archival Documents: Providing Accountability through Recordkeeping*, Ancora Press, Melbourne, pp. 55–97.

Linton, J. E. 1990, *Organising the Office Memory: The Theory and Practice of Records Management*, University of Technology, Sydney, Kuring-gai Campus, Centre for Information Studies Publications, Chapter 11.

Osburn, W. D. 1989, 'The power of a records retention programme', in International Records Management Council in association with the Records Management Association of Australia, 2nd International Congress, Perth, 11–14 December, *Papers Presented*, Promaco Conventions for the RMAA, Perth, pp. 95–105.

O'Shea, G. 1994, 'The medium is not the message: appraisal of electronic records by Australian Archives', *Archives and Manuscripts*, vol. 22, no. 1, pp. 68–92.

Parer, D. & Terry, R. (eds) 1993, *Managing Electronic Records: Papers from a Workshop on Managing Electronic Records of Archival Value*, Sydney, 30 October 1992, organised by the Electronic Records Committee of the Australian Council of Archives.

Parker, E. A. & Emmerson, P. 1989, 'Establishing retention control', in P. Emmerson (ed.), *How to Manage Your Records: A Guide to Effective Practice*, ISCA Publishing, Cambridge, Chapter 4.

Penn, I. A., Pennix, G.B. & Coulson, J. 1994, *Records Management Handbook*, 2nd edn, Gower Publishing Co., Aldershot, Hants, Chapters 8 & 9.

Picot, A. 1991, 'Appraisal of electronic media', in Records Management Association of Australia, Victorian Branch, 1991 State Conference, Melbourne, 11–12 April, *Managing Records: Strategies for Records Managers and Archivists into the 1990s*, Longman Professional, Melbourne.

Picot, A. 1995, 'From "search and destroy" to "design and dispose"—the interventionist records manager', in Records Management Association of Australia, 12th National Convention, Melbourne, 18–21 September 1995, *Redefining Records Management*, RMAA, Melbourne, pp. 56–63.

Poynton, T. 1992, 'Get active or get archived', *Informaa Quarterly*, vol. 8, no. 3, pp. 26–32.

Reed, B. & Roberts, D. (eds) 1991, *Keeping Data: Papers from a Workshop on Appraising Computer-Based Records*, Australian Council of Archives and Australian Society of Archivists, Sydney.

Ricks, B. R. & Gow, K. F. 1988, *Information Resource Management: A Records Systems Approach*, 2nd edn, South-Western Publishing Co., Cincinnati, OH, Chapter 3.

Robek, M. F., Brown, G. F. & Stephens, D.O. 1996, *Information and Records Management*, 4th edn, Glencoe/McGraw-Hill, New York, Chapters 2 & 3.

Sanders, R. L. 1987, 'Records inventories and scheduling for small organisations: a case study', *Records Management Quarterly*, vol. 21, no. 3, p. 2.

Saul, L. 1988, 'Records disposal—towards a new methodology', *Informaa Quarterly*, vol. 4, no. 4, pp. 21–2, 27–37.

Smith, M. 1986, *Information and Records Management: A Decision Maker's Guide to Systems Planning and Implementation*, Quorum Books, New York, Chapter 9.

Standards Australia 1996, *Australian Standard AS 4390–1996: Records Management*, Homebush, NSW, Part 4: Control, pp. 5–9, 7; Part 5: Appraisal and Disposal.

Stephens, D. O. 1988, 'Making records retention decisions: practical and theoretical considerations', *Records Management Quarterly*, vol. 22, no. 1, pp. 3–7.

Theodore, C. 1991, 'Electronic recordkeeping in the MMBW', *Informaa Quarterly*, vol. 7, no. 3, pp. 51–58.

chapter five

Creating and capturing full and accurate records

Overview

To implement an effective recordkeeping strategy, organisations must develop systems and practices which will enable them to capture **full and accurate records** of their business activities. These systems and practices should also ensure that the records:

- Can be readily retrieved when needed
- Can be readily disseminated to those who need the information
- Meet security requirements
- Are retained for the appropriate period of time.

  Additional goals of a recordkeeping strategy are as follows:

- To control the volume of information being produced. The more information that managers need to sift through and assimilate, the more cumbersome the decision-making process becomes.
- To improve the cost effectiveness of information processing.
- To control the standard of presentation of information. The standard of presentation affects not just the efficiency with which staff can assimilate information but also the image that the organisation projects to its clients or customers.
- To ensure information is timely.
- To minimise the duplication of information (e.g. production of multiple photocopies of documents for distribution).
- To ensure uniform procedures for records processing. Clearly defined procedures and rules improve performance at all stages—creation, retrieval, use, and maintenance.
- To control record sizes and media types. Use of different paper sizes can introduce extra costs in storage equipment and in reprographic processes. The use of different media types such as microfiche, roll film, computer tape and disk, means increased costs in storage equipment and systems. Some variations in record sizes and media types may be necessary but they should be properly managed.[1]

To achieve these goals and depending on business needs, a range of processes should be applied to the records. For example, as a general rule, they should be registered, classified and indexed, linked (physically and/or electronically) to other records related to the same business activity, stored in a suitable media and location, made accessible to those with a need to know, secured from those who should not have access to them, and tracked so that their location is known at any point in time. In addition, organisations need to develop processes to ensure that the records themselves display the characteristics which will make them reliable evidence of business activity.

This chapter focuses on the characteristics of full and accurate records, and the business rules and procedures which organisations may implement to ensure their records display those characteristics. Other chapters deal with some of the other processes. In particular, Chapters 6 and 7 deal with classification, indexing, and thesaurus construction, and Chapters 8 and 9 deal with registration and tracking and associated systems and practices.

Implementing recordkeeping strategies in an age of transition

To some extent the very rapid and diverse range of developments in computer and communications technology in recent decades, while bringing many benefits to organisations, has also made the task of maintaining complete and accurate evidence of their business activities more difficult. The majority of business records are now produced electronically. But they are likely to be produced on a range of systems and may be stored on a range of media, including paper. They are also easily copied and transferred from one medium to another, so different versions of records may be stored on different media and in different locations (e.g. on a paper file, in an online directory or folder, or in an archives database on tape). Consequently, organisations must develop strategies to manage records across media and systems, using business rules, operating procedures and other controls which take into account the special characteristics of the different media and systems.

There is no doubt that organisations (both government and private sector ones) are in a state of transition from the use of paper to dependency on electronic storage. Many medium to large organisations have been investigating for some time whether they should store their internal documents electronically and not treat paper copies as the primary records, also whether they should convert incoming paper documents to electronic formats, and whether they should seek to receive information from their customers in electronic format. As more organisations implement electronic document management systems (discussed in Chapter 9), the option of storing a lot of their information electronically will become more attractive. In the meantime, while the range of formats and media in which records may be created and disseminated keeps diversifying, so the complexity of implementing business rules and controls grow. On the positive side, while more and more functions are being performed on the desktop (i.e. on employees' personal computers), there is an increasing recognition in organisations of the need for rules and controls, and a willingness to invest time and money in strategies to implement them.

Characteristics of full and accurate records and strategies for capturing them

Part 3 of the Australian Standard AS 4390–1996 lists a number of general requirements for records related to their useability and then proceeds to specify the essential characteristics which make records full and accurate.[2] The rest of the chapter takes each characteristic in turn, reproducing in full the relevant clauses of the Standard (Standards Australia 1996, pt. 3, pp. 6–7, 5.3) and using them as the basis for discussing the types of business rules, operating procedures and other controls that organisations may implement to ensure their records display those characteristics. (The role of records management software in capturing full and accurate records is discussed in Chapter 9.)

Records must be compliant

Compliant Records must comply with the recordkeeping requirements arising from the regulatory and accountability environment in which the organisation operates. Thus, the organisation should be aware, at the corporate and program level, of the accountability requirements that bear upon it and how they affect recordkeeping. Employees must understand how they are affected.

Once recordkeeping requirements for each of the business functions of the organisation have been identified, rules and procedures for compliance must be built into the business processes for those functions.

Take for example, the *Income Tax Assessment Act 1936* (Commonwealth). Section 262A of the Act requires:

- A person carrying on a business to keep records;
- The records must record and explain all transactions and other acts engaged in by the person which are relevant for the purposes of the ITAA;
- The records must include any documents relevant for ascertaining the person's income and expenditure;
- They must be kept in writing in the English language, or in a manner where they can be easily converted into English;
- They must enable a person's tax liability to be readily ascertained;
- They must be kept for five years after the records were prepared or obtained (or the transaction or act to which the records relate was completed).[3]

The Australian Taxation Office issues published information to further explain the requirements, including the media in which taxation records may be stored. Business rules and procedures for ensuring compliance with taxation legislation requirements may be implemented in a number of ways, for example:

- Rules and procedures covering what records must be created, who is responsible, and how the records must be created, filed and maintained, may be set out in a practice manual (or section of a manual) which covers all matters relating to the processing of taxation requirements.
- A sign-off routine may be utilised whereby each step in the processing of taxation requirements, including records creation, is checked for completion and signed off by a nominated officer.
- The retention periods specified in the taxation legislation and other regulatory documents or codes of practice should be documented in the records disposal schedule of the organisation.

- System software such as workflow may be implemented to automate compliance; here the process of generating a particular record is built into a pre-defined workflow. (Workflow is discussed in Chapter 10.)

Organisations which are quality endorsed under the International Organisation for Standardisation's ISO 9000 series of quality assurance standards (Standards Australia AS 3900 series) present another example of where rules and procedures must be developed to ensure compliance with recordkeeping requirements. In this case the recordkeeping requirements are set out in the standards and monitored through an external audit process. The quality assurance standards as sources of recordkeeping requirements are discussed briefly in Chapter 3, however it is useful to reiterate the key points in the context of this chapter.

The quality standards require that all the elements and provisions to support the quality system of an organisation must be documented in the form of policies and procedures. A quality manual must be developed which describes or makes reference to the quality system procedures, including the procedures for document and data control. The manual must be controlled and must incorporate an approved process for revisions and additions.

The quality standards also require that quality records be maintained to demonstrate conformance to specified requirements and effective operation of the quality system. The organisation must document the procedures for the control of these records, including their identification, collection, indexing, access, filing, storage, maintenance, and disposition. The records themselves must be legible, dated (including revision dates), clean, readily identifiable, retrievable, and protected from environmental damage.

All of the characteristics of records listed in the Australian Standard AS 4390–1996 are important in the quality environment and the development of rules and procedures to achieve those characteristics are part of the quality process. Figure 5.1 is an extract from a quality manual developed for an Australian business.

XYZ Company Quality Manual

Document and Data Control Section

Purpose: This Section outlines the policies and methods by which all documents and data are controlled.

1 General provisions
- 1.1 All documents created for distribution shall bear the company's logo and relevant business unit branding
- 1.2 All documents shall be concise and grammatically correct
- 1.3 Documents which have visible signs of deterioration or other activity which may detract from the professional image the company wishes to maintain, will either be reprinted or repaired
- 1.4 Draft documentation will not be retained following the release of the next version, unless the customer has received a copy.

2 Electronic documentation
- 2.1 Electronic documents shall be created using the company's Document Style Guidelines. The Central IT Group is responsible for ensuring that templates based on these guidelines are available.

2.2 They shall be named according to the company's Document Naming Standard.

2.3 They shall be stored on the appropriate group server in the structure provided by the Group IT Coordinator [following the path principle: Customer: Activity: Document].

3 Paper-based documentation

3.1 A printed copy of final versions of all documentation will be retained.

3.2 The company will provide appropriate locations (onsite and offsite) for preservation and storage of paper-based documentation.

3.3 Access to the Records Office will be controlled. Files will not be issued outside the relevant business unit without the authorisation of a manager.

3.4 The company will provide an electronic catalogue/index to paper-based documentation in onsite and offsite storage.

4 Packaging

4.1 The company will provide packaging techniques as appropriate to the deliverable.

4.2 Due care will be taken in delivering products to customers' premises and only reputable and professional delivery agents will be employed for this purpose.

4.3 The company will provide file covers to store all working documentation. Each file is identifiable by a unique barcode. All necessary precautions will be taken to protect documents and files from loss, destruction, unauthorised access, which may introduce undetermined risk elements or media exposure. File types are:

Type	Purpose	Location	Records
File types are listed in this column	Summary of why and when particular file types are created and what type of documents are filed on them	Information on where files are stored at the various stages throughout their existence	Sets out the role of the Records Office in managing the files

5 Document types

- The following table lists the main document types created by the company and distinguishes between those which are vital and non-vital to the particular business activity.

Document type	Description	File location	Status	Action
Document types are listed in this column (e.g. proposals, reports, correspondence about particular jobs for customers, contracts, invoices, filenotes, drafts)	Brief description of document types, including their purpose, whether the original signed copy should be on file, etc.	Information on what type of file the documents are held on	The status of documents is given here, e.g. vital and non-vital classifications	Action to be taken at the completion of an activity, e.g. retain on file, destroy, transfer to another file

6 Lifespan of files

   6.1 Minimum retention periods are set by the company and ratified by the Managing Director. Changes to retention periods shall be based on considerations such as legal requirements, customer needs, risk considerations, and space availability.

   6.2 For each file type (paper and electronic), there shall be in place a system of file review, transfer to secondary storage, and destruction as follows:

Stage (i.e. active, inactive, destruction)	Description	Retention period	Location	Retrieval process	Authorisation for next move (i.e. from office to storage to destruction)
Information on each file type is presented in these columns					

7 Quality system documentation

7.1 A register/index of controlled documents shall be maintained by the Quality Management Representative. These records are retained to demonstrate conformance to the quality system. Details to be recorded about each document include:

- document reference
- document description
- effective date of document
- document authority (release notes and authorisation)
- details of version changes.

7.2 Obsolete documents shall be removed from the system or noted as 'reference only' or 'superseded'.

7.3 Access to all pertinent information shall be provided for the review and approval of document changes if the originator is unavailable.

7.4 Records supporting the quality system:

Document	Description	Controlled by	Authorised by	Status	Expiry date/ destruction
Information on each document is presented in these columns					

8 Data systems security

8.1 Access to the following systems is determined by passwords:

- file servers
- electronic mail
- customer information system
- practice management system
- records management system
- quality manual
- telephone services
- Internet services.

Provision of access to all systems is authorised by a senior manager and actioned by the relevant Group IT Coordinator. Access to all systems will be terminated immediately a staff member leaves the employ of the company unless contractual arrangements are made and copies of instructions are passed from the senior manager.

8.2 Passwords should be changed frequently and should not be on or near computers that provide access to any of the systems noted above. This is the individual staff member's responsibility.

Figure 5.1 Sample document and data provisions in a quality manual

Records must be adequate

Adequate Records should be adequate for the purposes for which they are kept. Thus, a major initiative will be extensively documented, while a routine administrative action can be documented with an identifiable minimum of information. There should be adequate evidence of the conduct of business activity to be able to account for that conduct.

Rules and procedures at both the corporate and business function level need to be developed to control the amount of detail that is recorded for particular activities and transactions. Practice manuals or other procedural documentation should spell out the steps involved in each activity, including the points at which documentation needs to be prepared, its purpose, audience and format. This type of approach ensures the right type and amount of documentation are created to form the necessary evidence to show how the business has conducted its activities.

Records must be complete and meaningful

Complete A record must contain not only the content, but also the structural and contextual information necessary to document a transaction, as follows:
(A) The *structure* of a record, that is, its physical format (if it has one) and the relationships between the data elements comprising the record, should remain intact.
(B) The *context* in which the record was created and used within business should be apparent in the record (including the business process which the transaction is part of, and the participants in the transaction).

Meaningful The contextual linkages of records must carry necessary information to correctly understand the transactions that created and used them. It should be possible to identify a record within the context of broader business activities and functions. The links between records which document a sequence of activities should be maintained. The date (and the time, if necessary) of a transaction should always be part of the record.

As far as possible the collection of the structural and contextual information about records (metadata) should be automated through system controls. For example, systems may capture history details such as document creator, creation and modification dates, identification of who has copied, modified and even viewed documents, version numbers and dates. They may also capture, through links to other systems, information on the positions and responsibilities of the employees working on particular documents, and information on the business activity or transaction which led to the generation of the documents. For example, a useful solution which some organisations have adopted is to link their records management system to their human resource system; this enables them to provide direct access from the records management system to information on document creators and other participants in a business activity (position in the organisation, role in the business activity, previous projects, skills, qualifications, etc.). Another useful link that may be made is between a records management system and a customer database which documents information such as customer details, work done for customers, contracts and billings. With this link, documents can be viewed in the context of the relationship between the organisation and the activity which led to their creation.

There are other tools which can be used to facilitate the capture of complete and meaningful records but which require more manual input from document creators and adherence to rules and procedures.

Forms

For many business activities, forms play a critical role in capturing complete and accurate records of transactions.

Technology is revolutionising the way organisations produce, disseminate and use forms. The use of online forms is growing rapidly as a way of speeding up information collection, reducing data entry workloads, reducing the volume of paper that needs to be stored, and streamlining information processing in general. Improved accuracy is being achieved by structuring forms so that questions must be answered in a set order, certain fields are made mandatory, and defaults can be supplied from files of common data for particular individuals or groups completing forms.

Information on the management of forms is provided in Appendix E.

Profiling

When creating a document through a document management system or a word processing system, the document creator may be presented with a profile screen where essential information must be provided in accordance with the organisation's business rules. Required fields may include document name, document type, a classification which links the document to other documents, indexing terms, a retention date for online access, a destruction date according to a disposal schedule, the name of the manager for the activity. Defaults may be set for groups of documents relating to a business activity, thus making the task of completing the profile screen easier. (Document management systems are discussed in more detail in Chapter 9.)

Document style guidelines

Document style guidelines are generally prepared and adopted by organisations for their word processed documents, however they may be developed for other types of documents as well. They are designed to ensure consistency in the way information is presented to the target audience, both external and internal, and to help ensure all the necessary structural and contextual information is captured.

Document style guidelines may include information on styles and fonts to be used within the word processing system and may also include rules on grammar, punctuation, document naming conventions and addressing protocols.

The style should be disseminated to staff as an inclusion in a general office procedures manual, or it may be issued as a separate document or part of a correspondence manual. Any staff orientation program should include a segment on the importance of using the style.

Document layout and style
Use of logo
Addressing
Salutations
Drafts
Headings
Graphics
Page numbering
Justification
Paragraph format
Signing
Tables
Fonts
Borders
Page numbering

Document types and use of templates
Letter
Memorandum
Bill/invoice
File note
Report

Fax
Meeting agenda
Minutes

Grammar and punctuation
Punctuation
Dates
Addresses
Proper names
Quotations
Abbreviations
Ellipsis marks
Parentheses and brackets
Ampersands
Numerals
Prefixes
Capitalisation
Preferred phrases
Active versus passive
Word usage

Document naming standards

Correct editing of documents

Figure 5.2   Sample topics for a document style handbook

Training programs for document creators on the use of the document style guidelines may also include training in business writing skills.

The ability of document creators to communicate the appropriate information in the appropriate way is critical to successful business transactions and also to ensuring records are complete and meaningful. For many people poor writing skills are a major barrier to promotion; for others who have reached management level, poor writing skills then become a burden for the organisation. Opportunities for improvement should be presented in a non-threatening way through techniques such as workshops and individualised instructional programs. There should be structured follow-up with individual staff members to ensure results are being achieved.

Poor writing skills are a burden to an organisation

Templates

Templates support document style guidelines and make document creation easier and consistent. Templates may be provided for all major types of documents produced within an organisation (e.g. letters, invoices, facsimiles, memoranda, file notes, agenda, minutes, reports). Business applications such as word processing and document management systems can be configured so that users must select a template in order to create a document.

Figure 5.3 shows how a sample letter template might be presented in a document style handbook.

Key points

Styles used

[Company letterhead – logo, address details, telephone and fax number, etc.]

1 February 1997 ②

Ms P Cooktown
General Manager

open ☞
punctuation

ABC Carpet Limited ②
203 Hand Street
MELBOURNE VIC 3000

① Our ref   Document name

① Contact   Peter Johns, 9zzz zzzz

① Your ref   ABC-Doc143.97

① *ref/contact*

Dear Ms Cooktown ②

Proposed visit of carpet importer ③

Capital ☞
first word only

I am writing in response to your request to bring a visiting carpet importer from Britain to see us on Friday 14 February 1997. We would be delighted to give you and your visitor a tour of our factory and hope you will also join us for a light lunch. ④

no ☞
justification

② *plain*

③ *subject*

We will expect you at 10.00 am. Please go to Reception on Level 2 and ask for me. ④

1 return ☞

Yours sincerely

④ *Normal*

4 returns ☞

shift return ☞

Mary Young
Public Relations Manager

title italics ☞

2 returns ☞

Enclosure

1 return ☞

cc: ②
Mr A Castle, ABC Carpet Limited

bottom margin ☞
5.5cm

Figure 5.3   Sample letter template

Form letters

Form letters are useful aids for situations where a standard response is appropriate. These may be pre-printed or, more commonly, set up as glossaries on the word processing system. They may also be pre-formatted to merge with a list of names and addresses for mailing purposes.

Guide letters and paragraphs

Providing guide letters and paragraphs on matters regularly dealt with in an organisation can also be worthwhile. These give suggested responses for routine letters and mean that correspondence can often be handled at a lower level in the organisation than would otherwise be the case.

Naming rules

Naming rules for both electronic documents and the directories/folders in which they are filed are essential aids in ensuring records are complete and meaningful. In addition rules are required for controlling where documents are filed (e.g. on business unit servers or individual employees' hard disks), and in which directories/folders. Naming and filing rules facilitate retrieval and the linking together of documents relating to particular activities.

Rules may also specify where document names are to be positioned on the different types of documents, such as reports, memoranda, letters. As well, there may be rules requiring that version number, date, and even time, are placed on some types of documents, such as financial reports.

It is important to note that naming and filing rules may become less important in organisations which use a document management system based on a searchable database. Retrieval of documents can be by a range of elements according to corporate needs, and the document name may be a simple numeric identifier.

Documentation maintenance rules

Other rules for ensuring contextual and structural information is captured may include documentation maintenance rules. For example, to ensure records are kept intact and are an accurate record of business activity, the employees responsible for working on a particular activity may also be made responsible, in conjunction with the records staff, for ensuring the following:

- A file (paper and/or electronic) is created at the start of the activity and that all documents related to the activity are attached to the file
- All drafts and file notes are removed from the file at the completion of the activity (depending on the policy of the organisation)
- All documents are named according to the organisation's naming rules and/or allocated the appropriate key terms, and other relevant information categories
- A retention period is allocated to the group of documents related to the activity, according to the disposal policy of the organisation.

The rules may specify that the supervisor for the activity must sign off that all documentation maintenance tasks have been completed.

A useful strategy for organisations to ensure that all steps in an activity have been completed, including those related to documentation, is to implement a **job completion form**. A separate form can be designed for each of the major business activities in the organisation and list all the critical steps in the activity for sign-off at the appropriate authorisation level (see Figure 5.4).

JOB COMPLETION FORM

Part 1: General information

Client:
Job description:

Part 2: Job activities

Activities	Signatures and dates			
	Business unit manager	Job manager	Job supervisor	Records manager
1.				
2.				
3.				
4.	(In this column is listed each activity which must be completed to ensure that the job has been carried out in accordance with risk management, legal and other business needs criteria established by the organisation. Activities subsequent to completion of the main part of the job should include a number of steps to ensure the appropriate records have been preserved, for example, unnecessary file notes and documents have been deleted/removed from the file, electronic documentation to be retained has been named and filed according to office procedures.)			
5.				
6.				
7.				
8.				
9.				
10.				
11.				
12.				
13.				
14.				
15.				
16.				

Figure 5.4 Sample job completion form showing sign-offs by authorisation level for each stage of a business activity. The form may be in paper format with handwritten signatures or in electronic format with electronic signatures.

Guidelines for managing electronic mail messages

Electronic mail has brought many benefits by facilitating the rapid and easy flow of information within organisations, and between organisations and the outside world. However it has also created difficulties for organisations attempting to ensure they have complete records of business activities. Studies within particular organisations often indicate that at least some managers and other staff are using electronic mail for communicating information which is a link in the chain of significant information relating to a particular business activity. If the information is communicated as an attachment to an electronic mail message, the problem is more easily addressed because the attachment is likely to have been saved according to rules for filing and printing documents. The problem arises with the messages themselves and the messaging backwards and forwards on a particular matter. Questions arise such as: How is the decision made as to what messages should be retained? Who makes the decision—the sender or the receiver? At what point is the information saved? Is each message saved? Or just those messages that are considered to contain information significant to the matter in hand? Or just the final collection of messages when it is assumed that the communication on the matter is completed? And who has responsibility for saving the information? And is it printed and put on a file with the other information related to the business matter or is it stored electronically according to electronic filing rules? Or as a somewhat extreme solution, are all electronic mail messages monitored by the records staff for any that should be extracted and filed?

There is a tendency by users to consider that the documents they produce on their computers are 'private' and that they can dispose of them as they wish

Developing guidelines for handling electronic mail messages is becoming increasingly important as electronic mail is used more and more extensively to communicate significant business information, not just internally but also between organisations and their customers and other contacts. The successful implementation of the guidelines may largely depend on how effectively the records manager has led the way in convincing staff of the importance of capturing the information. The main barrier is the attitude that information sent via an electronic mail message is personal, informal and confidential. Employees find it hard to acknowledge that if it relates to their work, it is potentially part of the corporate memory and needs to be assessed for retention as with any other business information. In addition to guidelines, it is helpful if the electronic mail system itself is designed so it is quick and easy for users to save messages to the appropriate location, or to print them, depending on the filing policy. Unfortunately in many systems saving documents to specific locations is quite time consuming, for example, messages may need to be electronically cut and pasted into documents. For organisations with an electronic mail system fully integrated with a document management system, it should be possible to streamline the process of saving messages. The electronic mail system should give an option to save the message and then present a profile screen to register the message into the document management system.

Records in business information systems

Developing rules and controls for capturing records in business information systems such as accounting systems, human resource systems and client information systems, is complex. One option is to ensure that the systems have reporting functions built into them which capture the records, including as much relevant contextual and structural information as possible. The reports may be stored in paper, electronic or microfilm format. Whichever way they are stored, they will probably need to be accompanied by further explanatory information about the system itself to clarify what the records are, including their purpose, function within the system, and relation to other records. If producing reports is then followed up by deletion of those records from the system, then storing records this way has limitations because it means the information can no longer be manipulated for further analysis.

Organisations such as Australian Archives have been working extensively for some years on the problem of managing electronic records in business information systems. The Australian Archives' solution is to put the onus back on government agencies to maintain the necessary hardware and systems to enable access to the records as required.

The Australian Standard AS 4390–1996 makes the point that business systems and processes, and communication systems should be designed so that the appropriate records of business activity can be easily and, as far as possible, automatically captured (see under Accurate below.) Most electronic business information and communication systems were not designed with recordkeeping needs in mind. For this reason there has been substantial discussion in the archives and records management literature on the sorts of controls that need to be introduced into information systems to ensure the capture of complete records, and certainly general agreement that archivists and records managers need to bring pressure to bear on vendors of business information systems to incorporate recordkeeping functions into their systems.

Records must be comprehensive

Comprehensive Records must document the complete range of the organisation's business. Records should be made for all those business transactions for which any kind of requirement for evidence exists.

The analysis of the business functions and activities of an organisation and the development of a business classification scheme are valuable processes in identifying any gaps in the recordkeeping practices of the organisation. The steps involved in undertaking such an analysis are outlined in Chapter 4.

Records must be accurate

Accurate Records must accurately reflect the transactions that they document. Business rules and codes of conduct should require employees to make records that accurately reflect the transactions that they are intended to document. Business processes and systems should be designed to make it easy, or even automatic, to make accurate records of transactions.

The rules and other controls for ensuring records are accurate should address business needs from two angles. Firstly, the need for organisations to develop codes of conduct which include clauses covering employees' obligations to make accurate records of the business activities they are responsible for. Secondly, the need to provide system controls which ensure the capture and maintenance of accurate information.

The requirement for high quality information, including accurate information, must be taken into consideration in the evaluation, selection, and ongoing maintenance of systems. For example, an organisation needs to feel confident that its information systems are operating properly and not causing any data corruption or loss.

If organisations upgrade their systems (whether the upgrades are simply to new versions of a product or to entirely new products where data or document conversions are necessary), they need to be sure they can access their earlier records with no loss or corruption of information, including the contextual information captured with records. Attempting to recreate records that were created using a system that has been entirely replaced continues to cause a lot of headaches for organisations. The data files or documents may have been kept but often the hardware, programs and even the software documentation have gone. It may be possible to access some of the information in the files but the difficulties of retrieving full and accurate records may be insurmountable.

The level of accuracy required is an important issue for organisations implementing technology which converts information from digital to text format. Software systems used in this context, such as Optical Character Recognition (OCR) and Intelligent Character Recognition (ICR) systems, do not yet achieve 100 per cent accuracy in the conversion process. If total accuracy is required (e.g. in processing handwritten forms containing information critical to the business activity), then the editing facilities of the systems need to be evaluated carefully, and operating procedures need to be established to ensure editing is undertaken to required standards. (OCR is discussed in more detail in Chapter 10.)

Records must be authentic

Authentic It must be possible to prove that records are what they purport to be and that their purported creators have indeed created them. The recordkeeping system must operate so that the records derived from it are credible and authoritative. It should be possible to show that the recordkeeping system was operating normally at the time the transactions were documented by the records. The authorised creators of records, and their authorised roles in business activity, should be documented and kept up-to-date.

The ability to link business transactions to the participants and their roles in the organisation is helpful in establishing the authenticity of records. This type of linkage is discussed in more detail above. There also needs to be clear policies within the organisation which deal with the levels of authorisations required for particular activities and transactions, and how those authorisations are to be obtained and documented. Figure 5.4 is an example of how authorisations may be documented for each stage of a business activity. For transactions which are processed electronically, the collection of authorisations is still often a cause of concern for managers. A common solution is to maintain a policy whereby copies of relevant parts of a transaction must be printed and stored with an original signature. Some organisations do not see *digital signatures* built into systems as meeting business or legal needs and obligations.

Records must be inviolate

Inviolate Records must be securely maintained to prevent unauthorised access, alteration or removal. No information in a record should be deleted, altered or lost once the transaction that it documents has occurred. Where information is added to an existing hard copy record, for example, by annotating it, (this adding is really part of a new transaction) the added information should be initialled and dated. To maintain the integrity of electronic records, changes and additions should be identifiable through audit trails. Information should never be added to a record so that it appears to be part of the original record. Organisations that have migrated records across changes in technology need to ensure that the evidence so preserved remains authentic and accurate.

Rules and controls for managing access requirements are vitally important to any organisation. They have become even more important as many organisations are implementing systems to allow remote access to their networks.

Security controls may be labour intensive to implement and maintain, depending on the sophistication of the security features of the particular system. However, business rules, operating procedures and system controls should be introduced to achieve the following:

- Only approved participants in an activity can edit documents and data related to that activity.
- Once a final version of a record has been produced, the record cannot be altered.
- If for some reason, it is necessary to annotate a record, the annotations should be authorised and dated.
- In the case of electronic documents an audit trail of access to the documents should be created.
- Unauthorised access to computers is prevented. Measures may include rules which forbid employees from leaving unattended computers which are logged on to systems or which contain sensitive information on the hard disks, and automatic log-off from computers where no work has been done in a pre-set time.
- Use of storage media which offer the best protection against tampering and deterioration.

- Access to paper and other records in a physical format should be restricted to approved persons. Measures may include use of security systems on file rooms, locked cupboards, rules forbidding staff from leaving files in cars and other vulnerable locations, and rules forbidding staff from granting access to records by unauthorised persons. These types of rules may be included in the organisation's code of conduct covering all aspects of professional behaviour.

Exercises

1 List some performance measures that could be applied to test if an organisation is capturing full and accurate records of its business activities.

2 Locate an example of a blank form, equivalent to at least an A4 page in length, which is designed to be completed by members of the public. Write a critical analysis of the form, including comments on the relevance of the information sought to the form's stated purpose, the clarity of the captions and instructions, the adequacy of layout and space provided, and the physical format. If you have any negative comments about the form, suggest improvements or design an improved version.

You will find it useful to read Appendix E before doing this exercise.

Case study 5.1

The XYZ Refrigeration Company has an electronic mail system (e-mail system) which enables its staff to create, send, receive, delete and file electronic messages (with or without attached documents). Most of the office staff, including senior staff, use the system quite extensively. They use it to send messages to individuals and groups on matters ranging from critical business issues through to organising work meetings, social events and advertising items for sale. In addition a number of the company employees use Internet E-mail to communicate externally with customers and colleagues.

Currently there are no company guidelines for how information in e-mail messages should be presented (titling, content, language, etc.) or for the retention and disposal of messages. The records manager is concerned that:

- Important business communications are occurring on the e-mail system but are often not presented in a way which will make them meaningful records when linked to other documents related to the same business activity
- Messages are simply being deleted from the system without adequate thought being given to their possible future importance to the company as part of the documentation of business activity.

Your task

Develop some draft guidelines for e-mail users in the company covering:

- How to present information on the e-mail system
- How to make decisions on what messages should be retained
- At what point messages should be captured.

1 What are the structural and contextual information elements about reports that may need to be captured in order to fully document the business activities which led to the generation of those reports?

2 In what ways are the problems in capturing full and accurate records of transactions which are processed as data in information systems different from those which are processed in document-based format?

3 The chapter suggests some measures that can be taken to ensure the authenticity of records. Can you suggest some more?

4 A records manager in a large organisation wishes to supplement the formal documentation on business rules and procedures related to recordkeeping with a training program on recordkeeping for employees. What should be included in such a program? Who should it be aimed at? In what context should it be offered? For example, as a stand-alone program in recordkeeping, as part of an induction program for new employees, as part of specialised training in a particular business activity?

5 What impact do you believe the increasing trend to communicate, collaborate, and process transactions electronically will have on the way we use forms to capture information?

Notes

1 This discussion of the need for controls over the creation and generation of records is based on Ricks & Gow (1988), pp. 411–14.

2 The Standard includes a footnote stating that the clause 'full and accurate' is derived from 'the functional requirements for recordkeeping', published in Richard Cox (ed.) 1995, *Recordkeeping Functional Requirements Project: Reports and Working Papers —Progress Report Two*, University of Pittsburgh, March.

3 Batskos, M. 1996, 'Legal requirements of document retention', in Records Management Association of Australia, Victorian Branch, 1996 State Seminar, Towards 2000, 6–7 May, *Papers Presented*, Melbourne, 26p.

Additional information

The most important reference for this chapter is Part 3 of Australian Standard AS 4390–1996 (Standards Australia 1996). The Standard not only defines what is meant by full and accurate records but also presents strategies for capturing them.

There have been a number of valuable government reports issued in recent years on electronic recordkeeping. These reports are an acknowledgement of the urgent need for policies and strategies to manage electronic records so that they are full, accurate and accessible into the future. Examples of such reports are those of the Information Exchange Steering Committee (1993 & 1995), Roberts (1995), and Australian Archives (1995).

The principles and practices associated with managing business rules and policies and procedures, and information tools such as forms, are included in some of the records management textbooks; one of the better treatments in this area is Penn, Pennix & Coulson (1994, Chapters 12 & 13). The two articles by Southwood (1994 a & b) are both useful for information on forms. Some of the general office management texts also provide information on forms management and on correspondence management and business writing, for example, Saville & Callender (1991). Garside (1986) is useful for its coverage of business writing.

References

Australian Archives 1995, *Keeping Electronic Records: Policy for Electronic Recordkeeping in the Commonwealth Government*, Exposure draft version 2, Canberra.

Corporate Memory in the Electronic Age: Statement of a Common Position on Electronic Recordkeeping, May 1996. (Available on the Internet at the Australian Council of Archives address, http://www.aa.gov.au:80/AA_www/ProAssn/ACA/ACA.HTM)

Garside, L. 1986, *Modern Business Correspondence: A Comprehensive Guide to Business Writing and Related Office Services*, 4th edn, Pitman, London.

Information Exchange Steering Committee (IESC) 1995, *Electronic Document Guidelines in Australian Government Agencies*, prepared by the IESCs Electronic Data Management Subcommittee, Commonwealth of Australia, Canberra. (Available from the Office of Government Information Technology.)

Information Exchange Steering Committee (IESC) 1993, *Management of Electronic Documents in the Australian Public Service*: a Report prepared by the IESC's Electronic Data Management Subcommittee, Commonwealth of Australia, Canberra.

McDonald, J. 1995, 'Managing electronic records in the modern office', *Informaa Quarterly*, vol. 11, no. 3, pp. 8–15.

Penn, I. A., Pennix, G.B. & Coulson, J. 1994, *Records Management Handbook*, 2nd edn, Gower Publishing Co., Aldershot, Hants, Chapters 12 & 13.

Ricks, B. R. & Gow, K. F. 1988, *Information Resource Management: A Records Systems Approach*, 2nd edn, South-Western Publishing Co., Cincinatti, OH, Chapters 16–18.

Roberts, D. 1995, *Documenting the Future: Policy and Strategies for Electronic Recordkeeping in the New South Wales Public Sector*, The Archives Authority of New South Wales, Sydney.

Saville, J. & Callender, G. 1991, *Managing the Australian Office*, 3rd edn, Macmillan, South Melbourne, pp. 213–19, 230–38.

Southwood, G. 1994a, 'Study guide: forms management', *Records Management Journal*, vol. 4, no. 2, pp. 95–107.

—— 1994b, 'Study guide: forms under control', *Records Management Journal*, vol. 4, no. 1, pp. 51–62.

Standards Australia 1996, *Australian Standard AS 4390–1996: Records Management*, Homebush, NSW, Part 3: Strategies.

chapter six

Classification and indexing for retrieval

Overview

This chapter deals with available classification and indexing options and methods employed to retrieve records when they are needed. The capacity to successfully locate and retrieve records needed in the course of business is a key component of a records management program. Australian Standard AS 4390–1996 deals with the role of classification and indexing in part 4 of the Standard, entitled 'Control'. The Standard states that control systems and processes encompass records registration and tracking of the location of records, as well as classification and indexing. 'Classification ... allows for appropriate grouping, naming, security protection, user permissions and retrieval'; and 'indexing ... allocates attributes or codes to particular records to assist in their retrieval (Standards Australia 1996, pt. 4, p. 3,1)

While information technology and retrieval techniques have been developing rapidly, recordkeeping arrangements in organisations will nevertheless remain, for the foreseeable future, a hybrid of practices dealing with paper and electronic documents. There has been enormous interest and debate at conferences, in printed publications, and in discussions and publications on the Internet about the challenges presented by current and future information retrieval needs and methods.

It is impossible in a single chapter (or perhaps even in a single book!) to provide a comprehensive overview of issues of relevance to classification and indexing which relate to the retrieval of files or documents when they are needed. This chapter sets out to highlight some of the main concepts and approaches relating to the classification and indexing of records for the purpose of retrieval. Chapter 4 outlines the steps needed to create a classification of the functions and activities of an organisation prior to undertaking the process of appraising records for their evidential value and retention requirements. This functional classification is viewed by the Standard as the basis also for setting up retrieval approaches. Chapter 8 discusses the physical arrangement of paper records and document/file tracking systems. Chapters 9 and 10, which deal with automated systems and electronic document management technologies respectively, contain elements which are highly relevant to the theme of classification, indexing and retrieval.

Retrieval is a key component of a records management program

Chapter 7 provides broad guidelines for constructing a thesaurus and classification scheme using the technique of facet analysis. These guidelines are most commonly applicable to situations in which the records manager has to devise classification and indexing approaches for documents which need to be accessed via their intellectual content. However, the principles outlined may be useful in many contexts in which categories have to be established.

Classification

Viewed very simply, classification is the process by which the records of an organisation are categorised or grouped into retrieval units. The process applies equally to paper and electronic records. The groupings may be primarily organised by business functions and activities—as recommended by the Standard, or by other characteristics, such as by originating department, or by the subjects dealt with in the records. Departmental divisions and subjects may well coincide with functions and activities in certain contexts.

Business classification

Australian Standard AS 4390.1–1996 Part 1 defines classification as:

> … the process of devising and applying schemes based on the business activities which generate records, whereby they are categorised in systematic and consistent ways to facilitate their capture, retrieval, maintenance and disposal. Classification includes determining document or file naming conventions, user permissions and security restrictions on records (Standards Australia 1996, pt. 1, p. 6, 4.8).

The Standard views functions/activities as the primary criterion by which documents are organised for retrieval, and is concerned not with the totality of documents created in, or received by organisations, but with those which have been identified as 'records', that is, as having evidential value. The functional approach ensures that in large, complex organisations records of evidential value will be retained in an order which consistently reflects the activities which led to their creation. The classification 'provides linkages between individual records which cumulate to provide a continuous record of activity' (Standards Australia 1996, pt. 4, p. 5, 7.1). This approach helps to identify those documents which should be given high priority within record-keeping systems.

In practice, records managers may have to set up retrieval systems for documents of evidential value and documents being maintained because of their intellectual content or relevance to the knowledge-base of the organisation. Some documents will have both kinds of value attached to them, for example, documents containing proprietary information, such as the chemical formulae and techniques of a chemical manufacturing company. Hence records managers need to be flexible in their approaches to classification and indexing.

Constructing a business classification

Suggested steps for developing a business classification for an organisation were outlined in Chapter 4 which dealt with the appraisal of records. In summary these steps are:

- Gather documentary sources of information and conduct interviews with appropriate personnel
- Gain an understanding of the overall mission or objectives of the organisation
- From the above steps, derive and list the broad functions by which the organisation's objectives are achieved
- Identify the hierarchies of activities of groups and individuals which support each function
- Identify the specific transactions which operationalise each broader activity
- Identify processes or activities which are common across more than one function, and position them within their respective hierarchies, and
- Produce a map of the hierarchies for each function, filling in as much detail as possible in the timeframe available.

The Standard, pt. 4, p. 7, 7.2 states that business classification schemes should have the following attributes—labelled (A) to (H):

A Consist of sufficient classes and subclasses (often called keywords and descriptors), to include all of the business functions and activities being documented;

B Derive their terminology from the business functions or activities being documented, not from names of organisational units;

C Consist of unambiguous terminology;

D Contain discrete classes (or keywords);

E Be hierarchical, moving from the most general to the most specific concept, e.g. Finance–Audit–External;

F Be specific to each organisation;

G Be devised in consultation with the users; and

H Be maintained to reflect changing business needs.

The Standard notes that the classification should be updated and modified as changes in the functions and activities of an organisation occur. The need to consult with users in devising the scheme is also very important.

The differences between business and knowledge-base classification

Business or functional classification differs from knowledge-base classification in the following ways:

1 The purpose of the business classification process is not only to create a scheme by which records may be arranged and retrieved, but more importantly to provide a basis for developing other key program components as well, such as the consideration of what documents might need to be captured into the recordkeeping system for evidential purposes, deciding retention periods, and defining and assigning security levels.

2 The process of constructing a business classification scheme starts with the broad core functions and activities of the organisation, rather than the records and other documents of the organisation, or the needs of current personnel. In the knowledge-base approach, literary warrant (the document content/subject matter) and user warrant (the needs of the main user group) are the overriding criteria in the categorisation process.

3 Business classification is limited to activities which have accountability implications for the organisation, and only to documents which relate to such accountability—called 'records' in Chapter 2. With this perspective, other kinds of documents which are not of evidential value are of secondary importance.

4 The names of organisational units/structures and terms representing subject content may be mapped into (or added as additional layers to) the business classification, but the primary criterion for categorisation is activity/task-based. In many cases, though, organisational terms will be the same as the appropriate functional terms, because the organisation's structure reflects its functions. Subject terms too will often coincide exactly with functional terms.

The rest of this chapter assumes that records managers may need to be familiar with both functional and knowledge-base classification approaches. Guidelines for the construction of a knowledge-base classification and indexing system using the technique of facet analysis are provided in the next chapter.

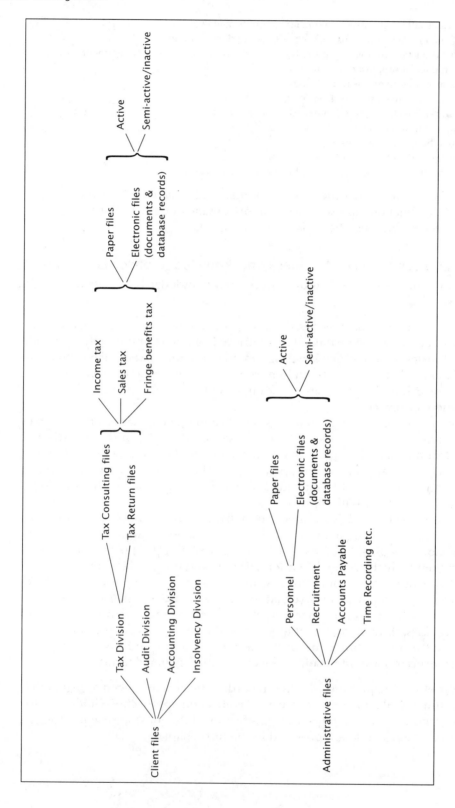

Figure 6.1 Examples of record series that might be managed in a firm of chartered accountants

Series, files and documents

In organisations it is common for records to be divided into, or categorised as series[1] and subseries; these series and subseries are then divided into files; and files may be divided into separate retrieval units consisting of individual documents. Functional analysis as described above will be helpful in this categorisation process. For example:

Series:	Community services
Sub-series:	Youth services
File:	Case management for a particular client
Document:	Case notes on the client

The grouping process is discussed further below.

Series

Records are commonly grouped into series by functions, such as accounting records and personnel records, and by the elements around which activities are organised, such as client files or project files. In a firm of chartered accountants, for instance, the taxation files may be an important subgroup within the primary series of client files, and the taxation files themselves may then be further subdivided into sales tax, fringe benefits tax and income tax. The medium of the records (paper, electronic) and the level of activity of the records are other commonly applied criteria. Figure 6.1 provides examples of record series that might be managed in a firm of chartered accountants.

Files and documents

Series are further subdivided into individual retrieval units. These are commonly either files or documents. A file is a group of related documents, usually located within a file cover or folder. A file may have a number of separate parts, stored within the same file cover, or in separate covers. Applying a business classification approach, the file may relate to an activity which supports a broad function. A document is the smallest unit of filing, for example, a single letter, a memo, or a photograph. Documents record transactions within a particular activity.

Decisions as to when to create a new file will depend greatly on an understanding of how documents are used in the organisation. A file should ideally contain records relating to one specific activity or subject. A new file is opened if no file exists on that activity or subject; also if a new issue which requires action has developed out of an older one, and the information required by the user has been scattered in a few different files. If a newly established file contains some information of particular relevance to the issue dealt with in another file, appropriate cross references between the files should be made in the indexing system.

Chapter 8 deals with procedures for establishing and maintaining paper files, for example, such issues as who should be responsible for establishing new files; whether records staff need direction as to what files to place documents on; and how the workflow in the records area should be organised.

Registration

Australian Standard AS 4390–1996, pt 4, p. 4, 6.1 stresses that the purpose of registration is 'to provide evidence that a record has been created or captured in a recordkeeping system'. In section 6.2.2 the Standard lists the minimum two data elements (a unique identifier, and date and time of registration) and offers a list of data elements which might be entered with respect to a new record in a computerised registration system. These elements include the document name or title, a text description or abstract, the date of creation, the date and time of communication and receipt, the author and sender, links to related records documenting the same sequence of business activity, application software and version under which the record was captured, details of embedded document links, including the applications software and version under which the linked record was created, etc. Registration is discussed further in Chapter 9.

Registering at the file or document levels

Classification and indexing are common processes in the task of registering a new file or document.

Filing systems are designed to manage either files, or individual documents, or a combination of the two. In some filing systems both the file and the individual documents on the file are classified. On the other hand, for example, a government department may classify individually all letters of complaint received from the public.

Files provide the ongoing history of a subject or event as related material is accumulated together. Depending on the policy of the organisation, a file may have its index terms changed, or added to, several times during its active life. Correspondence that starts as a complaint by a taxpayer X, comparing the tax owed with that owed by taxpayer Y, may evolve into an investigation of either taxpayer, or even into an industry-wide investigation. A proposal for the amalgamation of two health agencies may later become a ministerial review of all such agencies. This point stresses the essential difference between indexing a discrete document, which is done once, and indexing a file of documents, which is likely to be an ongoing process.

In a **document-based**, or document/correspondence management system, when a document arrives to be classified, the document is registered as a discrete item, and given its own number and/or classification terms. In most paper-based systems, each document also needs to be labelled with the number of the file in which it is stored. The classifier/indexer thus has to ascertain whether or not there is a previously established file relating to the broad activity or theme of the document to which the document should be attached. If there is not such a file, a new file needs to be opened to contain the document.

In a **file-based**, or files management system, when a document arrives to be classified, the classifier/indexer must ascertain whether or not a file has already been opened on the activity or subject to which the document relates. If there is a file on the same activity or subject, the document is attached to the file, and, if necessary, the file title or classification terms may be modified to cater for any overall change in the activity or subject relating to the file. If there is no file on the activity or subject of the document, a new file needs to be opened.

Indexing

The Australian Standard AS 4390–1996, pt. 4, p. 10, 8.1 defines indexing as: 'The process of establishing and applying terms or codes to particular records by which they may be retrieved. Appropriate allocation of indexing terms allows retrieval of records across classifications or categories'. When a record is classified, it is slotted into a position within a particular hierarchy. Indexing compensates for this by making it possible to give each record as many labels as might be needed for its retrieval.

A single document, stored at its given address or file number, often contains multidimensional information. If the same document belongs logically in each of several differently titled files, it might be an option (though a time-consuming one), to copy the document as many times as required, and attach it to the appropriate files, with a note indicating the location of the original document. Automated retrieval systems make it easy to assign multiple search points or attributes to each item description or profile. A search on one attribute will reveal all the files and/or documents labelled with that attribute.

In the context of records management, indexing has commonly been thought of as a manual process. However, powerful retrieval software (discussed later in this chapter) can search the whole, or selected parts of electronic documents, in which case the words in the document become the index or search terms, without the intervention of a human indexer.

Thus index terms may be derived from a document by the computer or assigned by a human indexer to enhance retrievability. Human indexing may consist of labelling of concepts using pre-established categories (e.g. from a thesaurus, classification scheme or metadata repository—see below), or it may augment record content with additional semantic elements (e.g. adding the spelled out form of an acronym), so that search engines have an optimal chance of retrieving a required document in whatever category or database it is situated.

In the practical situation, classification and indexing are processes which are closely interdependent. Often the category name by which a retrieval unit has been classified is also used as the label or index term by which the unit may be retrieved. Thus the titling or labelling of files and the registering of new files or documents are tasks which employ both grouping (or classification) and labelling (or indexing) processes. These tasks are described below.

File titling

It is common records management practice for each new file to be allocated a title, or a title and a set of index terms, which act as a label for the file. Titles 'should be representative of a record's context as well as its content' (Archives Authority of New South Wales, Records Management Office 1995, p. 8). The title acts as a summary or concise statement of the contents of the file, for example:

PARKS AND GARDENS—MAINTENANCE CONTRACTS—TENDERS.

The elements in the title may additionally be translated into a coded classification scheme so that a multiple number—such as 24/061/008—is created by which the file may be arranged on a shelf or searched on computer. If a sequential or running number which has no inherent meaning is used instead, retrieval will be even more dependent on the file title. File numbering approaches are discussed in Chapter 8.

As noted in Chapter 8, effective file titling will help to minimise confusion over what file to place a document on.

NIGHTINGALE AMALGAMATED HOSPITALS							
KEYWORD: PERSONNEL				FILE REFERENCE: P93/146			
DESCRIPTOR/S: STAFF APPRAISAL; PERFORMANCE EVALUATION; AWARDS							
NARRATIVE: TQM; QUALITY ASSURANCE							

1 Folio No.	2 Referred to	3 Date	4 Action Officer's Initials	1 Folio No.	2 Referred to	3 Date	4 Action Officer's Initials
	J. BURGER	1/2/93	J.B				
3	R. Phillips	8/2/93	R.P				
	M. white	12/2/93	MW				

INSTRUCTIONS FOR USING THE FILE COVER

WHEN ACTION IS REQUIRED: Action Officers should initial column 4 and return the file to station to which it belongs.
TO REFER TO ANOTHER OFFICER:
1 Where applicable, write the relevant folio number in column1.
2 Enter the officer's name.
3 Enter the date on which you send the file in column 3.

2 0 1 1 5 6

PART:

6 4 1   3 9 P

Figure 6.2 Example of a file title

In automated retrieval systems, the entire title in its given word order, and/or each individual word within the title can be searchable, depending on the software and indexing design used.

The words used in titles or as index terms may be:

- Selected from a thesaurus, an alphabetical list of terms which have been specially authorised for the purpose;
- Or they may be natural language terms, which are simply selected from the documents or elsewhere, but not from a controlled list.

Many online file retrieval systems use a combination of both controlled and natural language vocabularies to obtain good retrieval results. The vocabulary used in classifying documents is discussed in more detail later in the chapter. In Figure 6.2, the keyword and descriptors have been selected from a controlled vocabulary; the narrative comprises natural language terms.

File title structures

There are a number of different approaches to file titling. For example:

1 The file title may consist of a combination of controlled vocabulary in hierarchical order, and then a number of natural language terms:

   COMMUNITY SERVICES – YOUTH SERVICES – RECREATION SERVICES – BAND EVENTS BATTLE OF THE BANDS; HIGH STREET PARK, SOUTHFIELD, 1996

2 The file title may consist of a natural language summary statement, for example:

   DISPUTE BETWEEN GREENWOOD SECONDARY COLLEGE AND FIRE PROTECTION SYSTEMS LTD REGARDING INSTALLATION OF FIRE DOORS

3 The file title may be constructed as two separate statements, a natural language summary statement, and a set of controlled vocabulary terms in no particular order, for example:

   AMALGAMATION OF REPATRIATION CENTRES
   LINKSIDE REPATRIATION CENTRE, NIGHTINGALE HOSPITAL REPATRIATION CENTRE, MERGERS

4 The file title may consist of two controlled vocabulary components, that is, an initial broad class term called a keyword, and a set of more detailed terms, in no particular order, called descriptors, for example:

   TRANSPORT (KEYWORD)
   MOTOR VEHICLES, TRANSFER, OWNERSHIP (DESCRIPTORS)

5 The file title may follow Linton's Keyword System (Linton 1975; 1990) which uses a controlled vocabulary broad class term called a keyword, and up to four more detailed descriptors, set out in a hierarchical order from general to the specific, for example:

   COMPUTERS (KEYWORD)
   IBM : SOFTWARE PACKAGES : DATABASE : DBASE 4 (DESCRIPTORS)

Linton's Keyword System (Linton 1975; 1990, pp. 67–70) influenced the development of the Keyword Classification System of the New South Wales Records Management Office mentioned below.

Keyword AAA thesaurus

In 1995 the Records Management Office of the Archives Authority of New South Wales released a fully revised version of its original *Thesaurus of General Administrative Terms (GADM Thesaurus)* which was developed in 1978–79 and used by approximately 140 public sector organisations. It was originally based on a classification approach called the Keyword Classification System.

This new version of the thesaurus entitled *Keyword AAA: Accuracy, Accessibility, Accountability,* conforms to Australian Standard 4390–1996, being based on an analysis of common administrative functions, activities and transactions rather than subjects, and having a tighter hierarchical structure, with three levels of terms. It may be used to classify and index both electronic and hardcopy records. A useful feature of the thesaurus is that many of the keywords and activity descriptors correspond with activity-based classes in the recently revised *General Records Disposal Schedule—Administrative Records* produced by the Archives Authority of New South Wales.

Like its predecessor, this thesaurus covers terminology of a general nature i.e. terms which are common to the business of most organisations. The thesaurus must be used 'in conjunction with functional terminology, that is, those terms that are unique to the individual organisation's business functions and content ... The organisation's functional thesaurus may be merged with *Keyword AAA* term by term using word processing software or by merging using thesaurus management software' (Archives Authority of New South Wales, Records Management Office 1995, p. 4).

The thesaurus uses a hierarchical titling approach comprising one broad, functional keyword, followed by one activity descriptor (occasionally two) and one or two specific subject descriptors and/or some free text terms, for example:

FINANCIAL MANAGEMENT – ACCOUNTING – CASH BOOKS
[KEYWORD – ACTIVITY DESCRIPTOR – SUBJECT DESCRIPTOR]

FINANCIAL MANAGEMENT – ACCOUNTING – MISAPPROPRIATED CHEQUES
[KEYWORD – ACTIVITY DESCRIPTOR – FREE TEXT]

Advantages and disadvantages of hierarchical file titling

An advantage of hierarchical file titling is the ability to print and/or browse alphabetical listings with file titles grouped together within their broad class terms (or keywords) and activities. Other advantages are that both broad and specific terms are allocated to each file which, in an online retrieval system, can all be searchable, and that the hierarchy makes it possible to represent both contextual and content aspects of the record.

A disadvantage of the hierarchical approach is the need, for the sake of consistency among classifiers, to specify as many of the hierarchies as possible in advance, which is a time consuming process. Also, the hierarchies force each title into some kind of hierarchical order; this is not always logically possible, since the terms may, for example, be in an associative, but not a genus–species, thing–instance, thing–type or whole–part type of relationship.

An alternative to the hierarchical approach is to place a broad class term (or keyword) in one field and then to allocate as many specific descriptors as needed in any order in a separate field. Browsing of titles by broad category can thus be achieved, as well as online searching on highly specific terms.

Metadata and electronic records

Metadata is a description or profile of a document or other information object which may contain data about its context, form and content. Many archivists and records managers are concerned that because of the virtual nature of electronic records they are more susceptible than hardcopy forms to being lost. Ideally, in an electronic environment, metadata are attached to, or form an integral part of, each record. Some metadata elements might be automatically recorded by the computer, such as the date of creation, the author, the software application and version under which the document was created. Other elements such as the document name or title may need to be assigned manually. In this sense metadata is simply an extension of the concepts of classification and indexing.[2]

As with records in any format, electronic (or more specifically, digital) records need to be classified and indexed to facilitate their retrieval at a later date. The indexing principles which apply to a wide range of record formats apply also to electronic records. The main record series held electronically need to be identified and grouped logically into folders or libraries. And a search for information on an issue should ideally retrieve relevant records in all formats held by the organisation.

Just as paper records are allocated a file number or file series by which they can be retrieved, so the location of electronic records needs to be specified in an indexing system. It is essential to specify what file server, tape, cartridge or disk a record is held on; depending on the system, it may be important to specify what library or folder it is located in.

It is also important to ensure that each electronic record is assigned a meaningful and specific name so that it can be identified and retrieved by anyone with a genuine need, not just the originator. The records manager should ensure that standards and procedures for the storage and naming of electronic records are developed. A naming standard will have a fixed or maximum number of characters (depending on the type of software used). It may be a computer-allocated sequence, or it may be a user-friendly name assigned by the document originator and containing search elements such as a specific activity or subject name for the document, the type of document, the date of creation and the initials of the originator.

Steps in the indexing process

In very general terms, the process of assigning indexing terms to individual documents and files is made up of three main steps: examining the document, identifying key retrieval concepts, and translating the concepts into the system vocabulary. (For simplicity, these are called indexing steps, although, as explained earlier, classification is also a part of the process.) These steps are described below.

1 Examining the document

Parts of a document that may be helpful include its title (if there is one), names of originating persons or organisations, opening and closing paragraphs, and groups of words underlined or printed in different typefaces.

2 Identifying useful retrieval concepts

The next step is to identify those elements in the document or file that are of potential value as retrieval keys to the users. Questions about the document or file that may be helpful in this task are:

- Does it record a transaction?
- Does it record an activity or course of action?
- Does it refer to methods for accomplishing a course of action?
- Does it deal with a particular product, organisation, or condition?
- Does the subject contain an action concept, i.e. an operation or process?
- Does it deal with the effect of one thing on another?
- Appropriate search elements may include:
  —subject terms, such as 'annual leave' or 'public hospitals'
  —proper names, for example, names of people and organisations, and titles of reports or submissions
  —document types, such as 'reports', 'applications' and 'minutes', and
  —identifying numbers.

The number of retrieval elements which are assigned to a record is referred to as the exhaustivity or depth of the indexing. In theory, there should be no arbitrary limit as to the number of headings which may be assigned to a record, but in practice, factors such as file titling structures, user needs, and available software will impose limits.

3 Translating the concepts into the indexing vocabulary

The concepts selected must then be translated into the vocabulary of the indexing system. This process takes place both at the stage of file titling and at the stage of indexing individual documents or adding extra index entries for files. It also takes place when the indexer is determining whether a file already exists on a particular topic.

The indexing vocabulary

The selection of an indexing vocabulary will include issues such as:

1 Whether controlled or natural language vocabulary will be used, or a combination of the two
2 How proper names are to be indexed
3 Whether a pre-coordinate or post-coordinate method of indexing will be used
4 How specific index headings will be, and
5 How consistency in indexing will be achieved

These indexing decisions are explained below.

1 Controlled and natural language vocabulary

Human indexing is generally based on some level of controlled vocabulary and, increasingly, on some additional use of uncontrolled or natural language vocabulary as well.

The English language offers many alternative ways of expressing a particular idea or concept. With controlled vocabulary indexing, the indexer translates the identified concepts into the standardised or authorised 'allowed' terms listed in an alphabetical thesaurus. Thesauri and classification schemes are both forms of controlled vocabulary. A thesaurus of terms should refer the indexer from the non-allowed term(s) for a concept to the allowed term. The index terms should reflect terminology usage in the records and the usage of terms by users. It is of little use for a document about budgeting to be indexed under 'monetary procedures' if all the people who use the document refer to it as 'budget procedures'.

There are different approaches to thesaurus construction—the thesaurus may be a simple listing of allowed terms, developed as the filing system grows, or it may contain detailed cross references, including references between related allowed headings. Often the thesaurus is supplemented by sets of rules for formulating headings, particularly proper name headings. The thesaurus is a dynamic tool. As terms are needed, they are added to the list. A method for constructing thesauri and classification schemes is outlined in Chapter 7.

Many automated indexing systems allow the thesaurus to be stored, developed and displayed online, and assist the indexer and searcher by automatically replacing non-allowed/invalid terms with allowed terms.

Non-thesaurus (natural language) terms and phrases are often assigned by the indexer as well, for example, in an extra field called the 'Narrative', 'Identifier', or 'New terms' field. Proper names are frequently too numerous to list comprehensively in a thesaurus, and the indexer may be required to supply these, sometimes using special rules to maintain consistency of choice and form of name.

Summaries or abstracts are also sources of index terms, since with text retrieval software (software specially designed to retrieve text via terms found within it), the terms in any field can be searchable online.

2 Indexing proper names

Personal, organisational and other proper names are common indexing terms. In many organisations, case files (e.g. client files, student files, patient files, and project files) form the major category of records held. File titles may consist only of a name, or the titles may consist of a name and several additional indexing terms.

Names can be very successful retrieval keys because they often uniquely identify items. However, consistency in name indexing is not easy to achieve, because names often have variant forms; in addition, they are composed of elements that can be cited in different orders, and they have a tendency to change over the years.

For example, how should a personal name such as *Mary Watson Higgs* be recorded and filed? How should names in different languages be treated? Corporate names require even more thought. They often change, as in the case of amalgamations and changes of government. *True Blue Books Ltd* might be taken over by *The Southern Publishing Company*. The *Department of Agriculture and Rural Affairs* might become the *Department of Food and Agriculture*. Acronyms and abbreviations can also present difficulties. The *Municipal Association of Victoria* is also known as the *MAV*. The *Department of Employment, Education and Training* is also known as *DEET*. *J. B. Smith and Co.* could be entered as such, or as *Smith, J. B. and Co.*

Consistent rules are needed for entering different kinds of name, and for establishing preferred forms of name. Authorised forms of name may be listed as a separate authority list, or as part of the controlled vocabulary used with the indexing system. References are required from the variant form(s) of a name to the authorised form.

Alphabetical name arrangements for files and filing rules are discussed in Chapter 8, and Appendix A provides a list of filing rules for alphabetical name arrangements.

3 Pre-coordinate or post-coordinate indexing

An organisation must choose whether it will use pre-coordinate or post-coordinate indexing for its files and documents. These two indexing methods are described below.

With **pre-coordinate indexing**, the terms in a multi-aspect (compound/complex) topic are pre-combined into a single subject heading, for example:

INDUSTRIAL RELATIONS – STRIKES – TRANSPORT STRIKE OF 1987.

This approach is suited to printed (or microfiche) indexes.

To achieve consistent indexing each time that the same multi-aspect subject appears, an established word order is needed. Also, for the user who searches in the printed index under *Strikes* rather than under *Industrial relations* in the above example, it would be necessary to make a see reference:

STRIKES *SEE UNDER* INDUSTRIAL RELATIONS – STRIKES.

A reference would similarly need to be made from *Transport Strike of 1987* to *Industrial Relations – Strikes – Transport Strike of 1987*.

To avoid the need for these kinds of references in printed indexes, the terms in each heading can be rotated, so that each term in a heading gets a chance to be the first filing word in the heading.

Pre-coordinate index headings are also often used in online indexing systems. Online, the pre-coordinated headings may be searchable as complete headings, or by a word(s) within a heading, in the same way that post-coordinate headings are searched (see below).

With **post-coordinate indexing**, each term in a multi-aspect topic is entered singly, as an individual indexing unit, for example:

INDUSTRIAL RELATIONS;
STRIKES;
TRANSPORT STRIKE OF 1987.

The terms may be entered in any order.

The searcher may search by a single word or phrase, or by words in combination, using Boolean logic (Boolean operators are explained on pp. 130–31.) This kind of indexing has fewer problems in relation to word order. It is better suited to an online searching environment than to printed indexes, which usually need to be economical in the number of entries or access points provided.

Indexing methods frequently employ a combination of both pre- and post-coordinate approaches. For example, the file title may consist of a pre-coordinate statement plus a set of more detailed post-coordinate descriptors.

4 Specific and/or broad indexing

To maximise success in retrieval, the set of terms assigned by an indexer for a particular document should include terms which are as specific (i.e. at the same generic level) as possible to the concepts being represented in that document. This is to ensure that a document retrieved through a search on a specific term will be highly relevant to that term. A rule of specific indexing also helps in achieving a consistent approach to indexing.

Thus the indexing for a file about safety reviews of the Newtown Passenger Rail Network should include terms for the concepts *Newtown Passenger Rail Network* and *safety reviews.*

Subjects consisting of unique proper names are usually highly successful as retrieval keys, as long as the searcher is aware of the form and spelling of the indexed name.

One or more generically broader terms are often supplied in addition to the specific terms. For example, *train services* might be added as a broader term in the above example, if types of service are a category of relevance to the functions of the organisation. Broad terms enable file titles to be grouped together in large categories, which are especially helpful in computer-produced listings. In some systems, the broad class term or keyword is placed in a field of its own, and the searcher can decide whether to include it in a search or not.

5 Indexing consistency

The use of a thesaurus and rules for formulating names, and also clear guidelines on how to translate a required concept into the most specific thesaurus term available, will facilitate consistent indexing and hence predictability in retrieval. Clear indexing guidelines are particularly important where more than one person is doing the indexing, or where there are changes of indexing personnel. Without a degree of vocabulary control, problems are likely to include:

- The scattering of documents on the same topic in different files
- Incomplete files
- Low retrieval rates and difficulty in locating individual documents, and
- Resulting problems in carrying out reliable and efficient retention and disposal procedures.

Full text databases and networked information: indexing and searching approaches

The information technology environment

Chapters 9 and 10 give an overview of how automated records management systems are changing to meet the challenges of electronic document management and the networked information environment.

The growth of the Internet in recent years has encouraged the development of a range of sophisticated software indexing and search engines and navigational mechanisms. Local area networks and increasingly, intranets (private networks on the Internet), offer yet further challenges in regard to retrieving documents from within and across a number of different types of databases connected by networks. On these networks client/server computer configurations facilitate the requesting of information by one computer program (the client) from document collections stored by means of a computer program elsewhere on a network (a server). Users across geographically dispersed organisations can have access to corporate document collections stored at different points on the network.

Intranets are a potent form of collaborative information technology. The term 'groupware' also expresses the notion of digitally-based team collaboration in organisations. Groupware has until recently often been used to refer to collaborative software such as Lotus Notes which initially developed in non-TCP/IP environments (refer to Chapter 10 for more details). Inexorably, however, the market has demanded inter-operability between different groupware products, and no groupware product that cannot be incorporated into an intranet architecture for an organisation is likely to remain commercially viable. Workflow software, which automates the flow of tasks and information around an organisation, is another mechanism which assists in the linking of information systems, whether at the individual, workgroup, business unit or corporate level. The roles of groupware and workflow software systems are described in Chapter 10.

The very nature of the 'document' is changing. Hypertext links within electronic documents enable the searcher to jump from information in one document to related information in another, and may be thought of as a form of cross referencing.

Compound documents are digital documents which may be a combination of text, audio or graphic 'objects'. All the elements comprising such documents need not necessarily be stored together on one server. They can be brought together on demand through hypertext links. Compound documents may require indexing at the level of individual objects (e.g. a logo within a letter, an advertising jingle), or the document as a whole may be treated as an object requiring indexing. Such indexing is achieved through selected metadata which categorises and/or identifies the object.

The PICS system (Platform for Internet Content Selection) developed by the Massachusetts Institute of Technology's World Wide Web Consortium (W3C), is a set of technical standards to enable Web site authors to attach labels, descriptions (or metadata) to their sites to make it possible for filtering software to block access to that site. Future applications may use the labelling system for information searching purposes. (See Web site http://www.w3.org/pub/WWW/PICS/ for further information on this.)

Australian Standard AS 4390–1996, pt. 4, p. 10, 8.1 makes the point that retrieval may be required at different levels within a recordkeeping system—at the level of 'recordkeeping systems as a whole, collections of records such as physical or virtual files; or individual records or documents'. In computer network environments, reliable retrieval of documents will depend on classification and indexing being applied at each of these levels and across all the levels. The appearance of menus[3] of alternative categories often signifies reliance on a classified order from broad classes to specific items within those classes. The application of classification and indexing will be reflected in systematic directory structures and standardised document naming conventions. The nature and extent of human classification and indexing required will depend also on the storing, indexing, and searching software used by the system.

Evaluating retrieval performance

The performance of retrieval is often evaluated by two measures, recall and precision.

- The recall measure of a search is the number of relevant documents retrieved as a percentage of all the relevant documents in the database(s) searched. Recall essentially measures how successful the system is in retrieving all of the broadly and partially relevant items in the database.

- The precision measure is the number of documents found to be relevant out of all those that were retrieved in a search. Precision is more concerned than recall with the quality of what is retrieved, the extent to which the retrieved items are actually of relevance to the search.

The two measures tend to have an inverse relationship—features of the retrieval system which increase recall will decrease precision. For example, the use of the Boolean *or* operator (described below) is likely to increase recall while decreasing precision; the *and* operator will increase precision and decrease recall.

Many authors have criticised these measures because of the subjective nature of judging 'relevance'. However the two concepts are helpful in categorising the kinds of results which particular searching and indexing approaches are likely to achieve. Depending on the requirements of target user groups, different indexing and searching mechanisms may emphasise precision over recall, or vice versa. For some kinds of enquiries, it may be essential to have as high a recall rate as possible; for others, precision may be more important. Over the years there have been many debates in the literature as to whether controlled or natural language systems give better retrieval performance. Some augmenting of natural language retrieval systems with human indexing has been seen to be helpful in increasing the precision of searching. See, for example, Tenopir & Ro (1990, Chapters 5 and 9). There seems to be considerable consensus at this point in time that a combination of both approaches achieves good results with respect to recall and precision.

Indexing and searching technologies

Retrieval from both profile and full text databases commonly depends on a match taking place between the terms used by the searcher when undertaking an inquiry and the terms from each database record. These terms are usually placed by the software program in an alphabetical index (called an inverted index) to facilitate matching. The computer searches character by character and word by word, so that a small difference in spelling, punctuation or spacing can prevent a 'hit' or a match from occurring. A set number of characters may have to be searched from left to right in a particular field. With free text searching, the computer searches for the occurrences of a word or phrase in one or more fields within database records or in the full texts of documents stored on the system. All terms not on the system's stoplist (very common words such as *he, the, those, in, of, between,* etc.) are searchable.

Other search methods which are particularly relevant to full text databases are dependent on different computer indexing approaches. Summarised very briefly here from Koulopoulos & Frappaolo (1995, pp. 166–90), they include:

- Free text scanning in which there is no index—the computer sequentially scans the terms in each document of the database to find matching terms to the query.
- N-grams or suffix arrays in which an index stores word fragments on which matching takes place.
- Pattern recognition in which an index stores binary representations—the words in the database and the words in language queries are encoded by the system into their binary representations, i.e. as sets of 0s and 1s in order to obtain matching. While being helpful in relation to spelling errors, its fuzzy searching can also return documents with terms of similar patterns which are not related to the query. Pattern matching has exciting prospects in relation to non-text formats such as sound, video clips and images.

- Document clustering in which a document's words are examined and the document is assigned one or more themes suggested by sets of terms or subject profiles in the document. Each theme is stored virtually as a dimension of the document and gives the document an index value. Natural language queries are processed in the same way, and judgements about relevance are based on the closeness of the document's location to the query's location within the virtual storage area. With concept-based clustering, the initial assessments of subject clusters are made by humans. With statistic-based clustering subject clusters are selected by means of algorithms applied to the words in the documents; and

- Hypertext systems which comprise semantic networks in which nodes or chunks of information (including text, images, sound, etc.) are stored and connected by means of links or pathways from one node to another. On an Internet web site, for example, the searcher connects to a node or piece of information by clicking on an icon or on highlighted text (called buttons).

Particular products are likely to use more than one of these methods.

Searching approaches

Boolean and other searching techniques

The very common Boolean searching method is based on the query term either occurring or not occurring within a database record. Boolean algebra can be used to express statements in logic mathematically. The most frequently used Boolean operators or search patterns are explained below.

The '**and** search' looks for the occurrence of documents containing both headings, thus a search on **Accommodation** *and* **Elderly** is likely to produce documents about accommodation for the elderly.

The '**or** search' looks for the occurrence of documents containing either term individually or containing both headings. Thus a search on **Accommodation** *or* **Elderly** is likely to produce documents about accommodation, documents about elderly people, and documents about accommodation for the elderly.

The '**not** search' looks for the occurrence of documents containing the first heading, but not the second, nor the second in combination with the first heading. Thus a search on **Accommodation** *not* **Elderly** is likely to produce documents about accommodation, but not about elderly people, nor about accommodation for elderly people. Other searching mechanisms include the following:

- Wildcard searching uses a character like * for more than one letter and an @ for a single letter within or at the beginning/end of a word when one is searching an automated system and one is not sure of its exact spelling, or one needs to locate all words with the same root. Many software products only offer truncation, i.e. wild cards at the ends of words, as explained below.

- Truncation makes it possible to search the index file on the first few letters of a heading. It is helpful if one is unsure of the form of a word or of its spelling. For example, searching on PARK* would retrieve all documents indexed under headings beginning with those four letters, thus PARKER-J., PARKER-S., PARKING, PARKING PERMITS, PARKINSON-H., PARKS, etc.

- Various proximity operators make it possible to stipulate that nominated terms must, for example, be adjacent to each other, or must occur in the same sentence, paragraph or within a certain number of terms in the document. Thus, to locate records containing the phrase 'alcohol consumption' the searcher might enter ALCOHOL ADJ CONSUMPTION.

- The application of fuzzy logic by which a search engine makes the search specifications more vague than that input by the searcher. For example in some relevance ranked searching approaches (defined below), for an AND search, the computer will undertake both an OR search as well as an AND search, but the AND search result will receive a higher ranking.

Relevance ranked searching

Manual (or human) indexing is a time-consuming, and therefore relatively expensive process, particularly if a controlled vocabulary is used. It is very appealing for indexing to be undertaken partially, or even completely, by computer. Powerful software systems are able, for example to:

- Eliminate stop words
- Automatically stem terms, so that *hous* may be the root or stem of *housing, houses, house* and *housed*
- Generate pairs of adjacent stems within a sentence, for example from the sentence, *The small boy played with his mother*, the computer can extract, *small_boy, boy-play*, and *play-mother*, techniques which give improved results over searching all the words in the text (Salton 1983, 1989).

An increasing number of searching software systems on the market and the search engines on the Internet make use of relevance ranking algorithms. These algorithms enable the computer to display documents relevant to a query in a ranked order from most to least relevant to the query. Ranking is most helpful as a precision device in relation to searching full text databases, but it can be applied also to profile databases which contain fields for manually assigned terms.

Efforts to use the computer to support or replace human effort in constructing and or searching textual databases date back to the 1950s with the work of Luhn (1957) and others. Since the 1960s Salton researched and published extensively on the theme of machine processing of text, both of document texts (usually abstracts) and of questions entered in natural language (e.g. Salton 1971, 1989; Salton & McGill 1983). Salton obtained good results using automatic indexing and ranking techniques, but it has taken nearly twenty years for computer hardware and software to develop to the current stage where the methods he pioneered are being widely used.

Two popular ranking approaches are outlined below. Kouloupoulos & Frappaolo (1995, pp. 205–06) have referred to them as **term summing** and **weighted term summing.**

With **term summing**, the computer counts how many times each of the terms in the query occurs within each document. The document which contains the largest number of query terms is ranked as the most relevant. The least relevant document contains the least number of occurrences of the query terms. The hypothesis on which this approach is based is that the more frequently a term appears in a document, the more likely it is that the document is relevant to the term.

With **weighted term summing**, the summing or totaling is based not only on the frequency of occurrence of the query terms in the document, but also on a weight value assigned by the computer on the basis of the *uniqueness* of the term. The hypothesis here is that query terms which occur *least often* in the database are more unique, and hence documents with the least-frequently occurring terms are more likely to be highly relevant to the query. The more occurrences of the term in the database, the less likely it is that the document containing the term is of relevance to the query. A popular variation of this weighting approach is to allow users to indicate weightings for each of their query terms, and to trial different sets of weightings. This variation helps the search results to be more targeted to the needs of the user.

These two basic algorithms do not take into account either:

- The possible large differences in the lengths of documents—longer documents with more occurrences of query terms will be given higher rankings; or
- The fact that terms placed next to each other in a query may match on terms which are far apart from each other within large documents, and thus have little relevance to the user's query.

It is thus important for the algorithms to additionally allow for the bias created by the size (i.e. the number of words) of the documents, and also to assess documents as being of greater relevance if the query terms are close to each other within the document.

Internet search engines

Finding aids on the Internet include Web search engines and subject directories. The search engines (e.g. AltaVista) use computer programs to automatically move through Web addresses, titles/headers and certain numbers of words on Web pages, collecting addresses and words, and placing them in a full-text index. The search engines then apply one or more algorithms to rank the relevance of sites to the search query.

The subject directories (e.g. Yahoo) are catalogues of Web sites which have been manually categorised by subject. Henninger (1997) has produced a most useful 'in a nutshell' book about surfing the Internet. She points out that, in fact, a number of subject directories are using search engines, and some search engines are being enhanced with manual categorisation of selected Web sites.

Each engine uses slightly different combinations of ranking approaches. Henninger (1997, p. 64) provides the following list of commonly applied ranking criteria, from most to least common:

1 The word(s) present in the title
2 The number of times word(s) are present in the first part of a document
3 The word(s) present in meta-tags [words assigned to some Web sites by their authors to facilitate searching—these may include synonyms, etc.]
4 The word(s) present in a short document often have more weight than the same words in a long document
5 The number of times word(s) are present in [the] entire document.

Notess maintains a Web site on the subject of Internet search tools which contains a selective bibliography on search engines
(URL:http://www.imt.net/~notess/search/index.ht).
Miller (1996), Black (1997), Weinberg (1996) and many other authors have noted that the resulting rankings can be extremely helpful to searchers, but at times can also be very frustrating. For succesful Internet searching, it is necessary for searchers to become familiar with what is indexed by particular search tools, and to study whatever information is provided in their FAQs (frequently asked questions) and search guides about searching approaches and the bases of ranking which have been applied.

Many projects have been set up to research and implement the attachment of metadata to resources on the Internet, for example the Dublin Core project by which resources are described in terms of fifteen core data elements, including subject, title, publisher, object type, relation, coverage. Information about this kind of metadata can be found at: http://www.oclc.org/metadata/dublin_core/.

Exercises

1 Suggest two synonyms or near-synonyms for the term *accommodation*.
2 Suggest a hierarchical file title which begins with the keyword, *Safety*.
3 Arrange the following terms in hierarchical order: *Records Management Association of Australia*, *Membership*, *Applications*, *Associations*.
4 For a file about the purchase of Holden Camira motor cars, suggest:
   a A pre-coordinate hierarchical file title, and
   b A title made up of post-coordinate index terms.
5 How are client files in an accounting firm or government department likely to be titled?
6 Suggest two categories of documents in an organisation which are likely to require subject indexing of a complex nature.
7 Suggest two tangible benefits of a successful indexing system.
8 Consider whether the following searching techniques would increase recall or precision:
   a Boolean *or* searching
   b Boolean *and* searching
   c Proximity searching
   d Wildcarding
   e Fuzzy logic
9 Concepts quiz. Suggest concise definitions for the following terms and phrases:

- Indexing
- Classification
- Business classification
- Record series
- Metadata
- The indexing process
- Case files
- Free text searching
- Inverted index
- Full text searching
- Pre- and post-coordinate indexing
- Controlled and natural language vocabularies
- Broad and specific indexing
- Functions
- Precision and recall
- Relevance ranking
- Document clustering

Practical indexing exercises

Part 1   File titling exercise without a thesaurus

For letters 1a and 1b (p. 134), imagine that you are the records manager at the Boralian Taxation Office. Provide one precise statement to serve as a title for the new paper file containing these letters.

For letters 2a and 2b (p. 135), imagine that you are the records manager at the Boralian Council of Secondary Colleges. Provide one precise statement to serve as a title for the new paper file containing these letters.

Would a controlled vocabulary be justified for this kind of correspondence? Give reasons for your answer.

Now imagine that all four letters were stored in a word processing format (with no manual indexing) and you needed to retrieve a particular letter. Assuming that a suitable text retrievable software package was available, how successful do you believe a full text search is likely to be?

Letter 1a

DEPARTMENT OF TAXATION OF BORALIA
134 Blue Street, Burke Town, Boralia, 3J22

Phone (04) 303 822
Fax. (04) 303 820
Address all correspondence
to the Commissioner

18 January 1997

Town Clerk
Burke Town Council
Technical Services Department
Transport Unit
Burke Town Hall
Main Street
Burke Town
Boralia 3K99

Dear Sir/Madam,

Re: Application for Parking Permit in the Main Street Mall

Owing to the limited parking facilities for commercial vehicles in the area of the General Post Office, and the large volume of our mail, this Department seeks approval for our Courier to park in Main Street to collect daily mail. We would appreciate your approval of a parking permit for this purpose.

Thank you for considering this matter.

Yours faithfully

Pat Smith, Department of Taxation

Letter 1b

Burke Town Hall
Main Street
Boralia 3K99
GPO Box 299
Boralia 3K97
Phone: (04) 603 345
Fax: (04) 603 346

26 January 1997

Ms Pat Smith
Department of Taxation
134 Blue Street
Burke Town
Boralia 3J22

Dear Ms Smith,

I refer to your letter of 18 January 1997 applying for permission to park in Main Street to collect mail for the Department of Taxation.

I regret to inform you that we are unable to issue the permit as it would be contrary to the Council's policy of keeping Main Street a traffic-free zone. You might consider contacting the General Post Office for permission to park in their loading zone.

Yours sincerely

J B Mathews
Town Clerk

Letter 2a

Boralian Council of Secondary Colleges
21 High Street, James Town, Boralia, 6K51

Phone (07) 307-211
Fax. (07) 307-210

20 February 1997

The Commissioner
Department of Taxation
134 Blue Street
Burke Town
Boralia 3K22

Dear Sir/Madam,

At our last Council meeting a number of members instructed me to ask for clarification concerning the issue of tax deductibility for donations to our member secondary schools. A recent article in the Boralian News suggested that the issue is currently under review.

Would you kindly provide the Council with a statement of the current guidelines on this issue at your earliest convenience?

Yours faithfully,

Kate Browne
Director

Letter 2b

DEPARTMENT OF TAXATION OF BORALIA
134 Blue Street, Burke Town, Boralia, 3J22

Phone (04) 303 822
Fax. (04) 303 820
Address all correspondence
to the Commissioner

3 March 1997

Kate Browne
Director
Boralian Council of Secondary Colleges
21 High Street
James Town
Boralia 6K51

Dear Ms Browne,

Re: Request for statement concerning guidelines on deductibility of donations to secondary schools

Provision is made under Section B312(V6) of the Boralian Income Tax Act for a donor to a registered secondary college to claim the value of the gift or donation as a deduction for income tax purposes. For claims to be accepted, colleges are required to be registered as a secondary college with the Boralian Ministry of Education, and to then have lodged their registration form with our department.

Yours sincerely,

Barry Ferguson
Assistant Commissioner
For The Commissioner

Part 2   File titling exercise with a thesaurus

Imagine that you are the Records Manager at the Alcohol and Drug Research Association (ADRA) of the country of Boralia. It is your task to index, on an automated correspondence management system, letters published in the *Boralian Times* 'Letters to the Editor' section, and other Boralian newspapers, which have responded to a new report your organisation has published, entitled *Alcohol Consumption in Boralia*. This report proposes increasing the liquor licence fees paid by the liquor industry in order to fund treatment and rehabilitation programs for victims of alcohol abuse.

The following two letters are to be placed in one file. Suggest a suitable, broad, phrase-type file title for the file, using natural language. Then, using the thesaurus on pp. 137–40, assign a set of more detailed index terms to each individual letter. Prepare a worksheet so that for each letter there is a folio (letter) number, a file number (92/35), the source and date of publication of the letter, the author, the author's affiliation, the (given) letter title, the file title, the index terms relating to the letter, and any additional non-thesaurus terms or proper names not in the thesaurus that might be required.

In order to do this exercise, you will need to decide how detailed the indexing should be. You will also need to decide whether terms in searchable fields such as the letter title and the file title should be repeated in the index term field(s) or not.

Folio 1

Boralian Times, 'Letters to the Editor' Section, 19 June 1997

ADRA's liquor proposals are misguided.
from H. Pembroke, Director, Distilled Spirits Industry Association

The recently published ADRA report misses the crucial point that alcohol-related social problems are in any case on the decrease, and that over the past five years, the consumption of alcohol has been falling. Consumption has dropped from a high of 10.5 litres per capita in 1987 to 7.9 litres per capita in 1997. The report fails to mention this important trend, and greatly overstates the social costs of alcohol abuse.

The alcohol industry has had a generous and open attitude towards government and health professionals' initiatives to reduce the problems of alcohol abuse. Two million dollars are spent annually on education and research to prevent and reduce alcohol addiction. One brewery, Hodges Ltd, for example, has supported an expensive publicity program against underage drinking, and has contributed to several of the highly effective government-sponsored drink-driving advertisements of the government's Alcohol Abuse Campaign.

The proposed liquor levy would inevitably result in increased liquor prices, so that the moderate and responsible drinker would inevitably bear the brunt of ADRA's misguided proposals. Increased liquor levies are not needed to reduce alcohol-related harm.

Harry Pembroke, Bluehill

Folio 2

Boralian Times, 'Letters to the Editor' Section, 24 June 1997

Proposed liquor tax is inappropriate.
from K. James, Director, Boralian Council of Brewers

The ADRA report on alcohol consumption appears to have been accepted at face value, in editorials in both the *Boralian Times* (20/6) and *The Boralian Weekly* (22/6). Previous studies, such as 'Social costs of alcohol' by the Department of Health and the 1996 study commissioned by the Hofmeyer Foundation estimated the social costs of alcohol addiction to be in the range of $700 million to $5 billion nationally. ADRA's estimates of a national cost of $7–$14 billion do not appear to be based on hard evidence, and their lack of substance raises doubts about the research methods used in the study.

Statistics on the alcohol-related road toll have been misinterpreted in the ADRA report. The South Boralian Police Enforcement Review in fact shows a steady decrease in road fatalities directly related to alcohol, and this trend has been noticeable in official statistics over the past four years.

The Boralian Council of Brewers and the DSIA allocate generous funds each year towards education of the community. Both organisations have a sincere commitment towards decreasing the harm resulting from alcohol abuse. Education is clearly steadily reducing the immoderate use of alcohol. Legislative controls, such as the introduction of new taxes will be harmful to the industry, and will ultimately hurt the responsible and moderate drinker.

Kenneth James, Roseville

Thesaurus for practical indexing exercise, Part 2

Note: Proper names and new terms for concepts not in the list may be used if needed, but must be tagged so that they can be authorised by the Chief Indexer of the ADRA Records Management Unit. Terms in upper case are allowed terms. 'Use' refers the indexer to the allowed term(s); UF stands for 'Used for' and reminds the indexer of the non-allowed terms for the allowed term. BT stands for 'Broader Term' and RT stands for 'Related Term(s)'. SN stands for 'Scope Note', a note which defines the term for the purpose of indexing.

ADRA
    UF   Alcohol and Drug Research Association

ALCOHOL
    NT   Beer
             Wine
             Spirits

ALCOHOL ABUSE
UF   Alcohol addiction
       Alcohol misuse
       Alcoholism
BT   Alcohol consumption
NT   Underage drinking

Alcohol addiction
Use   Alcohol abuse

Alcohol and Drug Research Association
Use   ADRA

ALCOHOL CONSUMPTION
NT   Alcohol abuse

ALCOHOL CONSUMPTION IN BORALIA (REPORT)

Alcohol industry
Use   Liquor industry

Alcohol misuse
Use   Alcohol abuse

Alcoholism
Use   Alcohol abuse

BEER
BT   Alcohol
RT   Spirits
       Wine

BORALIAN COUNCIL OF BREWERS
BT   Liquor industry
RT   Distilled Spirits Industry Association

COMMUNITY COSTS
SN   The social, economic and/or personal cost to the community relating to alcohol
       consumption
UF   Social costs

DISTILLED SPIRITS INDUSTRY ASSOCIATION
UF   DSIA
BT   Liquor industry
RT   Boralian Council of Brewers

DSIA
Use   Distilled Spirits Industry Association

EDUCATION PROGRAMS
BT   Public health programs
RT   Prevention programs
       Rehabilitation programs
       Treatment programs

Fatal road accidents
Use   Road fatalities

FATALITIES
NT   Road fatalities

Financial support
    Use   Funding

FULL STRENGTH ALCOHOL
    SN   Traditional strength prior to introduction of light alcohol substitutes; not pure
            alcohol in the 10% proof category
    BT   Alcohol

FUNDING
    UF   Financial support

GOVERNMENT
    SN   Use where term incorporates both national and local levels of Boralian government
    NT   Government (National)
            Government (Local)

GOVERNMENT (LOCAL)
    BT   Government
    RT   Government (National)

GOVERNMENT (NATIONAL)
    BT   Government
    RT   Government (Local)

LIQUOR INDUSTRY
    UF   Alcohol industry
    NT   Boralian Council of Brewers
            Distilled Spirits Industry Association

LIQUOR LICENCES
    SN   A means of industry regulation and for collecting revenue/fees
    BT   Taxation

PREVENTION PROGRAMS
    BT   Public health programs
    RT   Education programs
            Rehabilitation programs
            Treatment programs

PUBLIC HEALTH PROGRAMS
    NT   Education programs
            Prevention programs
            Rehabilitation programs
            Treatment programs

REHABILITATION PROGRAMS
    BT   Public health programs
    RT   Education programs
            Prevention programs
            Treatment programs

RESEARCH
    NT   Statistics

ROAD FATALITIES
    UF   Fatal road accidents
            Road toll
            Traffic fatalities
    BT   Fatalities

Road toll
Use   Road fatalities

Social costs
Use   Community costs

SPIRITS
BT   Alcohol
RT   Beer
       Wine

STATISTICS
BT   Research

TAXATION
NT   Liquor licences

Traffic fatalities
Use   Road fatalities

TREATMENT PROGRAMS
BT   Public health programs
RT   Education programs
       Prevention programs
       Rehabilitation programs

UNDERAGE DRINKING
SN   Alcohol consumption by persons under 18 years
BT   Alcohol abuse

WINE
BT   Alcohol
RT   Beer
       Spirits

Case study 6.1

Imagine that you have been called in as a records management consultant by the government-funded National Organisation for Marine Safety in the country of Boralia.

Background information

The primary functions of this organisation are to:

- Undertake research relating to sea safety, including standards relating to ship construction and navigation aids
- Monitor accidents and rescues at sea, involving large and small vessels
- Monitor port pollution, and
- Coordinate maritime safety activities.

This research-based organisation employs a total of eighty-seven staff, of whom fifty are researchers who require access to the records held in the organisation. A part-time librarian maintains a small collection of published materials, (books, journals, etc.) to support the research function, but there is no position classification of Records Manager, and none of the clerical staff who currently organise and maintain the files (in addition to their other tasks) have had any RM training outside of the workplace.

There are approximately 11 000 file folders containing correspondence on administrative, policy, and sea safety issues; print-outs of statistics; working papers on subjects such as ship construction and navigation aids; published safety regulations and standards; and internal reports on sea rescues and port pollution. Much of this material is presently filed in filing cabinets under broad and overlapping alphabetical subject categories in bulging, tatty folders. There are also about 500 maps and plans of coastal and surrounding waters, stored one on top of the other in a set of drawers, and about 100 book registers of ships and seamen stacked together on some open shelving. There are no indexes to assist in the retrieval of required documents. The research staff say they have great difficulty finding correspondence on policy matters, or documentation on a particular sea rescue, waste disposal company, vessel component, regulation, etc.

You have been appointed for a three-month period to study and make recommendations on classification and indexing for the records which are causing so much concern.

Your task

Discuss approaches and options you would consider in relation to the following (make recommendations only if you feel you have enough information):

1 Bases for grouping the records into series
2 Which series should be indexed by records management staff
3 Which series might be indexed at 'file' and which at 'individual document' level
4 File titling structures
5 The indexing features that would be desirable in an automated indexing system, and
6 The nature and source of the indexing vocabulary(ies).

Case study 6.2

Imagine that you are the records manager at the Boralian Association of Trade Unions, and you have the responsibility of making accessible on a network a growing collection of approximately 3000 BATU press releases. All of these press releases are available in word processed form and they are approximately 300–500 words in length. Likely users of the system are the general public, especially researchers and students who are interested in obtaining information about events, people and policy changes.

Your task

Discuss the pros and cons of manually indexing this collection. Consider the cost–benefits of making the press releases searchable in full text form only. Would relevance ranking be helpful in this situation?

Questions

1 Suggest contexts in which each of the following might be appropriate:
   a Business (or functional) classification
   b Knowledge-base classification
   c A combination of both kinds of classification

2 Why is it important for metadata to be attached to electronic records in an organisation?
3 Consider the role of manual (human) indexing in the future. Do you believe that automated approaches will entirely replace manual ones in the next couple of decades?
4 How important is classification in the organisation of information resources on intranets? Give reasons.
5 What are the factors to be taken into account when considering the costs of manually indexing documents using a controlled vocabulary?
6 Consider in which contexts automatic indexing approaches might be more appropriate from a cost–benefit point of view than indexing methods requiring human input.
7 '...Doing the same search using different search engines will often give you wildly differing results' (Eagan & Bender 1996). Why is this?

Notes

1 A series or 'record series' is defined by Robek, Brown & Stephens (1996, p. 585) as 'a group of identical or related records that are normally used and filed as a unit, and which permits evaluation as a unit for retention scheduling purposes'.
2 Chapters 5 and 9 provide further discussion on the types of information related to the content, context and structure of records which may be referred to as 'metadata'.
3 Mayhew (1992) and Shneiderman (1992) are examples of books which deal with software user interface design.

Additional information

There is a vast literature on the subject of indexing and information retrieval. Apart from articles in the records management journals, there are many journals devoted to information retrieval and new technologies, such as *Online, Information Processing and Management, Journal of the American Society for Information Science* and *Annual Review of Information, Science and Technology*. In Australia, conferences and/or meetings of organisations such as the RMAA (Records Management Association of Australia), VALA (Victorian Association for Library Automation), and ALIA (Australian Library and Information Association) often focus on themes of relevance to the field.

Three of the many established authors in the field of subject analysis and indexing are Lancaster (1986, 1991), Foskett (1996) and Fugmann (1993). Fidel et al (eds.) (1995) have produced a useful collection of articles on the indexing of electronic text and images.

With the proliferation of electronic documents, there has been great interest from information professionals of different backgrounds in the area of metadata. The Internet is a rich source of information about research and different projects on the issue. See, for example, the OCLC web site, http://www.oclc.org/metadata/ dublin_core/ and the web site of the Resource Discovery Unit at DSTC in Queensland, http://www.dstc.edu.au/RDU/.

There are a number of indexing standards which, though dated, are still helpful conceptually, such as BS 6529 (BSI 1984), ISO 5963 (ISO 1985) and ANSI Z39.4–1984 (ANSI 1984). NISO (US) has publicised a draft standard Z39.4–1996 *Guidelines for Indexes and Related Information Retrieval Devices* which revises ANSI Z39.4–1984. Useful guidelines on the construction, format and management of thesauri are provided in ANSI/NISO Z39.19–1993 (NISO 1994). Australian and international standards are available via Standards Australia.

References

ANSI 1984, *Basic Criteria for Indexes* (ANSI Z39.4–1984), NISO Press, Bethesda, MD.

Archives Authority of New South Wales, Records Management Office 1995, *Keyword AAA: Accuracy, Accessibility, Accountability*, Records Management Office, Sydney.

Black, G. 1997, 'Organising the Web: the need for third party intervention', *CAUSE in Australisia '97: Information Technology—the Enabler, 13–16 April, Melbourne Australia: Conference Proceedings*, University of Melbourne, Melbourne. pp. 39–46.

BSI 1984, *British Standard Recommendations For Examining Documents, Determining Their Subjects and Selecting Indexing Terms: BS 6529*, British Standards Institution, London.

Eagan, A. & Bender, L. 1996, 'Spiders and worms and crawlers, oh my: searching on the World Wide Web', *Untangling the Web: Proceedings of the Conference, 26 April, 1996, University of California, Santa Barbara* (http://www.library.ucsb.edu/untangle/eagan.html)

Fidel, R. et al. (eds) 1995 *Challenges in Indexing Electronic Text and Images*, NISO, Oxon Hill, MD.

Foskett, A. C. 1996, *The Subject Approach to Information*, 5th edn, Library Association Pub., London.

Fugmann, R. 1993, *Subject Analysis and Indexing*, Indeks Verlag, Frankfurt.

Henninger, M. 1997, *Don't Just Surf: Effective Research Strategies for the Net*, University of New South Wales Press, Sydney.

ISO 1985, *Documentation—Methods for Examining Documents, Determining Their Subjects, and Selecting Indexing Terms: ISO 5963*, International Organization for Standardization, Geneva.

Koulopoulos, T. M. & Frappaolo, C. 1995, *Electronic Document Management Systems: a Portable Consultant*, McGraw-Hill, New York.

Lancaster, F. W. 1986, *Vocabulary Control for Information Retrieval*, 2nd edn, Information Resources Press, Arlington.

Lancaster, F. W. 1991, *Indexing and Abstracting in Theory and Practice*, 2nd edn, Wiley, New York.

Linton, J. E. 1975, *Keyword Filing: A Manual of Filing Procedures*, Sydney, Advance Industries.

—— 1990, *Organising the Office Memory: The Theory and Practice of Records Management*, University of Technology, Sydney, Kuring-gai Campus, Centre for Information Studies Publications.

Mayhew, D. 1992, *Principles and Guidelines to Software User Interface Design*, Prentice Hall, Englewood Cliffs, NJ.

Miller, P. 1996, Metadata for the masses, *Ariadne: the Web version*, issue 5, September (www.ariadne.ac.uk/issue5/metadata-masses)

NISO 1994, *Guidelines for the Construction, Format and Management of Monolingual Thesauri: an American National Standard* (ANSI/NISO Z39.19–1993), NISO Press, Bethesda, MD.

Robek, M. F., Brown, G. F. & Stephens, D. O. 1996, *Information and Records Management*, 4th edn, Glencoe/McGraw-Hill, New York.

Salton, G. (ed.) 1971, *The SMART Retrieval System: Experiments in Automatic Document Processing*, Prentice Hall, Englewood cliffs, NJ.

—— 1989, *Automatic Text Processing: The Transformation, Analysis and Retrieval of Information by Computer*, Addison-Wesley, New York.

Salton, G. & McGill, M. J. 1983, *Introduction to Modern Information Retrieval* (McGraw-Hill Computer Science Series), McGraw-Hill, New York.

Shneiderman, B. 1992, *Designing the User Interface: Strategies for Effective Human-Computer Interaction*, 2nd edn, Addison-Wesley, Reading, MA.

Standards Australia 1996, *Australian Standard AS 4390.6–1996, Records Management, Part 1: General and Part 4: Control*, Homebush, NSW.

Tenopir, C. & Ro, Jung Soon 1990, *Full Text Databases*, Greenwood Press, New York.

Weinberg, B. H. 1996, 'Complexity in indexing systems-abandonment and failure: implications for organizing the Internet', presented at the ASIS 1996 Annual Conference Proceedings, October 19–24, 1996. Web site: http://www.asis.org/annual-96/Electronic Proceedings/weinberg.html

seven

Constructing a thesaurus and classification scheme

Overview

It is fairly common for recordkeeping and other professional information work to be combined in one job role (e.g. a position of information manager). This chapter from the first edition of the book has been included here (with very minor changes) on the basis that a records manager may need to construct a thesaurus or classification scheme for the informational documents within an organisation, or may need to incorporate some aspects of 'knowledge-base' classification into a more functionally organised scheme. Chapter 6 explained that Australian Standard AS4390–1996 recommends the use of an activities-based classification and thesaurus for titling and indexing documents which have evidential value in a given context. However there may be situations in which future retrieval will need to be based on the intellectual or subject content of the documents.

This chapter also contains a section (pages 159–60) which provides some guidelines about the choice of a coding or numbering system which might be helpful in a wide range of contexts.

Chapter 6 discussed the need for titling and indexing of documents to be based, at least to some extent, on a thesaurus. A thesaurus is an alphabetical list of allowed and non-allowed terms, with some degree of cross referencing to link non-allowed and allowed terms, and related allowed terms. The thesaurus often also includes a set of rules for formulating the forms of name to be used for people and organisations. The use of a thesaurus or controlled vocabulary helps to facilitate predictability in retrieval.

A classification scheme may consist of terms (which represent concepts) organised into hierarchies. A thesaurus can be produced from the classified categories, each term being listed alphabetically and indicating its synonymous and related terms. This kind of thesaurus is often used in records management as a file titling tool. The hierarchical categories may also be used to produce a classification scheme by which documents may be arranged physically so that similar subjects are grouped together within a particular overall logical order. Detailed classification schemes of this kind are less popular than in the past. Arguments for and against constructing such schemes are outlined later in this chapter.

Increasingly, information stored electronically and in paper form is shared across several departments in the organisation, so that more staff than before are involved in the naming and retrieval of files and documents. A corporate-wide thesaurus is likely to be needed in large, complex organisations. Such a thesaurus may integrate into one alphabetical sequence the terms of a specialised nature contributed from individual departments with the terms reflecting the business of the organisation as a whole. For example, the management department of an aerospace engineering company might frequently use the term, *aircraft components*, but the manufacturing department might additionally need to use more specialised terms, such as *airframes, airfoils, control surfaces, ailerons*, etc.

In many situations, an available 'readymade' thesaurus can be purchased, e.g. the functionally-based *Keyword AAA* thesaurus described in Chapter 6, which is designed to be merged with the specialised functional terms of an organisation (Archives Authority of New South Wales Records Management Office, 1995). Often, however, it is necessary to construct the thesaurus inhouse to meet the particular needs of the organisation.

The tasks of thesaurus construction and development have been made easier with automated records management systems. With many systems, the records manager can view online (or obtain a print-out of) the index terms that have been assigned by indexing personnel, and can thus identify multiple approaches to the spelling of a term, or the allocation of a number of different terms or phrases which have the same meaning. The computer provides assistance in the human tasks of editing and of adding appropriate cross references, and by undertaking the alphabetical filing of the thesaurus terms. It is a good idea for those who are developing an inhouse thesaurus to purchase a thesaurus management software package, or to make use of the thesaurus module of an automated records management system.

This chapter is intended to assist those involved in designing or reviewing a thesaurus and/or classification scheme. The method used here for thesaurus and classification scheme construction is called facet analysis, which is based on the grouping of terms into facets or categories.[1]

The facet analysis approach

Constructing a thesaurus and/or a detailed classification scheme for an organisation requires an understanding of information organisation theory. The facet analysis approach incorporates many aspects of this theory. Examples of concepts or principles include:

- Selecting terms that reflect the usage of the authors and the users of the documents
- The need for rigour in analysing and defining terms
- The role of mutual exclusivity in creating categories by theme
- The grouping of terms into categories and subcategories that reflect contextual and hierarchical interrelationships
- The need for numerical and/or alphabetical coding systems that are easy to file and are expansible, and

- The linear, one-dimensional nature of any given classified shelf arrangement which groups together some subject aspects, while scattering others.

This theory is useful in reviewing and modifying an existing thesaurus or classification scheme, as well as in constructing detailed or broad indexing and classification tools.

Using thesauri

The indexer consults the thesaurus when translating the concepts from the file or document being indexed into the controlled vocabulary. The user/searcher consults the thesaurus to decide which words to use in looking for files or documents on a topic. The thesaurus is often stored as part of the automated indexing system. When indexing or searching, non-allowed terms can be linked automatically or via cross references with the appropriate index terms from the thesaurus. A thesaurus is a dynamic tool—terms will need to be added and deleted with the changing emphases of the organisation. When new terminology is introduced to replace a previous term, cross references may need to be made between the old and new terms.

Using classification schemes

Classification schemes establish categories, and an order within each category and overall, by which documents or files are arranged. A notation (letters, numbers or both) is a coding system which mechanises the chosen order, while providing each item with an address. A classification scheme will inevitably group together some aspects of multi-aspect subjects, and scatter others. The indexing system compensates by providing more than one index term or search point for each document/file containing multi-aspect subjects.

Constructing a thesaurus

The steps below provide a very brief summary of the facet analysis approach to thesaurus construction.

Step 1 Understanding user and organisation needs

It is important for the thesaurus compiler to understand the goals and functions of the organisation and, by observation and discussion, to become familiar with the search terms that users/action officers are likely to use when searching for files. It may be helpful to analyse available transaction logs recording searches made by users in the past. While user input is essential, sometimes the thesaurus compiler will have to make a decision as to the term that will suit most likely users. The thesaurus will also reflect the perspective of the organisation. For example, a tobacco industry association would view cigarettes as a valuable product; while an anti-cancer organisation would view them as a health hazard.

Step 2 Defining the scope of the thesaurus

The categories of records to be indexed with controlled vocabulary will define the scope of the thesaurus. Kinds of questions that may need to be asked are, for example: Are index headings required for internal administrative structures? What kinds of proper names will be included? Will the thesaurus include format terms, such as meeting papers and reports? Will headings for operational documents such as budgets and requisitions be needed on the system?

Step 3 Collecting terms

From a representative selection of records to be indexed, collect at random a large number of terms that appear to be likely search terms. Titles of files, letters, memoranda and reports tend to be useful sources of terms. Include terms from users' questions examined in Step 1. Proper names may be included and different versions of the same name should be noted. The number of terms collected will depend on the complexity of the records—ranging perhaps from 300 terms to 3000 terms. It is helpful to record each term or phrase, and to record under it a definition of the way the term was used. Initially, or as a subsequent step, it is necessary to break up phrases as far as possible into their component parts, for example, *government funding* would be better as two terms, *government* and *funding*.[2] In many cases a phrase may be regarded as a 'term' if it is often used to represent a particular concept. See Figure 7.1 for a list of examples of terms that might be randomly collected from files in a nutrition research organisation.

Step 4 Grouping terms into broad categories, subcategories and sub-subcategories

The next step is to divide the terms into broad categories (or facets). A category is a group of terms which share a common characteristic. For example, in the field of building, the broad categories might be *types of buildings*, *parts of buildings*, *operations*, *materials* and *equipment*. In the field of nutrition, some categories might be *nutritional problems*, *nutrients (food elements)* and *food operations*. It is not important what the categories are called, as long as it is possible to identify what the shared characteristic is within each grouping. A category entitled *hazards* or *problems* or *products* will appear to be perfectly logical within the given context. Such labels may often have to be added if they were not in the original collection of terms. Adding or supplying additional terms can only be helpful in the categorisation process. It is helpful to begin by grouping the terms according to the characteristics which appear to occur most frequently.

Each broad category should now be examined to see whether or not it may be grouped further into subcategories. Subcategories are derived by dividing a category by subordinate characteristics applicable only to it. Each subcategory may, in turn, be divided into 'sub-subcategories' in the same way, for example:

BUILDINGS
RELIGIOUS
EDUCATIONAL
RESIDENTIAL
CHURCHES
SCHOOLS
BRICK
TIMBER
WEATHERBOARD

ANAEMIA	FOOD ADDITIVES	METABOLIC DISORDERS
ANIMAL PROTEINS	FOOD CONTAMINANTS	MIDDLE AGE
ANOREXIA NERVOSA	FOOD DEFICIENCIES	MINERALS
ARTIFICIAL SWEETENERS	FOOD DISTRIBUTION	MONOSODIUM GLUTAMATE = MSG
ASPARTAME	FOOD ELEMENTS	NUTRITIONAL PROBLEMS
ATHLETES ACTIVE LIFESTYLE	FOOD EXCESS	NUTRITIONISTS
BACTERIAL FOOD CONTAMINANTS	FOOD HANDLING	OBESITY
BAKING	FOOD OPERATIONS	OESOPHAGEAL DISORDERS
BALANCED DIET	FOOD POISONING	ORGANISATIONS
BODILY SYSTEM DISORDERS	FOOD PRESERVATION	OVERWEIGHT
BOTTLING	FOOD PROBLEMS	PEOPLE
BREAD AND CEREALS	FOOD SANITATION	PESTICIDES
BULIMIA	FOOD SPOILAGE	PRESS CLIPPINGS
CANNING	FOOD STORAGE	PREVENTATIVE NUTRITION
CARBOHYDRATE DISORDERS	FOODS	PRITIKIN DIET
CARDIOVASCULAR DISORDERS	FREEZING	PROTEINS
CHEMICAL FOOD CONTAMINANTS	FRUIT AND VEGETABLES	RECOMMENDED DIETARY
COLOURING AGENTS	FRYING	ALLOWANCES (RDA)
CONSUMER PROTECTION	GOALS	RESEARCH REPORTS
COOKING METHODS	GOVERNMENT	RICKETS
CORONARY HEART	HEALTH	SACCHARINE
DISEASE	HEALTH DIETS	SALMONELLA
DESIRABLE WEIGHTS	HEALTH REGULATIONS	SLATING
DIABETES	HEALTHY	SANITARY STANDARDS
DIET	HIATUS HERNIA	SCARSDALE DIET
DIETITIANS	HISTORY	SEDENTARY
EATING DISORDERS	ILL	SMALL (BODY FRAME)
EDUCATIONAL VIDEOS	INFANCY	STANDARDS
ELDERLY	INVALIDS	STATISTICS
FOOD AND AGRICULTURE	IRON	THERAPEUTIC DIETS
ORGANISATION OF THE	IRRADIATION	VEGETABLE PROTEINS
UNITED NATIONS (FAO)	LABOURERS	VITAMIN D
FATS	LARGE (BODY FRAME)	VITAMINS
FEMALE	LEGISLATION	WEIGHT
FIVE FOOD GROUPS	LOW SODIUM DIET	WEIGHT REDUCTION DIETS
FLAVOUR INTENSIFIERS	LOW CHOLESTEROL DIET	
FOOD ADDITIVE REGULATIONS	MALE	

Figure 7.1 Examples of terms that might be randomly collected from files in a nutrition research organisation

After the process of creating subfacets:

BUILDINGS
(BY TYPE)
   RELIGIOUS
      CHURCHES
         CATHEDRALS
   EDUCATIONAL
      SCHOOLS
   RESIDENTIAL
      HOUSES
(BY MATERIAL)
   BRICK
   TIMBER
      WEATHERBOARD

It is a fundamental principle that the process should lead ultimately to categories and subcategories made up of arrays. An array is a list of terms in which the terms:

1 Are mutually exclusive of one another, and
2 Share a common feature or characteristic.

To test whether or not the terms in an array are mutually exclusive, try to envisage a compound topic made up from any two terms within the array. If such a compound topic is possible, the terms in the array are not yet mutually exclusive, and thus require further grouping: e.g., in a scheme on community information:

A Not mutually exclusive	B Mutually exclusive
People	People
Workers	By age
Unemployed	Middle-aged
Middle-aged	Elderly
Elderly	By socio-economic role
	Unemployed
	Workers

The terms in the array in A are not mutually exclusive. It is possible to envisage topics in the literature such as Unemployed middle-aged people or Elderly workers, etc.

Phrases such as *by type* and *by age* identify the common characteristic shared by each group and sub-group of terms. The preposition *by* should be omitted when compiling the alphabetical listing of thesaurus terms. In the grouping process *by* is always 'understood' as preceding each term which acts as a criterion of division, whether the preposition is explicitly supplied or not.

The process of deriving arrays also involves ensuring that the hierarchical (genus–species, whole–part, thing–instance, thing–type) relationships existing between the terms are clearly indicated.

For example, for an Office Administration thesaurus, the terms:
SWITCHBOARDS, ORAL COMMUNICATION, PABX, TELEPHONES, VOICE MAIL should be grouped as:

Oral Communication
   Telephones
      Switchboards
         PABX
   Voice Mail

NATURAL MATERIALS, SLATE, TIMBER, HARDWOODS, PINE, MARBLE, SOFTWOODS, STONE should be grouped as:

Natural materials
   Timber
      Hardwoods
      Softwoods
         Pine
   Stone
      Marble
      Slate

The relationships identified will depend on the given context as well as on naturally occurring interrelationships. Thing–type relationships may be more specifically defined, for example, as 'thing–purpose', 'thing–shape', 'thing–cause' etc.

An example of facet analysis for some categories derived in Step 3 from the collection of nutrition terms in Figure 7.1 (with a few added terms) is provided in Figure 7.2. It should be noted that different views of the field would result in different groupings.

The lay-out is particularly important. As can be seen in Figure 7.2, arrays are indicated by indentation. The levels of indentation will be extremely helpful when constructing the thesaurus, and the user of a resulting classification scheme will be able to tell at a glance how the terms relate to each other.

Synonymous terms which should appear in the thesaurus as non-preferred terms are placed here next to the preferred term after an equals sign. Scope notes beginning with the words 'Class here' may be included at this point or later on. A 'see also' note is used to refer the indexer to a related term in a totally different facet.

NUTRITION
FORM
   PRESS CLIPPINGS
   REPORTS
   MEETING PAPERS
PLACE
   AUSTRALIA
      VICTORIA
         MELBOURNE
      NEW SOUTH WALES
         SYDNEY
VIEWPOINTS
   LEGAL
      LEGISLATION
      REGULATIONS
      STANDARDS
   RESEARCH
      STATISTICS

AGENCIES AND SERVICES
  BY PURPOSE
    HEALTH PROMOTION Class here preventative nutrition
    CONSUMER PROTECTION
  BY TYPE
    ORGANISATIONS
      GOVERNMENT
        DOMESTIC
          STATE
            ANRF = Australian Nutrition Research Foundation
          FEDERAL
        OVERSEAS
          FAO = Food and Agric. Org. of the U.N.
  PROFESSIONAL SERVICES
    BY FUNCTION
      DIETITIANS
      MEDICAL PRACTITIONERS
      NUTRITIONISTS
FOOD OPERATIONS
  BY PURPOSE
    HANDLING
      STORAGE
      DISTRIBUTION
        SALES
    PRESERVATION
      BY PROCESS
        BOTTLING
        CANNING
        FREEZING
FOOD SPOILAGE
  BY CAUSE = Spoilage causes
    CONTAMINANTS
      BACTERIAL
        SALMONELLA
      CHEMICAL
        PESTICIDES
  BY RESULT = Spoilage effects
    CONTAMINATED FOOD Class here food that may cause poisoning
NUTRIENTS = Food Elements
  PROTEINS
    ANIMAL
    VEGETABLE
  MINERALS
    IRON
  VITAMINS
    VITAMIN D
  FATS = Oils
DIET = Food Therapy
  BY PURPOSE
    WEIGHT DIETS
      WEIGHT GAIN Class here diets for weight gain
      WEIGHT REDUCTION Class here diets for weight loss
    THERAPEUTIC DIETS Class here diets for particular medical conditions
  BY CONTENT
    LOW-SODIUM
    LOW-CHOLESTEROL
  BY NAME
    PRITIKIN
    SCARSDALE DIET

```
    BY GOAL
        BALANCED DIET
            RECOMMENDED DIETARY ALLOWANCES = RDA
PEOPLE
    BY LIFESTYLE
        ACTIVE
        INACTIVE = Sedentary
    BY OCCUPATION
        LABOURERS
        ATHLETES
    BY STATE OF HEALTH
        HEALTHY
        ILL
        CONVALESCENTS
    BY SIZE
        SMALL (BODY FRAME)
        LARGE (BODY FRAME)
    BY GENDER
        MALE
        FEMALE
    BY AGE
        MIDDLE AGE
        INFANCY
        ELDERLY
    BY GOAL
        DESIRABLE WEIGHTS = Ideal weights
NUTRITIONAL PROBLEMS
    BY CAUSE
        PSYCHOLOGICAL CAUSES
        HEREDITY = Genetic causes
        SOCIO-ECONOMIC
            SOCIAL FACTORS
            ECONOMIC FACTORS
    BY SYMPTOMS
        WEIGHT PROBLEMS
            UNDERWEIGHT
            OVERWEIGHT
                OBESITY = Obese
    BY TYPE
        BODILY SYSTEM DISORDERS
            CARDIOVASCULAR
                CORONARY HEART DISEASE
            OESOPHAGEAL
                HIATUS HERNIA
            METABOLIC
                CARBOHYDRATE DISORDERS
                    DIABETES
            GASTRO-INTESTINAL
                FOOD POISONING
        EATING DISORDERS
            ANOREXIA NERVOSA
            BULIMIA
        DEFICIENCY DISORDERS
            ANAEMIA
                RICKETS
```

Figure 7.2 Example of facet analysis for some nutrition terms

Step 5 Producing the thesaurus

Once all the categories or facets have been rigorously analysed as above, the thesaurus may now be produced. The procedure is to create a record for each term (including synonyms and any terms from a 'class here' note) in turn, documenting whether it is an allowed term or not. For each allowed term, appropriate cross references are noted. These are based on the final groupings and arrays. ANSI/NISO Z39.19–1993 describes this kind of structure which, for each allowed term displays other allowed terms at only one step up (broader) and down (narrower) in its hierarchy as a 'flat thesaurus structure' (NISO 1994, sect. 6.2.1). This is illustrated in Figure 7.3. It is suggested that these references (if relevant) should be set out under each term, using symbols as follows:

USED TERM

- **SN** (Scope Note) is used before a scope or inclusion note (i.e. a note explaining how the above term is defined in the thesaurus).
- **UF** (Used For) indicates, in alphabetical order, which synonyms for the above term are in the list as unused terms.
- **BT** (Broader Term) indicates the used single term that is super-ordinate (i.e. one step up from the above term).
- **NT** (Narrower Term(s) indicates, in alphabetical order, the used term or terms that are subordinate (i.e. one step down from the above term, indented inwards).
- **RT** (Related Term(s) indicates, in alphabetical order, the term or terms that are coordinate (i.e. on the same indentation level with the above term, under the relevant broad term).
- **A/RT** (Additional Related Term(s) indicates a term from a different facet that is related in some way to the above term (not commonly used).

Note that the symbols in the order given here are only a check list of the references you may require. Facet headings, for instance, will only have narrower terms listed under them in the list.

The symbol USE is used for the see reference referring the user from each unused term to a used (or allowed) term, as follows:

UNUSED TERM
USE
USED TERM

Note that once the terms have been faceted, the production of the thesaurus is a somewhat mechanical process, as the analysis of relationships has already taken place.

Different typographic styles may be applied to contrast the appearance of allowed and non-allowed terms; different symbols may also be used.

You might find that the thesaurus production stage results in some amendments to your classified arrangement. For example, you may realise that a concept, or an entire subcategory, has been inappropriately positioned.

Terminology decisions are made at this stage:

- The use of phrase-type headings may be found to be necessary to clarify the meaning of a term. One example of this is the addition of explanatory terms in parentheses to homographs in the list e.g. *letters (alphabet)* and *letters (correspondence)*.
- Occasionally the phrase for the concept in a facet might need to be expressed with the terms in a slightly different order to increase the chances of the searcher or indexer finding it in the list. Dividing characteristics beginning with the word *by* should be rephrased, for example, *By process* under *Preservation* might become *Preservation processes*. Other phrases beginning with *by* may be ignored as thesaurus terms. For example, *by function* under *Professional services* (Figure 7.2) is not a likely search term, and therefore it need not be incorporated into the thesaurus. In this situation, the narrower terms to *Professional services* are *Dietitians*, *Medical practitioners* and *Nutritionists*.

In addition, decisions will have to be made as to:

1 Preferring the noun or verb form of a term, e.g. *constructing* or *construction*
2 Preferring the singular or plural form of a term, e.g. *vitamin* or *vitamins*

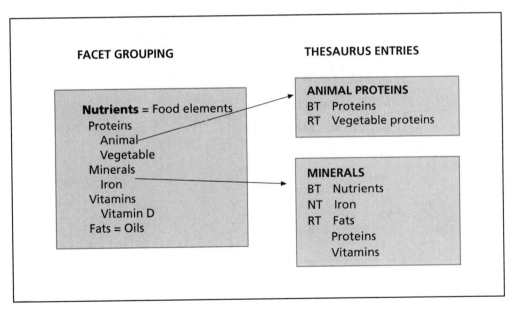

Figure 7.3 Thesaurus entries for *animal proteins* and *minerals* derived from facet relationships

Note: If there are two or more related terms, they are arranged in alpabetical order

Category based on facet analysis (classified grouping)

NUTRIENTS=Food Elements
PROTEINS
    ANIMAL
    VEGETABLE
MINERALS
    IRON
VITAMINS
    VITAMIN D
FATS=Oils

Thesaurus grouping
(terms not yet in A/Z order)

NUTRIENTS
UF   Food Elements
NT   FATS
       MINERALS
       PROTEINS
       VITAMINS

Food elements
Use
NUTRIENTS

PROTEINS
BT   NUTRIENTS
NT   ANIMAL
       VEGETABLE
RT   FATS
       MINERALS
       VITAMINS

ANIMAL PROTEINS
BT   PROTEINS
RT   VEGETABLE

VEGETABLE PROTEINS
BT   PROTEINS
RT   ANIMAL

MINERALS
BT   NUTRIENTS
NT   IRON
RT   FATS
       PROTEINS
       VITAMINS

IRON
BT   MINERALS

VITAMINS
BT   NUTRIENTS
NT   VITAMIN D
RT   FATS
       MINERALS
       PROTEINS

VITAMIN D
BT   VITAMINS

FATS
UF   Oils
BT   NUTRIENTS
RT   MINERALS
       PROTEINS
       VITAMINS

Oils
Use
FATS

Figure 7.4 Thesaurus entries for the category entitled NUTRIENTS

3 Using direct or indirect entry for phrases, e.g. *residential buildings* or *buildings, residential,* and

4 Preferring the abbreviated form of a topical term or proper name, e.g. *RSI* or *repetition strain injury,* and *US* or *United States.* For example, a records manager may

apply the rule that where an organisation is better known by an acronym than by its full name, the acronym should be used as an allowed thesaurus term.

Many of these decisions will have been made during the facet analysis stage. The main aim is to achieve consistency, and to select terminology that is commonly used in the organisation.

Once the entries containing the used terms and their references, and the synonymous terms and their references have been completed, it is then necessary to arrange all the entries in alphabetical order. Sets of UF, NT or RT terms within an entry are also in alphabetical order.

Examples of thesaurus entries term by term from the facet NUTRIENTS are provided in Figures 7.3 and 7.4. In the completed thesaurus all the entries would be arranged in alphabetical order. Within each entry more than two narrower or related terms are also arranged alphabetically. Note that by simply glancing at the BT, NT, and RT terms for each used term, the indexer/searcher is quickly able to mentally re-create the original hierarchies derived from the facet analysis process.

It is a good idea to test out the thesaurus with a pilot indexing project. Some amendments may need to be made at this stage.

A user guide or manual should be prepared to explain how the thesaurus should be used, whether proper names not in the list should be supplied by the indexer, and any rules for formatting such names.

The online thesaurus helps you select the right term

When to construct a knowledge-base classification scheme for files/documents

Textbooks such as those by Aschner (1983), Gill (1993) and Linton (1990) provide advice on the construction of knowledge-base classification schemes. Multiple numbering systems (which use a hierarchical coding approach for the primary, secondary and tertiary aspects of a subject) are examples of classification schemes. They are discussed with other file numbering approaches in Chapter 8. The advantages and disadvantages of multiple numbering systems outlined on p. 169 apply to all physical arrangements based on classification schemes.

Detailed knowledge-base classification schemes are declining in importance. Simple running number or sequential filing systems are very appealing to set up and maintain, and automated indexing systems make it easy to browse online the file titles of relevance to a topic.

A running number placed after a code for a departmental name or function (e.g. PER 001, PER 002, for the personnel files) is a common compromise approach which achieves a rough logical grouping with a minimum of effort. Linton (1990, p. 68) provides a list of mnemonic alphanumeric codes for the primary classes in his classification system.

However, there are situations in which a detailed knowledge-base classification scheme is required. For example:

- The records to be organised may comprise both published and unpublished documents which need to be arranged in subject themes. A collection of research materials, for example, would most logically be grouped for use by researchers in a subject arrangement.
- The records manager may be called upon to design a detailed classification scheme by which to browse and retrieve pictorial images stored electronically.

Constructing a classification scheme

If a classification scheme for physically arranging documents/files is required, the terms as grouped in Figure 7.2 of Step 4 on pp. 151–53 must now be arranged in a satisfactory schedule order. This is the order of categories and subcategories that comprises a subject classification scheme. This order is based on certain principles outlined below.

Order within the classification scheme

- Single-concept topics should stand logically next to similar or related topics— 'like' topics should be grouped together.
- Orders in array (coordinate terms within categories and subcategories) should be logical, for example: young to old, small to big, chronological, etc. Alphabetical order would be a last resort.
- The overall order of categories should go from least to most important from the viewpoint of the users of the files. Thus areas of vital interest to the organisation would be lower down in the final order of categories.

- Compound or complex topics will be built up, working from lower down (or more important categories) to higher up (less important categories). The order of combining elements from different categories and subcategories (lower to higher) using the order in the sample outline schedules in Figure 7.5 will be, for example:

  Deficiency disorders – Elderly – Victoria – Statistics
  Desirable weights – Male – Large-frame – Athletes

This reverse combining order will achieve a file arrangement of simple before compound/complex, or 'general before special'. Thus, documents on the *elderly* (general topic) and documents on *deficiency disorders* (general topic) will file before documents on *deficiency disorders in the elderly* (compound topic). The more important aspects of compound/complex topics will be grouped together in the file arrangement, while other less important aspects will inevitably be scattered.

Once the arrays of terms within each category and subcategory have been inserted in their correct positions, a coding or numbering system can be added to establish the arrangement.

The function of the coding system is to mechanise the preferred order of subjects and to act as an address by which a record can be retrieved.

Features of coding systems

The requirements of a coding system are as follows:

- It should have a self-evident order. This limits our choice to the alphabet in upper or lower case, or numbers, or a combination of these.
- It should be highly expansible. The expansibility of a notation is the capacity to insert a new concept into the scheme in its logical position in relation to other topics, rather than just tacking it on at the end of the scheme. To achieve this expansibility numbers may be treated as decimals, and thus filed digit by digit as if there were a decimal point after each digit, e.g. 6, 61, 616, 62, 624, 63 .... Letters may be treated in a similar way, e.g. K, Kf, Kfg, Kg, L ....

It is also desirable to leave some gaps in the notation. Avoid notation ending in zero, A or a as it is impossible to insert a code that will file in front of these symbols.

It is tempting to make the coding system expressive of the hierarchical relationships between terms. This can result in a loss of expansibility, as well as in extremely long numbers. Examples of expressive and non-expressive notations:

S	Buildings		
Sk	Residential		*expressive*
Skp		Private	*notation*
Skpd		Houses	
Skpdc			Detached

Sb	Buildings		
Sk	Residential		*non-expressive notation*
Sm		Private	(i.e. an ordinal
Sp		Houses	notation)
T			Detached

Brevity is a desirable feature of notation, particularly since multi-aspect topics will have numbers made up of several elements of notation in combination.

The notation should provide the mechanics for synthesis known as facet indicators. When elements of notation are combined, it should be easy to distinguish the beginning of each element of the notation, so that the desired filing order will be clear. Facet indicators often consist of:

- the use of a / (slash) or : (colon) or . (full stop) or some other symbol. These do not have a self-evident order, thus filing rules would be required;
- the use of capital letters contrasting with lower case letters or numbers. Synthesised numbers may thus look like this:
PFC/GDB/EDR,
74/43/21,
SptKfGd,
L23D78B51

Filing the assigned classification codes

It is important to explain in a user guide how the notation is to be filed. Single elements of notation must file before compounds starting with those single elements, thus:

B011; B121; B534; L023; L023/B011; L027; N542; N542/L023; N542/L023/B011 ... etc.

Example of a classification scheme

An example outline of a classification schedule follows in Figure 7.5 below. In this scheme, the notation that was added to the schedule order of categories is not expressive of hierarchies. The codes are integers. When classifying documents, a slash / is used to link two or more notations in a compound/complex subject. Linked notations are combined in 'Z to A' order. If two notations from the same array are required to express the topic, rather choose the broader number that encompasses both.

NUTRITION IN GENERAL	**A000**
FORM	**B000**
PRESS CLIPPINGS	B011
EDUCATIONAL VIDEOS	B121
RESEARCH REPORTS	B332
STATISTICS	B534
PLACE	**E000**
AUSTRALIA	E001
VICTORIA	E010
MELBOURNE	E341
NEW SOUTH WALES	E412
SYDNEY	E623
VIEWPOINTS	**G000**
LEGAL	G007
LEGISLATION	G107
REGULATIONS	G302
STANDARDS	G602

AGENCIES AND SERVICES	**J000**
BY PURPOSE	J002
HEALTH PROMOTION	J109
Class here preventative nutrition	
CONSUMER PROTECTION	J206
BY TYPE	J221
ORGANISATIONS	J248
GOVERNMENT	J321
DOMESTIC	J345
STATE	J356
ANRF = Australian Nutrition	
Research Foundation	J358
FEDERAL	J421
OVERSEAS	J429
FAO = Food and Agric. Org. of the U.N.	J456
PROFESSIONAL SERVICES	J501
BY FUNCTION	J503
DIETITIANS	J508
MEDICAL PRACTITIONERS	J601
NUTRITIONISTS	J606
FOOD OPERATIONS	**L000**
BY PURPOSE	L010
HANDLING	L023
STORAGE	L027
DISTRIBUTION	L032
SALES	L034
PRESERVATION	L111
BY PROCESS	L145
BOTTLING	L233
CANNING	L356
FREEZING	L467
FOOD SPOILAGE	**N000**
BY CAUSE = Spoilage causes	N038
CONTAMINANTS	N078
BACTERIAL	N155
SALMONELLA	N344
CHEMICAL	N468
PESTICIDES	N542
BY RESULT = Spoilage effects	N633
CONTAMINATED FOOD Class here food that	
may cause poisoning	N722
NUTRIENTS = Food Elements	**P000**
PROTEINS	P134
ANIMAL	P157
VEGETABLE	P167
MINERALS	P245
IRON	P249
VITAMINS	P324
VITAMIN D	P456
FATS = Oils	P789
DIET = Food Therapy	**R000**
BY PURPOSE	R001
WEIGHT DIETS	R020
WEIGHT GAIN Class here diets for weight gain	R102
WEIGHT REDUCTION Class here diets for	
weight loss	R124
THERAPEUTIC DIETS Class here diets for	
particular medical conditions	R156
BY CONTENT	R213
LOW-SODIUM	R218
LOW-CHOLESTEROL	R221

BY NAME	R310
PRITIKIN	R324
SCARSDALE	R346
BY GOAL	R421
BALANCED DIET	R435
RECOMMENDED DIETARY	R467
ALLOWANCES = RDA	
PEOPLE	**S000**
BY LIFESTYLE	S015
ACTIVE	S024
INACTIVE	S046
BY OCCUPATION	S126
LABOURERS	S178
ATHLETES	S188
BY STATE OF HEALTH	S233
HEALTHY = HEALTH	S242
ILL	S322
CONVALESCENTS	S362
BY SIZE	S435
LARGE (BODY FRAME)	S437
BY GENDER	S466
MALE	S468
FEMALE	S501
BY AGE	S504
INFANCY	S522
MIDDLE AGE	S532
ELDERLY	S542
BY GOAL	S678
DESIRABLE WEIGHTS = Ideal weights	S777
NUTRITIONAL PROBLEMS	**V000**
BY CAUSE	V030
PSYCHOLOGICAL CAUSES	V056
HEREDITY = Genetic causes	V101
SOCIO-ECONOMIC	V105
SOCIAL FACTORS	V129
ECONOMIC FACTORS	V167
BY SYMPTOMS	V202
WEIGHT PROBLEMS	V206
UNDERWEIGHT	V223
OVERWEIGHT	V257
OBESITY = Obese	V267
BY TYPE	V301
BODILY SYSTEM DISORDERS	V374
CARDIOVASCULAR	V368
CORONARY HEART DISEASE	V417
OESOPHAGEAL	V455
HIATUS HERNIA	V462
METABOLIC	V532
CARBOHYDRATE DISORDERS	V555
DIABETES	V567
GASTRO-INTESTINAL	V572
FOOD POISONING See also Contamination	V581
EATING DISORDERS	V701
ANOREXIA NERVOSA	V762
BULIMIA	V774
DEFICIENCY DISORDERS	V858
ANAEMIA	V862
RICKETS	V866

Figure 7.5 Example of an outline classification schedule on the subject of nutrition

Applying the above scheme, ELDERLY would be S542, DEFICIENCY DISORDERS would be V858, and DEFICIENCY DISORDERS IN THE ELDERLY would be V858/S542.

Index and user guide

A classification scheme is not complete without an alphabetical index to the schedules. This involves taking each term, in turn, and placing its notation next to it; then filing all the terms alphabetically. To avoid see references, synonyms would simply be indexed to the appropriate notation, for example:

FATS ...   P789
Oils ...   P789 etc.

A user guide should be prepared to explain how the classification scheme should be used.

Exercises

1 Using the grouping of terms within the *food spoilage* category on p. 161, produce a set of thesaurus entries for each term, showing relevant scope notes, and UF, BT NT and RT references under each term.

2 Examine the category *nutritional problems* on p. 162, and use this to create a keyword plus three descriptors style of file title for the following two topics (the keywords in each case will be *nutritional problems*):
   a Obesity as a symptom of nutritional problems
   b Social factors as a cause of nutritional problems.

3 Using the outline classification schedules in Figure 7.5, assign numbers for documents on the following topics. Then file them as they would file on the shelves. (Answers at the end of the exercise.)
   a Information about the Australian Nutrition Research Foundation
   b Information about health promotion
   c Consumer protection
   d Regulations concerning consumer protection
   e Regulations about nutrition in general.
   Answers: a—J358; b—J109; c—J206; d—J206/G302; e—G302
   Filing: G302;   J109;   J206;   J206/G302;   J358

4 Select eight short 'Letters to the Editor' on one broad theme from a newspaper and construct a small thesaurus for indexing the letters, using the steps outlined above.

Notes

1 The approach has its origins in the writings of Ranganathan and the index languages produced by the Classification Research Group in England. Ramsden (1974) and Foskett (1996 and previous editions) describe facet analysis principles.

2 Discussed further in, for example, ISO 2788, (ISO 1986) and ANSI/NISO Z39.19–1993 (NISO 1994).

Questions

1 Faced with an unindexed collection of knowledge-base documents in various forms (e.g. letters, e-mail, diagrams, Web pages), how would you:
   a Identify terms which might form the basis of a thesaurus?
   b Group those terms into categories and subcategories?
   c Deal with synonyms?
   d Derive an alphabetical thesaurus as the result of the above?
2 Discuss the advantages and disadvantages of constructing and using a detailed subject classification scheme for organising and retrieving documents.
3 What are the essential features of a successful coding system of a classification scheme?

Additional information

This chapter gives a very condensed account of thesaurus and classification scheme construction using facet analysis. Further reading, and examination of available published and unpublished thesauri and classification schemes would be helpful to gain insight into a range of thesaurus construction approaches. Standards on thesaurus construction such as ANSI/NISO Z39.19–1993 and ISO 2788 (NISO 1994 and ISO 2788) are invaluable sources of guidelines. They are available via Standards Australia. Aitchison & Gilchrist (1987; 3rd edition by Aitchison, Bawden & Gilchrist, in press), Townlee and Gee (1980). Ramsden (1974) is a useful text. Linton (1990), Gill (1993) and Aschner (1983) provide explanations and examples of subject filing arrangements. ANSI/NISO Z39.19–1993 provides a list of further reading which includes publications about thesaurus software ·and computer interfaces. A bibliography being compiled by Willpower Information on thesaurus construction and thesaurus software can be found at the Web site address: http://www.willpower.demon.co.uk/thesbibl.html.

References

Aitchison, J. & Gilchrist, A. 1987, *Thesaurus Construction: A Practical Manual*, 2nd edn, Aslib, London. A third edition by Aitchison, Bawden and Gilchrist is in press.

Archives Authority of New South Wales, Records Management Office 1995, *Keyword AAA*, Records Management Office, Sydney.

Aschner, K. (ed.) 1983, *Taking Control of Your Office Records: A Manager's Guide*, Knowledge Industry Publications, White Plains, New York.

Foskett, A. C. 1996, *The Subject Approach to Information*, 5th edn, Library Association Pub., London.

Gill, S. L. 1993, *File Management and Information Retrieval Systems: A Manual for Managers and Technicians*, 3rd edn, Libraries Unlimited, Englewood, Colo.

ISO 1986, *Guidelines for the Establishment and Development of Monolingual Thesauri*, ISO 2788: 2nd edn, International Organization for Standardization, Geneva.

Linton, J. E. 1990, *Organising the Office Memory: The Theory and Practice of Records Management*, University of Technology, Sydney, Kuring-gai Campus, Centre for Information Studies Publications.

Love, A. 1988, 'Thesauri: the essence of intellectual control', *Informaa Quarterly*, November, pp. 15–18.

NISO 1994, *Guidelines for the Construction, Format, and Management of Monolingual Thesauri: An American National Standard* (ANSI/NISO Z39.19–1993), NISO Press, Bethusda, MD.

Ramsden, M. J. 1974, *An Introduction to Index Language Construction*, Bingley, London.

Townlee, H. M.& Gee, R. D. 1980, *Thesaurus Making*, Deutsch, London.

chapter *eight*

Managing active paper records

Overview

In designing a system for managing active paper records, a number of major decisions have to be made. These include:

1 Will the location and day-to-day control of the records be centralised within a records unit or decentralised to the business unit which uses them the most?
2 What registration procedures will be adopted and what classification and indexing methods will be used?
3 In what sequence(s) will the records be held?
4 What will be the procedures for establishing and maintaining files?
5 What filing equipment and supplies will be used?
6 Will a document and/or file tracking system be implemented?
7 How long will the records be kept in the system and how will they be culled?
8 What use will be made of technology in the design and operation of the system and in the way the records are stored?

This chapter focuses on questions 1, and 3–6. Chapters 6 and 7 are devoted to classification and indexing methods, including file titling; Chapter 4 includes information on disposal procedures; and Chapters 9 and 10 discuss the role of technology in records management. Chapter 9 also includes information on the registration of records.

It should be noted that a discussion of filing sequences is equally relevant to a study of classification and indexing principles (as presented in Chapter 6) as it is to the processes discussed in this chapter.

Centralised versus decentralised management of active records

With any record series, two decisions have to be made:

- Whether to store the records in a central records area or with/near staff who use them the most
- Whether to centralise control over the records or to leave control with the staff in the particular business unit concerned.

Factors bearing on these decisions are:

- Who uses the records? Is it just one group of users or is it users from across the organisation?
- How often are the records accessed and how quickly do they need to be retrieved? Are they used for reference purposes on a regular basis or are they used intensively for a while and then only occasionally?
- Should users have free access to the records or should access be restricted to the records management staff and accredited persons? (Examples of records which may have restricted access are staff records containing tax file numbers.)
- If there are security considerations, what facilities are there for securing the records? (There would need to be either a lockable area or lockable equipment.)
- Can users readily retrieve information direct from the record series or does an index need to be maintained to enable access?
- Are there space considerations? Is there room to store the records centrally? Is there a suitable space in the relevant business unit?
- How much maintenance is required on the records? Do they need to be reviewed regularly to see if they should be sent to offsite storage or be destroyed?
- Do the records move around the organisation very much? Is it necessary to keep track of where they are at all times?

In an organisation-wide records management program, even though different record series may be in different locations and be stored and retrieved using different methods, they should all be subject to the organisation's standards and rules on such matters as:

- Registration, classification, indexing and filing
- Records retention and disposal
- The purchase of filing equipment and supplies.

It is certainly important that business units are discouraged from setting up their own mini-filing systems as and when they choose. Coordination across the organisation is essential to minimise duplicate filing and to ensure the most efficient use of existing records.

Some examples of record series which are commonly filed, stored and retrieved using different methods include the following:

General correspondence files

These are commonly held in a central records area and are filed in classified subject, alphabetical or numerical order. They are usually controlled by registration and tracking systems, manual or automated.

If an organisation is large or geographically spread, there may be correspondence file stations in various locations. There are obvious advantages in maintaining centralised control in such situations:

- Staff throughout the organisation can be aware of what correspondence files exist, wherever located
- A file can be moved from one file station to another and still be tracked at any time.

Records of periodic transactions (forms, related correspondence, etc.)

These are frequently filed near, and maintained by, the personnel using them the most. They often have a natural filing order such as invoice number and are referenced via specialised systems within the operational area, such as accounting systems.

Project records (project documentation such as research reports, survey results, correspondence, file notes)

These are usually filed by project name or number, and located with project personnel while the projects are current.

Case files (e.g. personnel, student, medical, client and property records)

These may be located near the staff using them the most or in a central records area; the location is often determined by quantity and availability of space. They may be controlled by specialised systems within the operational area, such as student record systems, or by separate registration and tracking systems.

In the past, case files were most commonly filed alphabetically by name. Increasingly, where large numbers of records are involved and economical storage methods are essential, they are filed numerically using a sequential numbering system or a self-numbering system such as insurance policy number.

Filing sequence

In this context filing sequence refers to the physical arrangement or ordering of files. It is always necessary to give each file some kind of unique identification number or address to enable it to be stored and retrieved. This is achieved through a coding system based on notations which have a self-evident order, such as the alphabet (upper/lower case), Arabic numerals used as decimals or as integers, Roman numerals, or date (day, month, year).

Since all filing arrangements are linear 'one-dimensional' systems, it is often necessary, for efficient file retrieval, to supplement those arrangements with indexes that will lead the user from one or more of the index terms that have been applied to the file to the appropriate file location number address.

The most important question to answer before choosing a filing sequence is: whose needs come first—the users, or the records management staff? Should the system enable the users to go direct to the files they are after, or should it be designed around the needs of the records management staff for simplicity and efficiency? Client files, for example: if they are filed in name order, users can go direct to the file they want. If they are filed in a sequential number order, users will have to check an index first for the relevant number. From the records management staff's point of view, it is easier and quicker to maintain files in a sequential number order, particularly if there is a lot of filing to be done on a regular basis. In addition, filing in alphabetical order means that banks of files have to be moved periodically to make space for newly opened files in the sequence, whereas in a sequential numbering system new files are simply added to the end of the sequence.

The following is a summary of the most commonly used systems for arranging files. Needless to say there are all sorts of variations of these.

Multiple numbering systems

Examples:

L/06/08
(L = Leave; 06 = Recreation; 08 = Applications)
G/02/096
(G = Grievances; 02 = Hearings Process; 096 = Education Ministry)

Multiple numbering systems were common in the past when file indexing systems were manual and, in many cases, less than adequate. They enable browsing on the shelves or via a list in file number order. The primary, secondary and tertiary numbers/letters may be listed in separate schedules, or, as is more frequent, the codes for the headings and their particular subheading codes are spelt out one by one in a single list.

Advantages of this approach are:

- Related files are grouped together.
- The file numbers are translatable into their subject categories.
- Relocation of particular groups of files is facilitated since all files sharing a function or subject category will have the same initial code.
- In some cases, detailed keyword or descriptor indexing is dispensed with, since the classified schedules can provide the searcher with the number for a subject.

Disadvantages of this approach are:

- There is a constant demand for space around existing files to house new files opened in the same subject area. There is a substantial burden involved in carrying out periodic major reshuffles of files to allow for growth.
- The classification schedules or sets of headings can be complex and difficult to maintain. Unless the classification scheme is extremely well constructed in the first place, allowing for infinite expansion of the numbering system, it is very easy for problems to arise as organisations branch into new areas of operation.

Sequential numbering systems

Examples:

000001–999999 (straight sequential)

97/0001–97/9999 (new sequence started each year)

CP/0001–CP/9999 (file series incorporated into number;

CP = Curriculum Proposals)

Advantages of this approach are:

- It enables a far more efficient use of space. Gaps do not have to be left for additions within the sequence, and there is no periodic shuffling around of files to free up space.
- It is much simpler for records management staff to allocate new file numbers.
- It is easier and quicker to file using such a simple numbering system.

Disadvantages of this approach are:

- Users always need to check the file index to ascertain the number of an existing file or to see whether a file has already been opened.
- Related files are separated. (Some would argue that this is not a disadvantage as there is no need for browsing on the shelves; browsing can be done more efficiently on an automated registration and tracking system where all files on a topic can be scanned, including those on loan.)
- The most frequently used files tend to be at the end of a filing sequence and congestion around that area can result.

Variations on filing by sequential number are **middle digit** and **terminal digit** arrangements. These are used to spread files across the system instead of having all the most recent ones at the end of the sequence.

Terminal digit filing is reasonably widely used in Australia for large collections. Numbers are read from right to left in small groups beginning with the terminal group. For example, in file number 295634, the digits are divided into three groups of two digits each:

tertiary	secondary	primary
29	56	34

The files whose number ends in 34 are filed first; then subfiling is by 56 then by 29. Numbers of less than six digits are brought up to that figure by adding zeros to the left of the file number.

In middle digit arrangements, filing is firstly by the middle two digits, then by the digits on the left and the right.

The main advantage of terminal and middle digit filing is that as files are added to the system, they are distributed across the sequence. There is not the same likelihood of congestion around the most recent files as can occur with straight sequential numbering systems. The main disadvantage is that banks of files may have to be moved periodically to make space for new files.

Self-numbering systems

Another system for arranging files is to use an already existing sequential numbering sequence within an organisation, for example, an insurance company might use its policy numbers.

Alphabetical name arrangements

Case files, that is, files where a name is the subject of a file, are often simply filed by name as in a telephone directory. Examples of such names are clients, staff, organisations, buildings, municipalities, and streets. Alphabetical arrangements are most successful with collections of files of up to about 1000.

Advantages of this approach are:

- No intervening steps are needed to locate a file
- Files relating to the same person, organisation, or other entity are kept together.

Disadvantages of this approach are:

- Space has to be constantly made for new files at the appropriate position
- Words are slower and more cumbersome to file by than numbers.

Files can also be arranged alphabetically by subject category but this is only successful with small collections such as personal filing.

With alphabetical arrangements a set of filing rules has to be developed and followed strictly. Such rules should reflect the style of name usage within the particular organisation, however, there are published rules that can be used as a guide. The Records Management Association of Australia has published a list of filing rules and these are reproduced, with some minor amendments, in Appendix A.

Procedures for creating and maintaining files

Whatever decisions are made regarding how files are to be created and maintained, it is important that the procedures are, firstly, clearly documented, and secondly, adhered to.

Decisions need to be made on the following issues:

- **Who is responsible for creating files?** What is the role of the users? The records management staff? The relative roles need to be clearly delineated. A typical scenario might be that the users are responsible for initiating new files by completing a 'Request for a New File' form (see Figure 8.1); the records management staff then make up the file and create any database or index entries required. Alternatively, the records management staff may be responsible for deciding when a new file is needed from their daily processing of incoming correspondence. A third option is that the users actually make up new files according to set guidelines. This may be the case in small organisations with no full-time records management staff.
- **How should both external and internal documents move around the organisation?** For example, at what point should correspondence arrive in the records area? Should the records management staff sort and process incoming mail, or should it go direct from the mail room to the business units or individuals concerned? What special controls are needed to ensure paper documents received by facsimile machine are processed along with other incoming mail? Should correspondence move around the organisation as loose papers, or on file?

    Factors such as the potential confidentiality of information, and the speed with which matters have to be considered are important here. Is there time for mail to go to the records area to be sorted, and to be placed on the relevant files prior to distribution? Is it important that new documents are presented in the context of all other documents held on the same topic; that is, is it important to present the whole file?

- **What is the best way to ensure that copies of internal documents and outgoing correspondence are directed to the records area to be placed on files,** if, in fact, this is what is required?
- **Do the records management staff need direction as to what files to place documents on?** With internal and outgoing documents, the typing of the relevant file name or number on every document will provide the records management staff with the required information. Another technique is for users to highlight filing names on documents which are to be filed in an alphabetical arrangement; and yet another technique is the use of a simple stamp on each document which users complete to indicate file destination.

VG SUMMS & LEGERS

REQUEST FOR NEW CLIENT FILE(S)

Please complete this form and return to Jane Smith, Central Records.
Attach any documentation to be placed on the file(s). For new clients, ensure files are opened prior to the commencement of client work.

CLIENT NAME _____

_____

CLIENT SHORT NAME (if varies from full name e.g. ABC) _____

_____

FILE TYPE (please tick)

      Tax Return   [ ]

      Correspondence   [ ]

      Fees   [ ]

      Audit   [ ]

      Accounting   [ ]

      Permanent   [ ]

CLIENT MANAGER _____

CONTACT NAME FOR QUERIES _____ PH _____

DATE _____

Figure 8.1 Sample form for requesting that a new file be opened

- **What links can be made between paper documents on files and the electronic versions of the same documents, and between paper documents on files and electronic documents on the same topic?** This is becoming a critically important question for organisations as the volume of documents stored in electronic format continues to grow.
- **What is the best way of organising the workflow in the records area for such tasks as the following?**
  — Creating new files
  — Indexing
  — Data entry
  — Preparing and sorting papers for filing
  — Filing
  — Repairing files.
- **Who is responsible for doing the filing?** Should users file loose correspondence on files they currently hold or should all loose correspondence be sent to the records management staff for filing? Should users file files away or should this be left to the records management staff?
- **What procedures can be established to minimise the misfiling of documents and files?** The cost of misfiling to an organisation can be substantial, both in terms of staff frustration and potential embarrassment, and in dollar terms. Retrieval costs of a misfile can quickly reach hundreds of dollars if both records management staff and users are involved in searching for the file or document.

  Clearly, staff training plays a major role here. The consequences of careless filing need to be stressed. Effective file titling will also help by minimising confusion over what file to place a document on. And the introduction of other techniques such as colour coding will aid in the battle against misfiling. Colour coded number and letter labels, used to represent file numbers, can be placed along the tabs of files to create bands of colour. If a file is misfiled it is highlighted because it does not fit into the band where it is located (see Figure 8.2).
- **What procedures will be established to ensure only active records are kept in the office?** It is important to develop procedures to regularly transfer files which have predetermined active periods to secondary storage or destruction. Once the initial decision as to how long files need to be kept in the office is made, then there are a number of techniques that can be used to facilitate the transfer process. For example, colour coded year labels on the tab of the files will help rapid identification of annual files ready for transfer. Also many of the automated records management systems available allow reporting on dates when files are due for action, such as transfer to secondary storage or destruction.

  Files which are not limited by period need to be regularly reviewed to ensure they do not become too thick and cumbersome to handle. New parts need to be opened as required.
- *What special procedures are needed for the filing of non-paper records* (such as magnetic media, microfilm, photographs)? Are these to be integrated with paper records or filed separately?

There are no hard and fast answers to any of the questions listed here. The records manager must study the needs of the particular organisation or business unit carefully and assess what will be the best solutions.

Records management

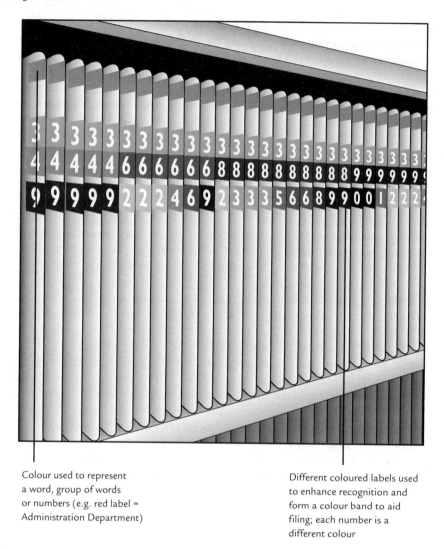

Colour used to represent
a word, group of words
or numbers (e.g. red label =
Administration Department)

Different coloured labels used
to enhance recognition and
form a colour band to aid
filing; each number is a
different colour

Figure 8.2   Colour coding on files

Filing equipment and supplies

The selection of the most appropriate filing equipment and supplies is fundamental
to the successful storage and retrieval of records.

Filing equipment refers to the **hardware** (such as shelving units and cupboards)
which is used to house records. The term **supplies** refers to the **software** such as file
covers, binders, guides, colour code labels, file clips and index cards.

In Australia, equipment and supplies can be purchased through selected general
stationers, and through office and storage equipment suppliers. There are also
vendors specialising in records management needs and offering total solutions.
These vendors generally offer consulting services to assist in selecting equipment

and supplies. However, it is very important that the records manager has a good knowledge of available options and can make informed decisions about what is best for the organisation. It is also important that the records manager guards against being tied into a system where the vendor has gone out of business, and specialised supplies are no longer available. The issue of compatibility of available supplies needs to be considered.

Equipment

How to select equipment

Before evaluating available equipment, gather information about:

- The types of records to be stored, for example, A4 documents in file covers, microfilm, cards, audio-visual materials, oversize documents, large computer printouts, magnetic or optical media. Whether related records in different formats (such as a paper file and a set of diskettes) should be stored together or in separate storage units.
- How often the records are accessed. Whether there are different record series with different access rates.
- How quickly the records need to be retrieved.
- The likelihood of the records being transferred to another records area within the organisation at some time. And if so, whether the filing equipment in the other area is suitable or whether the equipment being selected needs to be easily transportable.
- Any security requirements on the records. Whether access is restricted to certain personnel. Whether the records need to be readily accessible during the day but secured after hours.
- Any environmental factors to be accommodated, for example, the need for dust-free conditions.
- The floor space available for the equipment. Whether extra space has to be rented or purchased to accommodate the equipment and to what extent the cost of floor space is an issue. (Cost is always an issue, but tends to become more or less so according to where the organisation is located. Also storage equipment which takes up more floor space may weigh up better economically in the long run than equipment which takes less space, but is slower and more difficult to access.)

Main types of equipment

This section does not attempt to describe in detail the range of filing equipment available to organisations in Australia. It simply presents a brief overview of the major types of shelving and other cabinetry. Where a need exists within an organisation for new equipment, it is important that the records manager investigates thoroughly the range available on the market and discusses, where possible, the merits and demerits of particular equipment with colleagues who are actually using it.

Vertical filing cabinets

These are available in one- to five-drawer sizes. They can be useful for personal filing; there is a definite trend away from them for filing large volumes of documents.

- They are expensive relative to some other types of storage equipment, and require more maintenance.
- The space at the back of the drawers is often wasted because it is difficult to access.
- They take up more space than other types of equipment in terms of amount of material stored per square metre and amount of space required for access (see Figure 8.3).
- They are slower to access than some other types of equipment simply because drawers have to be opened. This becomes a significant factor when there is a medium to large amount of daily filing.

Static shelving units

If these are open units, retrieval and refiling is quick and easy (see Figures 8.4–8.6). A minimum aisle width of approximately 800 mm is required; 900 mm provides good access. Maintenance is minimum.

A minimum of two metres is required between vertical cabinets if this situation is to be avoided

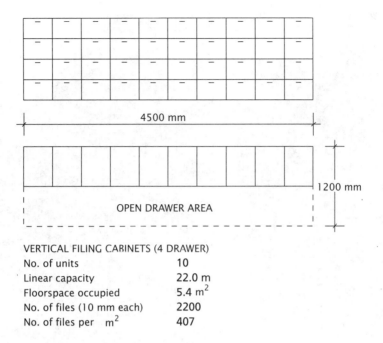

VERTICAL FILING CABINETS (4 DRAWER)
No. of units   10
Linear capacity   22.0 m
Floorspace occupied   5.4 m^2
No. of files (10 mm each)   2200
No. of files per   m^2 407

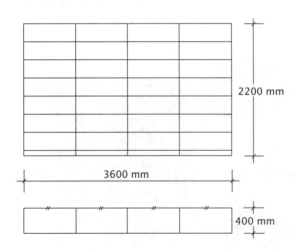

STATIC OPEN SHELVING
3600 LONG X 2200 HIGH X 400 DEEP
No. of shelves   7
Linear capacity   25.2 m
Floorspace occupied   1.5 m^2
No. of files (10 mm each)   2520
No. of files per   m^2 1680

Figure 8.3   Comparison of linear capacity of filing cabinets and static shelving in terms of floor space requirements

Figure 8.4   Filing the daily correspondence in an open shelving arrangement

Figure 8.5   Consulting colour coded lateral files in an open shelving arrangement

Figure 8.6   Consulting a file on a pull-out reference table

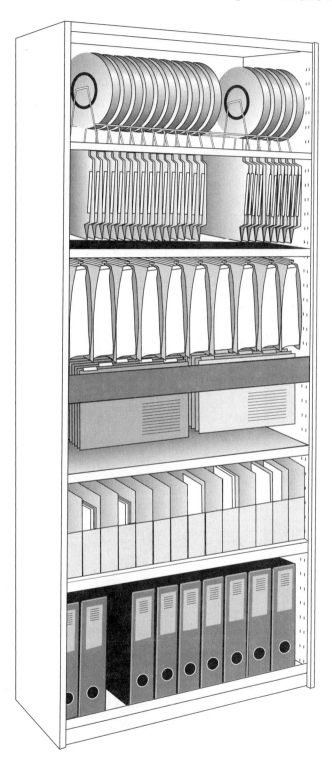

Figure 8.7   A cupboard set up for different types of record formats

Static shelving units may house binders, files stored laterally with identification aids such as guides, tabs and colour coding, files in suspension pockets, or non-paper media such as computer tapes stored in racks. They generally have adjustable fittings so shelves can be placed to take different sizes and types of records, and can also be replaced with racks for suspension filing (see Figure 8.7).

These types of units are also available with doors; these may be required for security, aesthetic or other environmental reasons. Such doors come in swing, folding or retractable style. However, the additional cost of doors is generally high and would represent an expensive solution for a large volume of records. Filing cupboards with shelves or racks for suspension filing are useful for personal filing; they are a good substitute for the four-drawer filing cabinet because they require less office space.

Mobile shelving units

Mobile shelving units move on tracks either manually or electrically and are of two types. The most common type has the tracks at right angles to the shelving bays (Figure 8.8); in the other, the tracks are parallel to the shelving. The following comments apply most particularly to the first type.

Figure 8.8 A manually operated mobile shelving unit

Mobile shelving is expensive—approximately double the cost of open static shelving. It is cumbersome to move; the bays can become very heavy if full. Access is slower than with static shelving; the bays have to be moved to get to the appropriate one and generally only one bay can be accessed at a time (see Figure 8.8). More maintenance is required than for most other types of storage equipment.

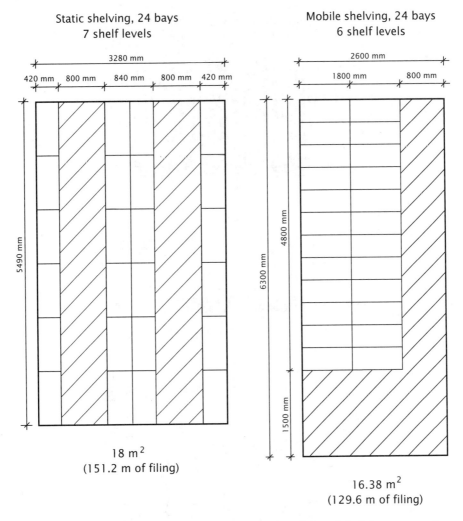

Figure 8.9 Two sample configurations of twenty-four bays of shelving, comparing area and amount of filing space available, using static shelving and mobile shelving

Its main selling point is that it takes up less floor space than static shelving, although skilful configuration of static shelving may reduce this to the point where it is not a major consideration (see Figure 8.9).

Another advantage of mobile shelving is that it can be locked. It should be noted however that a number of the locking devices commonly used are very easy to break.

Mobile shelving is a useful alternative for large collections of records which are infrequently accessed or which need to be secured in an otherwise poorly secured area.

Rotary units

Rotary (circular) shelving is a good option for binders held near work areas. It is expensive, but it takes less space than the mobile shelving discussed above, and is easier to use (see Figure 8.10).

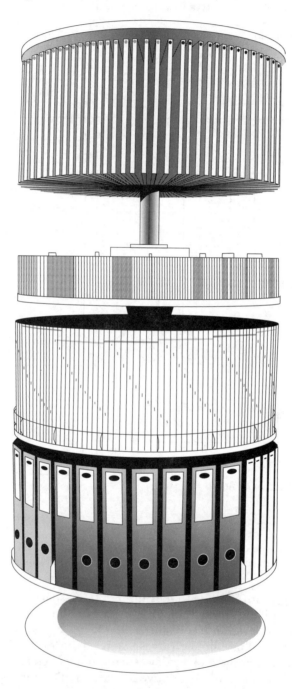

Figure 8.10   Rotary unit with adjustable tiers to accommodate different types of records

Automated filing systems

These operate on a ferris wheel system and usually incorporate a keypad for entering the code of the file and directing the appropriate tray or shelf to the access position. The greatest value of these systems is that the file is brought to the operator and there is no time wasted travelling around the shelves retrieving files. However, they are far more costly than other filing solutions and are only justifiable in situations where the retrieval rate is very high.

Specialised units

There are also specialised storage units designed for particular types of records, such as microfilm, plans, photographs, forms and cards.

Evaluating equipment

In evaluating equipment, look for equipment which:

- Is best suited to the record type, whether the records be paper or in some other medium. But consider also the need for compatibility with other equipment within the organisation to cope with the transfer of records from one location to another.
- Allows the best integration of different types of records which relate to each other.
- Meets security needs.
- Allows quick and easy access if the records are heavily used.
- Enables efficient use of space while at the same time meeting accessibility requirements.
- Is aesthetically pleasing and appropriate to the work environment.
- Makes users and records management staff feel good about using it.
- Will give most cost benefit. It is not necessarily the cheapest. The more expensive types of units may give better value in terms of space utilisation and retrieval speed.

Supplies

There can be a very substantial recurrent cost involved in purchasing filing supplies, depending on the volume of records and the filing method. For many organisations it is also one of the most difficult and frustrating aspects of a records system to get right.

A useful strategy is for organisations to standardise supplies such as file covers across the different business units. This enables these organisations to achieve cost savings from bulk purchasing and to facilitate transfer of records between units. It also means that it becomes relatively cheap to customise file covers with the organisation's logo, and whatever other information is required.

How to select supplies

Select supplies with the following criteria in mind:

- Are supplies readily available when needed? (Imagine the effect on a records system utilising colour coding if a particular colour label is out of stock for several weeks.)
- Is the item under consideration compatible with the storage equipment used?
- Has the quality of the item been proven with experience? (Carry out your own tests; check with colleagues who have used it.)
- Is the item the best choice to improve the efficiency of the records system?
- How does the cost of the item compare with alternative solutions?

File covers

There is a large range of file covers on the market, varying from flimsy covers for short-term files to lever arch binders.

When considering the type of file cover to use, look at issues such as:

- The weight and sturdiness of board required. Obviously a file of working papers that is used heavily for the span of a particular project is a candidate for a stronger cover than a holding file that is referred to infrequently.
- The type of clip required. An important consideration in this context is whether documents have to be inserted within a file rather than just added to the top of the existing documents. There are clips available which are designed for this purpose (see Figure 8.11).
- The cost of the components (folder, clip, labels). As an example of how the costs can add up very quickly, if an organisation with 50 000 files decides to convert to a file cover with a plastic two-pronged clip, it would be spending approximately $23 500 for clips alone for the first run.
- The storage space taken by the covers. Ring binders are sturdy but require more space than manila or cardboard covers. Suspension filing using file pockets requires more space than files placed laterally between shelf dividers. It is estimated that suspension filing uses up to 30 per cent more shelving space than lateral filing.

Colour coding

There has been a significant trend towards the use of colour coding on file covers in recent years. Colour coding is used in two main ways:

- Colour is used to represent a word, group of words or numbers. For example, a coloured stripe may denote a particular record series or business unit; files with that particular coloured stripe are very easy to spot.
- Colour is used to enhance recognition. For example, pre-printed labels of letters and numbers, with a different colour for each letter and number, can be attached to a tab along the side of a file cover to indicate the filing sequence.

These colour coding techniques are extremely effective in the battle against misfiling. A number of suppliers now market different sorts of colour coding systems. (See Figure 8.2, p. 174 for an illustration of colour coding.)

Document and file tracking systems

One of the most important features of records management software sought by many organisations is an effective **file and/or document tracking system**. Staff need to know where a file or document is at any one time, whether it is with a particular user, on the shelves, or in secondary storage.

Both manual and automated tracking systems are widely used. Alternative names to tracking system are **charge-out system** or **file movement system.**

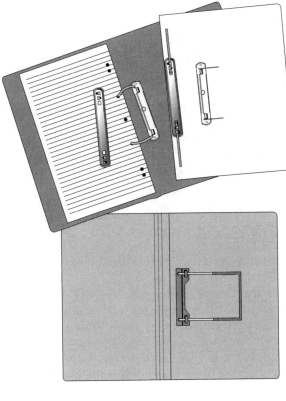

This spiral clip with transfer prongs is designed for heavily used files where it is necessary to add and remove pages within a file. It is an economical alternative to the two ring binder.

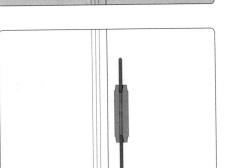

This plastic clip is also designed to simplify the process of adding and removing pages within a file, and photocopying documents on the file.

This clip is cheaper than the two clips above and is suitable for files where most documents are simply added to the top.

Figure 8.11 Three different types of file clips

Manual systems

Manual document tracking systems are time-consuming to maintain and are slowly being replaced with automated systems. In Australia, they are still used in some organisations to control unattached correspondence (i.e. correspondence which for a number of possible reasons is not moved on a file).

Manual file tracking systems are widespread. Common types of manual file tracking systems are:

- Use of a file movement book register to charge files out in date order. This is a hopelessly inefficient method because of the difficulty in tracking back through the pages to find who has a file. Book registers are gradually being replaced by more effective systems.
- Use of a separate file movement card for each file, these cards being held in one sequence by file name or number.
- File movement markers or 'file out' cards. These are left in the file storage area in place of a file when that file is taken by a user. File movement markers are still widely used in records systems of all sizes (see Figure 8.12).

Automated systems

Features of automated document or file tracking systems:

- Most systems cater for issues, returns and transfers, and for checking the movement history of files and documents.
- Many systems incorporate barcode tracking of documents and/or files.
- The electronic recording of document or file movements may be done centrally or at remote workstations by records management staff or users. Remote recording of file movements can eliminate the need for other less efficient methods of informing the records management staff that a document or file has been handed on to someone else (such as using the telephone or sending a file transfer slip).

Barcoding

Barcoding greatly enhances both the speed and accuracy with which file or document movements are recorded. Manual keying of borrower or location codes or names, and file and document identification numbers, is replaced by automatic reading of barcodes. Each user or location is allocated a barcode and a barcode label is attached to each document or file. By passing a **barcode wand** or **scanner** over both barcodes, the document or file is recorded against the particular user or location. Moldrich (1991, pp. 40–41) reports that tests have shown that a skilled keyboard operator will make one error out of every 208 to 230 characters read, whereas barcodes have a substitution error rate of about one in every 3.4 million characters scanned. He also states that scanning barcodes with a wand is at least twice as fast as data entry via a keyboard with a skilled operator.

A **portable barcode reader** can be used to carry out a **file census** or **audit.** The records management staff member enters each office with the portable barcode reader, wands or scans the user or location barcode (this may be attached to the desk) and then each file in the office; the information is later downloaded into an automated tracking system and the file movement records are updated. Every medium to large organisation experiences problems with missing files because staff members hand them on to others without informing the records management staff. The barcode file census helps keep track of files wherever they are located. An added bonus is that some types of barcode readers can be programmed to alert the operator when a missing file is located.

FILE MOVEMENT MARKER

TITLE: _____

_____ FILE NO. _____

CHARGED TO	DATE	RET'D DATE	CHARGED TO	DATE	RET'D DATE	CHARGED TO	DATE	RET'D DATE

Figure 8.12 File movement marker—reduced from A4 size

In a file census, the records staff member wands or scans both location and file barcodes

If barcoding is to be used, some important decisions need to be made in relation to equipment. For example:

- Will barcode labels be produced in-house or will pre-printed labels be purchased? Specially designed barcode printers are available. Good quality labels can also be produced on laser printers; even dot matrix printers can be used, although the quality is not as good. The decision to produce labels in-house may be justified if customised barcodes are required or if identical barcodes need to be produced to replace damaged labels. On the other hand pre-printed labels are easy to use, relatively cheap, and generally of a good quality.
- What sort of reading equipment will be acquired? A light pen or wand (a contact device) or laser scanner (a non-contact device which is more expensive but has a higher read rate)?

Decisions on equipment need to be based on such issues as workflow considerations, costs and efficiency, and the state of the technology.

Resubmit systems

Resubmit systems (alternatively called bring-up, call-up or diary systems) allow users to return files to the records area for recall on a predetermined date for follow-up action. They are a useful way of discouraging users from hoarding a lot of files in their offices.

Manual resubmit systems usually operate on a simple diary system.

Many automated records management systems incorporate resubmit systems. Details of the files to be resubmitted are entered as requested, and a printout or display of files due to be resubmitted is run each day.

Exercises

1 To complete this exercise you should study the filing rules reproduced in Appendix A. It would also be useful to read the rules spelt out in other texts, such as Ricks & Gow (1988, pp. 611–21), which deal with alphabetical filing arrangements.

1a Put the following names into alphabetical order:
- Robert O'Brien
- Aguk Gian Tan
- 130 Collins Street Pty Ltd
- A. C. Brown & Co. Ltd
- Liang Huong Lim
- Jan Arthur-Watson
- 21st Land Properties Pty Ltd
- A & J Smith Ltd
- B21 Pty Ltd trading as Autowheels
- Brown Brothers Pty Ltd
- The State of Play Co.
- Geoffrey Jones Family Trust
- Geoffrey and Alice Jones
- Peter Obruk
- P. J. and J. R. Black Family Trust

1b List the rules you followed in making your arrangement. These may be rules you gathered from published sources or rules you developed yourself.

1c List the problems associated with filing alphabetically by name.

2 Arrange the following file numbers in terminal digit order, using the system presented in the example on p. 170.

340291	823656
40389	30965
598768	498301
900231	263656
680191	530965
392677	923556

3 What filing sequences would you recommend for the following groups of records? Justify your answer in each case and explain what retrieval aids, if any, users would require to be able to locate particular files.
- 5000 files covering 500 different hospitals. For each hospital there is a file for the hospital board papers, a general correspondence file, and a file for each of the major services/divisions of the hospital. Some of the hospitals are branches of the bigger hospitals.
- 500 client tax files. These include files for individuals, family trusts, companies and other organisations.
- 2000 files belonging to a trade union. These cover all industrial topics and projects dealt with by the union.
- 100 personal files held by the managing director of a small company.
- Invoices received by the accounts payable department of a medium-sized organisation.

4 Accepting the limitation that you do not know what sort of records are housed in the filing equipment shown in Figures 8.13 to 8.15, list any inefficiencies you can observe in the way the records are housed. Make brief notes on the options you would consider to improve the filing method in each case.

Case study 8.1

Selection of filing equipment

You have been asked by the management of a research organisation to review the current methods and equipment used for storing its paper records. The organisation has a staff of 100 spread over three floors of a building.

Assume that the organisation does not wish to change the current locations of its records series. Current filing arrangements are:

1 The organisation has a central correspondence registry of 5000 files; these are filed in numerical sequence and are stored horizontally in pigeon-hole shelving in a mobile storage unit. The unit is full. The file covers have a tie-clip at the top left corner of the inside right cover. Many of the file covers are very shabby.

2 The organisation has several project teams and each team maintains its own project files. There can be 100 or more current project files in a team at any one time. These files consist of a mixture of A4 documents in manila folders, 38 mm x 28 mm and A4 computer printouts, collections of completed questionnaire forms in lever arch files, and computer cartridges and floppy disks.

Some of the teams file their hard copy records in four-drawer filing cabinets; some in suspension files on open shelves. Some interfile their computer printouts with their manila folders; in other cases the computer printouts sit horizontally on open shelves. The lever arch files are also filed on open shelves or wherever space can be found for them. Project files are generally filed alphabetically by project title, and roughly alphabetically under each title, depending on storage media and types of cabinetry used.

3 Administration files—accounts, personnel, payroll, purchasing, etc. These are mostly stored in lever arch files housed vertically on open shelving near the workstations of the staff working with them. There are also 38 mm x 28 mm and A4 computer printouts stored in binders wherever there is space for them—on open shelves, in filing cabinets, etc. Individual staff members keep

records such as correspondence and their own working notes and personal documents in manila folders in two- or four-drawer filing cabinets near their workstations. These are generally filed alphabetically by subject and housed in suspension pockets.

Figures 8.13–8.15   Three examples of inefficient filing arrangements

4 Non-current files which must be kept for legal and other reasons, are transferred in their existing covers or lever arch files to a mobile storage unit in the basement of the building. It is a dusty and dirty environment. The mobile shelving is currently full. Periodically, as space runs out, some clearing out is done.

Your task

Make checklists of:

- The issues you would need to take into account before recommending changes to storage methods and equipment.
- The type of filing equipment and supplies you would consider for the various categories of records, and the reasons for your choices.
- The points you would look for in selecting a supplier or suppliers.

To complete the second checklist you should scan through Australian office equipment and information management journals to gather information on what is available locally. If you have an opportunity to visit sites to see equipment in use this would be very useful too.

Questions

1 What factors would determine the choice of filing sequence for a collection of paper files?
2 Incoming mail may be sent direct to the addressees, or sorted and registered by the mailroom or records management staff prior to distribution as loose documents or on file. What factors will an organisation take into account in deciding how to handle incoming mail?
3 How would the records manager set about designing the work area for the staff responsible for managing a collection of paper files? What information would need to be gathered and what issues taken into account?
4 For an organisation moving into a new building, how will decisions be made about the type of storage to be used for paper records?
5 Under what circumstances might an organisation wish to track individual documents rather than files? What information might they want to be able to capture about the movement of documents?

Additional information

This chapter has presented an overview of the practical aspects of establishing a system for managing active paper records. It has not attempted to present solutions or hard and fast rules; it has not included a great deal of detail on such matters as the range of filing equipment available. Rather, it has focused on raising the issues that need to be addressed in developing a system. As has already been stressed elsewhere in this chapter and also in Chapter 2, it is most important that the records manager approaches the project with an open but well-informed and innovative mind; only then is it likely that effective solutions will be reached for the particular situation.

The best ways of gathering up-to-date information on options are to visit colleagues to view and discuss their solutions, contact suppliers for information on their products and to organise site demonstrations, attend workshops, visit trade exhibitions, and talk to other information professionals and to users. It is also useful to scan office equipment and information management publications, such as the *Complete Office Buyer's Guide*, *Office Products International*, and *Informaa Quarterly* (Records Management Association of Australia).

References

Hughes, S. 1994, 'Managing plans', *Informaa Quarterly*, vol. 10, no. 2, pp. 12–15.

Linton, J. E. 1990, *Organising the Office Memory: The Theory and Practice of Records Management*, University of Technology, Sydney, Kuring-gai Campus, Centre for Information Studies Publications, Chapters 1 & 2.

Moldrich, D. 1991, 'The role of barcoding in records management', *Informaa Quarterly*, vol. 7, no. 1, pp. 40–44.

Penn, I. A., Pennix, G. B. & Coulson, J. 1994, *Records Management Handbook*, 2nd edn, Gower Publishing Co., Aldershot, Hants, Chapter 15.

Ricks, B. R. & Gow, K. F. 1988, *Information Resource Management: A Records Systems Approach*, 2nd edn, South-Western Publishing Co., Cincinnati, OH, Chapter 6.

Robek, M. F., Brown, G. F. & Stephens, D. O. 1996, *Information and Records Management*, 4th edn, Glencoe/McGraw-Hill, New York, Chapters 5–7.

Smith, P. A. et. al. 1995, *Introduction to Records Management*, Macmillan Education Australia, Melbourne, Chapter 3.

Talbot, D. 1994, 'Managing photographs', *Informaa Quarterly*, vol. 10, no. 2, pp. 12–15.

chapter nine

Selecting and implementing automated records management systems

Overview

Automated records management systems are tools for supporting the recordkeeping process. If implemented in an organisation, they form an integral part of its recordkeeping regime.

The core purpose of an automated records management system is to manage the evidence of an organisation's business transactions through the systematised control of its records. The recordkeeping processes encompassed in records management systems include the registration, classification and indexing, retrieval, and disposal of records, also the tracking of action on those records, and control over who can access them. In general the more stringent controls the records management system enforces over these processes, the more effective it is as a recordkeeping tool.

Currently available records management systems include a range of capacities. They vary from simple paper files management systems, or systems which are devoted to particular processes (e.g. managing records in secondary storage), through to systems which manage all recordkeeping processes for records in all formats (paper, electronic, video, etc.). The most sophisticated records management systems available are evolving to manage both the records processes for all record formats and also the electronic records themselves.

Methods of implementing records management systems will differ with the needs of each organisation. Some organisations aim to implement one records management system across all business functions; others establish links between records management software and a variety of business applications software which capture and store part of the record of business transactions. For example, a purchasing system may be designed to capture the records of purchasing transactions but the copies of the orders sent to suppliers may be managed through the records management system. In other implementations, the records management software might be interfaced with imaging systems which store the record and/or its representation.

Records management systems can substantially reduce the labour involved in managing the records of an organisation and improve the efficiency with which those records are captured, stored, retrieved, and disposed of. As with the automation of any processes, they should only be introduced if existing systems are not meeting requirements, or if computerisation will lead to worthwhile productivity improvements or open up new and fruitful ways of managing information.

At the time of writing there were between twenty and thirty major records management software packages available in Australia, with a few dominating the market. The major systems range from database shells where the records manager can specify fields and other set-up aspects to suit the needs of the organisation, to systems with predetermined fields which require a minimum amount of configuration prior to operation. Some of the packages on the market are module-based; only those modules relevant to the organisation need to be purchased. Although it is commonly argued that the development of a records management system in-house can seldom be cost-justified, there are still plenty of cases where organisations find there are no records management systems which will both run on their particular platform and can be adapted adequately to meet their needs. This is particularly so in the private sector; a lot of the packages on the Australian market have been developed with government applications in mind.[1]

Some examples of commercially available records management systems are TRIM for Windows (Tower Software), RecFind (GMB Records and Information Management Solutions), Filemaster (DB Developments) and CARMS II (Ortex). Examples of systems devoted to managing electronic documents are DOCS Open (PC Docs Inc) and Mezzanine (Saros). These systems are simply mentioned as examples; their inclusion should not be seen as recommendations for particular products.

This chapter looks at the issues associated with selecting and implementing records management systems. In selecting systems, records managers need to have a very clear understanding not just of the current information management and recordkeeping requirements of their organisations, but also of the direction in which their organisations are heading in the way they create, distribute, use and store information. They need to work effectively with the software companies, either directly or through user groups, to ensure the two sides move forward in the most cooperative and productive way possible.

Records management and document management

There is a good deal of confusion between the records management and archives profession and the information technology community in the way the terms records management system and document management system are used. The information technology community tends to distinguish between records management systems as managing paper files and documents, and document management systems as storing and managing electronic documents. And when they refer to systems which manage both records and documents, they are referring to systems to manage paper and electronic documents.

The difference between a records management system and a document management system is best understood in the light of the difference between records and documents. The difference between records and documents is defined in Australian Standard AS 4390–1996[2] and also covered in the definitions in Chapter 1. Records represent evidence of business transactions; documents are any structured unit of recorded information, whether they are evidence of business transactions or simply information to support the business processes of the organisation.

Many document management systems manage the creation process associated with documents (e.g. by managing word processing input and output) and also facilitate collaborative working between members of designated workgroups. In addition, they provide increasingly sophisticated capacities to manage the product of the creation process, that is, documents. Documents become records when they form part of a business transaction and are linked to other documents relating to that transaction or process, when they are communicated beyond the person or workgroup which created them, and when they are registered into a management system for further use or reference.

For the purposes of this chapter, records and document management systems are treated together as records management systems on the basis that the discussion is about the management of records and documents as representations of business transactions, regardless of format. However it is also useful to distinguish between systems which manage the *information about records* (i.e. metadata) that is needed for records processes such as registration, classification, indexing, and disposal, and those which store the *electronic records themselves*. The functional requirements for managing records processes, outlined later in the chapter, are well recognised within the records management and archives profession; the functional requirements for managing the actual electronic records are only now emerging. While both sets of functions can occur within the one system, they require different but complementary functional specifications. Considerable confusion is avoided if the two concepts can be conceptually separated.

Development of records management systems

The history of the development of records management systems is one of fairly rapid change as software developers have tried to predict or respond to market demands—although it must be said that change never seems rapid enough for the organisation seeking the right system to meet its particular needs.

When records management packages first started appearing on the market in the early 1980s, they were largely computerised versions of existing manual processes for managing centralised registry systems handling hardcopy files and correspondence. Gradually their functionality and flexibility were improved in response to demands for features which would support more decentralised environments, enable more efficient processing and better capture of information about records (that is, metadata).

They also started to incorporate management of electronic records, the basis of this move being the push for integrated management of all types of records. At the same time electronic document management systems were appearing on the market. Although these systems were developed to manage electronic documents, in some cases they are now attempting to incorporate management of paper as well.

Most electronic document management systems were not developed with record-keeping requirements in mind. They were developed largely as responses to problems organisations were facing in locating poorly named documents stored on multiple file servers and hard disks. Some systems do incorporate certain features which are important to good recordkeeping (such as version, security and disposal controls) but in many cases these features cannot be implemented in a way which will satisfy recordkeeping requirements because they were developed for server administration rather than recordkeeping reasons. For example, disposal controls are aimed more at managing server space than ensuring records are kept for the appropriate period of time.

An alternative approach to managing electronic and paper records offered by some suppliers is to integrate a records management system with an electronic document management system. With this approach the records management system contains management data about records held in a variety of formats, and the electronic document system is used as a storage and controlling mechanism for electronic records. Users can search across both systems and can move from one to the other to gather information on records held in a variety of formats. Clearly this is not an ideal solution because the organisation choosing this option still has to maintain two systems and must rely on upgrades to the two systems being compatible. The most desirable solution is to have one system which manages the metadata about records in all formats, stores electronic records efficiently, and meets the needs of all types of users (enquirers, document creators, records management operators). While many records management systems are heading in this direction and thoughtful implementation can enhance capabilities of existing software, few are fully developed yet to effectively manage electronic records according to emerging functional requirements for electronic recordkeeping.

A parallel development has been the integration of records management systems with other types of information management tools and technologies, including imaging and workflow. These tools and technologies are discussed in detail in Chapter 10. Another development has been the insistence by organisations that records management systems should have the capacity to integrate with other internal business application systems and tools (such as practice management systems, human resource systems, customer name files, thesaurii of organisational terms) to reduce duplication of data and to promote consistency in the way information is presented across systems.

The point is sometimes made that the current type of 'catch all' records management systems should only be seen as interim solutions while the records management and archives profession, along with system developers, strive to better define how recordkeeping requirements should be met. At issue is the question of whether it is more logical to incorporate recordkeeping functionality into business application systems, or whether records should 'fall out' of business application systems to be captured and managed in records management systems. Whatever the answer, it is important that appropriate tools are selected and used that will link records to the business activities which created the records. Ensuring those linkages are created, and that they last, and are comprehensible over time, are challenges remaining for most records management systems.

Selecting a records management system

Before deciding on a records management system, the records manager must not only develop a good grasp of the current records management requirements of the organisation, but must also take into account the directions in which the organisation is heading in the way information is generated, processed and distributed.

Specific issues to be addressed include:

- The functional requirements of the system, including those that are mandatory and those that would be 'nice to have'.
- The type of records to be managed (e.g. paper documents, paper files, electronic documents, including word processing documents, spreadsheets and electronic mail messages, digital images, video, audio, compound documents, and any other types of materials such as library resources).
- The underlying systems architecture on which the application is based. This is of particular concern in applications where electronic records are to be stored. Options currently available in records management systems include: (1) 'capturing' a record and moving it as an image into a corporate store under the control of the records management system; (2) 'capturing' a record into a corporate store with pointers to the application software used to create the record, or (3) storing the pointers to records held in the native application which created them (e.g. a word processing or electronic mail application).

  These issues become crucial to how well the records management system can cope with the migration of records across upgrades within application systems or into new application systems.
- The degree to which electronic records to be captured into the records management system can be manipulated subsequent to their registration. It is desirable that once records are registered into the system, they cannot be added to or amended; however it should be possible to make a copy for re-use and manipulation within the creating software without affecting the integrity of the original record and its transactional context.
- The volume of records and documents to be managed.
- The need for integration with other systems.
- The availability of both financial and human resources to purchase, implement and maintain the system.
- The hardware, software and operating environment in which the system is to be implemented, and the degree to which the records manager is limited by, or can benefit from, the existing computer and communications facilities within the organisation.
- The level of computer support available within the organisation. This will certainly affect how adventurous the records manager can afford to be in using technology within the records management program.
- The quality of any existing manual systems that are to be computerised and the work needed to prepare the data for input.
- The need for conversion of existing records.
- The relative advantages and disadvantages of developing a system in-house and of purchasing a commercial package.

Developing a system in-house is seldom an easy option to justify. It is very expensive and it involves duplicating a lot of development effort that has already been expended by the software companies. However, there are situations where there is no package available that meets the needs of the organisation. The benefits of in-house systems are that they are tailor-made and can cater far more precisely for the information requirements and terminology usage within the organisation. They can also cater for a high level of interactivity with other systems. In addition, immediate technical support is available when needed, and there is likely to be in-built management support for the system.

Whatever records management system is selected, it should be seen as operating in a changing environment and should be either capable of future enhancement to meet changing needs or be capable of replacement without major conversion problems. An important task for the records manager is to prepare detailed specifications of exactly what the system will be required to do. Having detailed specifications to present to software vendors puts the onus on those vendors to show how their products can fulfil the requirements of the organisation. A helpful strategy for drawing up specifications is to frame them in terms of the processes and features that would be required to ensure the organisation complies with Australian Standard AS 4390–1996.

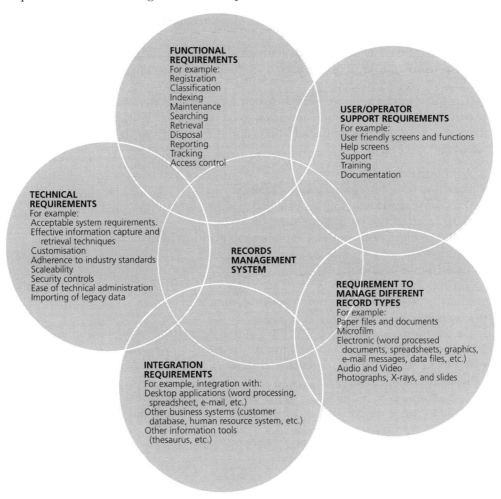

Figure 9.1   Records management system requirements

Functional requirements of records management systems

Functional requirements of records management systems include both those that apply to systems in general and those that are specific to a particular environment. Not all of the requirements discussed in this section will necessarily be relevant to a particular application, and certainly some will be seen as having higher priority than others. However, they can be used as a guide to help the records manager through the process of reviewing and evaluating records management software.

The core functional requirements of records management systems are to manage and record the registration, access, movement and disposal of records. Within those core functional requirements there are a whole range of features which may be relevant to particular organisations.

Registration

Registration provides evidence that a record has been captured into a record-keeping system.[3]

Organisations may need to register records in different formats, including paper and electronic. Links between files, and documents on files, may also need to be made at the registration stage.

The following list represents the type of information related to the content, context and structure of records which may need to be registered.[4] For any one organisation, there may be quite substantial additions and deletions from the list, depending on needs and record types.

- A unique identifier
- Date and time of registration/creation
- Data entry operator
- Date received (incoming documents)
- Author/originator/sender (by name and position held)
- Addressee
- Title (files and documents)
- Version (documents)
- Links between electronic and paper documents
- Location
- Physical format
- Abstract or descriptive information
- Other key terms or names to further describe the file or document
- Security classification
- Period to be covered or date of first correspondence (files)
- Links to other documents or files related to the same business activity (via file number or other referencing)
- Application (including version) in which the document was created (if in electronic format)
- Disposal status
- Details of compound document links
- Standard with which the record structure complies (e.g. SGML [Standard Generalized Markup Language])

The process of registering records into a records management system should be as streamlined as possible. This is particularly important where there are large volumes of registrations to be regularly processed, and also where the staff responsible for maintaining the system are not full-time or experienced records management staff. System features which help to streamline processing include:

- Automatic capture of contextual information about records (such as data entry operator, date and time of registration)
- Tables or lists from which information can be selected
- Ability to fill fields with default information related to particular record groups or types.

If the organisation uses a thesaurus or list of authorised terms to achieve consistency in the way in which its business functions and activities are described, it is likely that this tool will need to be incorporated into the records management system for use at the registration stage. The thesaurus or list of terms can be used to ensure consistency in file and document titling, and in the selection of indexing terms.[5]

There may be a similar requirement for the records management system to support various tables which control the changes in terminology, disposal provisions and organisational structures over time. For example, tables which record changes in the terminology used to name records—these are used to connect records labelled with older terminology to those more recently created; tables of organisational structures or groupings within the organisation which record the competence or authority granted to various officials to deal with certain business over time; and tables recording which staff members have occupied which positions over time. While increasingly seen as desirable elements of records management systems, few commercially available systems yet have these capabilities. Many systems have components of such tables, but few support the need to document changes over time; they assume that earlier contents in such tables can be overwritten. Such cumulative data becomes increasingly important when electronic records are 'locked' with metadata which describes the business context of their creation.

Access

Access refers to the ability and rights of users to retrieve the records they require. The features of a records management system which will determine the efficiency with which users can access records are:

- The indexing and searching techniques available
- The security functions, that is, the ability to set access rights for individuals and to set accessibility limits on individual records and documents
- The design of the storage database and the capacity and configuration of the computer hardware and network
- The integration with systems and tools to manage the distribution of information, for example, networking, electronic mail, intranets and Web pages
- The ability to redact electronic records, that is, to allow a limited view of records to users without full access privileges; and the ability to document who is able to see what sections of the record and when.

In evaluating both the indexing and searching features of a system, the key requirements in most environments are firstly, that there is minimal operator input at the indexing stage, and secondly, that searching is easy for the infrequent user but can be more refined and in-depth for the more experienced user. Some special features that organisations may require include the ability to do the following:

- Save often-used searches
- Search on specific fields or on the full text of a document, or a combination of both
- Search across record types (including metadata on paper and electronic records and on the contents of electronic documents)
- Use truncation and wildcard searching techniques
- Search on phrases
- Use Boolean operators
- Use fuzzy logic and/or proximity searching
- Search on unique identifier such as barcode or file number.

For documents stored in electronic form, some special features may include:

- The option to view the document only, or to open the application used to create the document (e.g. a word processing system). The 'view' function is valuable because it does not require that the user has access to the application.
- The option to display a list of documents recently created or edited by the user.

Indexing and searching tools and methodologies are discussed in Chapter 6.

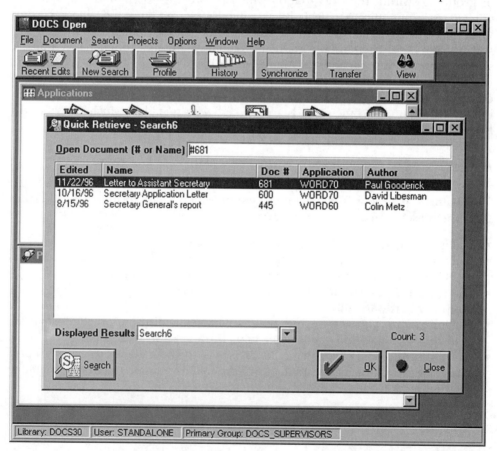

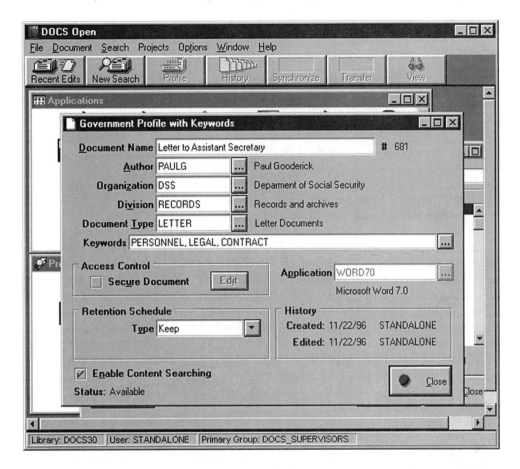

Figure 9.2 Sample screens from the DOCS Open document management system showing a search results screen and a profile screen

Source: Reproduced with permission of Educom, Sydney

In terms of security functions, the records management system should enable the administrator to take the following action:

- Set access rights by user to view, edit or delete records in the system
- Restrict user access to particular modules or features of the system
- Set access rights by workgroup as well as individual
- Allow users to belong to multiple user groups and have different access rights according to group
- Restrict the locations (electronic and physical) where users or groups can store records.

Movement

Recording the movement of records refers to the physical movement and location of records, and the tracking of action and use of records (both paper and electronic).

For many organisations a major requirement is to know where paper files or documents are at any one time; other organisations want to track other types of items such as diskettes. It should be possible to establish the location of a particular file, document or other item whether it is 'at home' in a filing system, with a particular user, in secondary storage, or whether it has been destroyed or is missing. Other questions that a tracking system may need to answer are:

- What items does a particular user have at any one time?
- What users are registered on the system?
- What users have seen or actioned a particular item in the past?
- What actions are pending or overdue?

A barcode interface may be used to facilitate the issuing and tracking of physical items. Barcoding enables significant improvements in the speed and accuracy with which records can be issued and returned and with which audits of records held in offices and workstation areas can be carried out.[6]

Organisations may also want to track their electronic documents. For example, where staff carry out a proportion of their work out of the office, the records management system should enable those staff to check copies of documents in and out; it should also record who checks them out and when, control whether checked-out documents can be edited by another person, and ensure that documents edited after being checked out are automatically entered as a new version at next login.

Records management systems should also enable organisations to set workgroup boundaries for use in determining when a document has been communicated beyond those boundaries and when a 'locked' version needs to be created as a record. Within the workgroup boundary, versions of documents may be collaboratively edited, and version controls are necessary to ensure that only the most recent version is used for action. Depending on needs, the system should be able to show versions created by date, time, and creator; also to identify the final version and lock the document. After a record is locked, all variations created during subsequent editing will not overwrite the original record, but will create a new record. Version control is therefore an important feature of records management systems which store and manage electronic documents. Systems should, at minimum, create an audit trail of document usage to enable organisations to establish who created, worked on, and viewed documents and when. Ideally such metadata should be linked to each record.

Some organisations have special requirements for managing incoming correspon-dence. They need to register an individual piece of correspondence and assign it to an action officer. They may also want to assign an action deadline and action proce-dures, track the correspondence and check on the progress made in dealing with it, issue regular reports on the status of correspondence, and distribute action reminders. Some records management systems include rudimentary workflow facilities which allow the allocation of action procedures to be automated according to the category of the document.

A final point to note about the ability of records management systems to manage the movement of records is the requirement to rapidly process change, for example, bulk transfer of records to a new location.

Disposal

A records management system needs to manage records from the time of creation right through to disposal. In other words, it needs to manage them throughout their existence, identifying infrequently used records which can be transferred to less accessible storage, records which have continuing value, and records which can be destroyed. It should be possible to include retention periods for records linked to tables supporting approved disposal agreements; also the flagging of individual items when they become due for transfer or destruction action.

Records physically removed from current offices into secondary storage usually change from being housed in a predetermined order on shelves in an active filing area, or on other equipment such as a file server, to being stored in a different or random order according to destruction dates in a container such as an archive box. Therefore, it should be possible to record on the system the new location of the records plus the total contents of each container. It may indeed be necessary to control records at three levels within the system—individual documents, documents within files, and files within containers.

The records manager needs to decide whether the system should delete all registration data about records when they are destroyed. Emerging consensus indicates that the registration data and details of the destruction dates and authorities should be retained on a continuing basis as evidence of the total records of an organisation. Another issue to resolve is whether access data should be retained for the same length of time.

Where there are both paper and electronic records documenting a particular business activity (whether they be different records or duplicate copies), it is essential that the disposal of those records be managed in an integrated way. For example, it may be very important for the protection of an organisation that all the records related to a particular business activity are destroyed simultaneously. Many organisations are currently grappling with how to use their records management systems to achieve this result.

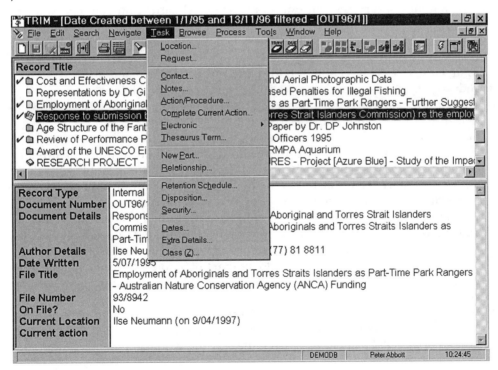

Figure 9.3 A sample screen from the TRIM records management system showing a search results screen and the detailed information on a selected item

Source: Reproduced with permission of Tower Software, Deakin, ACT

Technical requirements

In evaluating records management systems, the records manager not only needs to develop a thorough understanding of the functional requirements which will determine a suitable software solution for the organisation, but also a reasonable understanding of the technical requirements. Expert assistance should be sought in clarifying and documenting these issues prior to reviewing available packages.

Questions to be asked when reviewing a system relate to the following:

- Platform(s) and operating system(s)—which are supported? Does it operate across platforms? Is it client/server based?
- Networking environments.
- Server environments.
- System resources required—RAM, disk space for the software and for each record.
- Supported databases—does it rely on the organisation having a relational database system, and if so, which systems does it support? Or does it have a proprietary database?
- Ease of use—is the system easy for records management staff and other users to learn and operate? Does it cater for a range of users, from an infrequent enquirer to a records operator who is processing hundreds of transactions a day? Is the system interface either a GUI (graphical user interface) or text or character-based? Are the commands within the system functionally consistent with the standard techniques of the client operating environment (e.g. Windows 95)? Do all the 'buttons' appear in the same place on the screen at all times?
- Information capture and retrieval strategies—keyboard, mouse, touch pad, etc?
- Customisation—are there tools to customise profile (registration and enquiry) screens and field names? To add and delete fields? To set edit checks to minimise operator error (e.g. make some fields mandatory, restrict a field to all numbers or all letters, make selection of information from a table mandatory)?
- Industry standards—are the appropriate standards complied with?
- Support for compound documents (e.g. word processing documents with embedded spreadsheets, audio or video).
- Scaleability—can it be upgraded from a single workstation application to a single server to enterprise-wide? Are there limits on the total number of users or concurrent users or records? Number of databases and sites possible? Are there any performance issues related to the increase in number of users and records?
- Application integration, including provision of programming tools for writing integrations inhouse—can the system interface with other systems, both internal and external? For example, can information be downloaded from an internal customer information system or a practice management system, or from an external system such as the Internet? Can documents be copied to other information repositories (such as a server on an intranet) to facilitate distribution of information around the organisation?
- Importing of legacy documents—is conversion from the existing system to the new system possible? Are controls established to ensure no data or formatting is lost or corrupted during transfer from the existing system and between upgrades of the new system?

- Security controls through the organisation's network operating system and the records management system—can the system link to the organisation's security arrangements? Can it provide security down to user, menu and field level, and by class of records? Can it produce audit trails for actions on records?
- Technical administration of the system—what are the tasks?
- Online backup
- Disaster recovery/business continuity procedures
- Reliability and integrity (e.g. automatic recovery from corruption after a server crash, routine reporting of security violations).

Reporting and statistics

The system should have a standard set of reports as well as an inbuilt or third party report generator so that the records management staff can develop and run reports to suit the needs of the organisation.

The system may need to cater for the production of statistics. For example, in a correspondence system, management may want a statistical breakdown of correspondence processed by action officer or by originator. Statistics may also be useful in justifying more appropriate information management technologies such as imaging and workflow.

It should be possible to transfer reports or statistical information to a desktop product such as word processing, a spreadsheet system or electronic mail for further processing or distribution.

Help screens

Help screens are useful. The system should be supplied with help screens but these should be modifiable so that they can be adjusted to the set-up of the particular records management application and to organisational procedures.

Support and training

Software support must be readily available when needed. If there is no state representative for the software supplier, there should be at least a helpline number. Ready access to support is particularly important in the early stages of an installation, but it is also important that immediate help can be obtained at any time in working hours to deal with problems which are preventing people from using the system. One study of records management software in Australia found that a major problem is the large number of distributors on the east coast of Australia and the relatively poor servicing of sites in other states due to the lack of local representatives (Horsfall 1992, p. 13).

There should be a comprehensive but easy to use and well indexed manual for users; also good software support documentation.

There should be a clearly stated strategy for distribution and implementation of enhancements and upgrades.

Training should also be offered by the supplier. This should certainly be available at the installation stage but also for any major upgrades to the system, and on an ongoing basis as required.

When evaluating records management software, ask questions such as 'How long does it take for help line calls to be answered?'

In reviewing and evaluating records management software it is most important to look at the background of the supplier company. Factors to investigate are its financial viability, its performance in the market place, number of operational sites, its experience with records management systems, its product support history, its commitment to further developing the product. If the product has been on the market for a while, there should have been periodic and well-supported upgrades to the system.

It is also important to talk to other users of the system about their experiences with the product itself and about the quality of support provided. Useful questions to ask include:

- How long does it take for helpline calls to be answered?
- What type of assistance do you receive?
- How knowledgeable are the helpline staff?
- Have you ever had a system crash?
- How much does the technical assistance cost?
- How long did the technical assistance take? (Meyer 1989, p. 182).

It is a bonus if there is an established user group to act as a forum for discussion of all issues related to the system and to act as a pressure group for upgrades.

Costs

When reviewing packages, it is important to ensure information on all possible costs is gathered. The main costs are for the initial purchase of the software (commonly tied to the number of users), including any optional modules selected, hardware and other equipment, installation, annual or 'as required' maintenance, software modifications, and training.

Implementing a records management system

Once a records management system has been selected, an implementation program must be developed. A number of factors will be crucial to the success of that program.

Planning

An implementation timetable is essential. This should include tasks and timelines for a pilot phase in one business unit, then tasks and timelines for each of the other business units where the system is required. Scheduling will necessitate assessing each business unit in terms of the availability of staff resources, equipment and space for implementation. It will also involve assessing which existing records, if any, are to be converted to the new system, and whether the data on any existing automated records management systems can or should be converted to the new system. If manual conversion of existing records is to take place, it is preferable to employ people from outside the organisation for the task. Existing staff are generally busy and the conversion can drag on over a lengthy period. This can have a negative effect on the way both operators and users view the system.

User liaison

It is important to prepare potential users for the introduction of the new system and more importantly, to prepare them for the changes that will occur. Their support is essential and various strategies should be developed to obtain it, such as sending out information bulletins and keeping the topic on the agenda of regular business unit meetings.

A useful strategy is to try to get the potential 'knockers' of the system on side by giving them a direct role in the implementation program; this may be by involving them in a records management committee and giving them specific tasks.

Pilot phase

A pilot phase is essential. This is a period of implementation in which the records manager can adjust the system to meet the requirements of the organisation and iron out any problems such as user codes not being loaded, parts of the software not being available, poor response times, and hardware glitches. It is also a useful time to clarify any conversion procedures and adjust workflow patterns.

Maintenance and support

A good rapport must be established with the people who maintain and support both the software and the hardware associated with the system. This applies to both external support personnel and internal computer staff. It is important to communicate effectively with these people in order to be able to negotiate improvements and to provide them with the information they need to solve problems.

It is good practice to keep a diary and to record all problems and unusual occurrences; this is particularly useful in the implementation phase.

Training

While software vendors should provide training when the system is installed, the records manager will still have a significant task in training both the operators of the system and other staff users on how to use the system in the specific organisational environment. Pre-implementation training of operators should include the analysis of existing procedures and the changes that are to take place with the new system. Operators need to understand and support the reasons for change and be able to participate in the refinement of the system.

Manuals

Manuals are essential for any system. There are two categories of manuals vital to successful implementation.

Firstly, there are guides to using the system. The main guide supplied by the vendor should include a system overview and detailed explanations of the functions of the system. It may also be necessary for the records manager to produce a separate guide for the operators detailing procedures for using the system within the particular organisation.

Secondly, there are guides to the equipment such as the computer and its keyboard, printers and bar code readers.

Variations of the manuals include searchers' manuals for those users only searching on the system, and system administration manuals with more detailed technical information on the configuration and maintenance of the system.

'System down' strategies

Strategies must be developed for dealing with situations where the system is unavailable for use, whether this is because the system has crashed or because backups or modifications are taking place. It may be important to ensure that users have access to at least a paper copy of certain parts of the database.

Review

The system should be reviewed regularly after implementation to ensure it is still responding effectively to the records management needs of the organisation. The review may be after the first three and six months and then on an annual basis.

Exercises

For the following two exercises you will need to search the office and records management literature for advertisements and reviews of products, and articles on records management software. A number of the references at the end of this chapter will be helpful.

1 For each of the functions listed below, name at least one commercially available records management system which manages that function. The same system may be listed for more than one function.
    • Correspondence management, including action tracking
    • File and document tracking, with barcode interface
    • Structured file titling
    • Vocabulary control via an online thesaurus
    • Records disposal, including online disposal schedules
    • Management of electronic documents, including word processed documents and electronic mail messages.

2 Select a commercially available records management system and describe it in detail under the following headings:
    • Name of system
    • Supplier
    • Platform (operating system and hardware)
    • Network and server requirements
    • Brief description of product
    • Record types that can be managed (paper, electronic, both, etc.)
    • Versions and modules (if relevant)
    • System functions and special features
    • Customisation—degree to which purchaser can customise the system
    • Reporting capabilities
    • Opportunities for integration with other systems (e.g. with word processing, electronic mail, document imaging and workflow systems)
    • System administration tasks
    • Comments on user friendliness
    • Type of support provided
    • Availability of training
    • Documentation
    • Background information on vendor
    • General comments on the strengths and weaknesses of the system.

To attempt this exercise you will need to have lengthy access to a records management system plus its documentation.

Questions

1 What steps should be taken to prepare specifications for the selection of a records management system?
2 In what form should system requirements be presented to vendors in order to illicit the sort of responses which will provide the basis for a comparative evaluation of different systems?

3 In selecting and implementing a records management system, what factors will determine how the needs of the records management staff are balanced against the needs of the users?

4 What features of electronic documents make them different from paper documents in the way they must be managed in a records management system? What functions have records management systems introduced to deal with these differences?

5 What are the advantages in being able to integrate a records management system with other business systems in an organisation? Think of some examples of potentially useful integrations.

Notes

1 This is highlighted in Cowcher's (1992) historical overview of 'off-the-shelf' packages in Australia.

2 Standards Australia 1996, *Australian Standard AS 4390–1996: Records Management,* Homebush, NSW, Part 1: General, pp. 6–7.

3 Standards Australia 1996, *Australian Standard AS 4390–1996: Records Management,* Homebush, NSW, Part 4: Control, p. 4, 6.1.

4 *Australian Standard AS 4390–1996* Part 4, p. 5, 6.2.2 also includes a list of register characteristics.

5 The purposes and construction of thesauri are discussed in detail in Chapter 7.

6 Tracking systems, including barcoding, are discussed in more detail in Chapter 8.

Additional information

Records management software, and assessments of how it can assist organisations to maintain control over their records, has been covered in some detail in the literature over the last decade. Up until the late 1980s and early 1990s a high proportion of the journal literature on the topic consisted of case study presentations; a useful example included in the references listed below is Williams (1990). However, there were a number of papers which took a broader perspective and looked critically at the role of records management systems and how to select them. Some of these papers included information on specific products available in Australia—examples are Cowcher (1992), Horsfall (1992) and Meyer (1989)—but their main value is in encouraging records managers to rethink what they want from records management systems and how they can use them to meet organisational needs.

For records managers reviewing and evaluating records management software with a view to implementing a system, major sources of information are the advertisements and reviews in the office and information management literature, colleagues who are working with systems, and, of course, the software vendors themselves. The Records Management Association of Australia is making an increasing attempt through its publications and seminars to assist records managers to keep up-to-date with the application of technology to records management, including records management software.

References

Archives Authority of New South Wales, Records Management Office 1994, *Checklist for use in selecting records management software*, Sydney.

Attinger, M. L. 1994, 'Integrated information management', *Informaa Quarterly*, vol. 10, no. 1, pp. 4–8.

Cowcher, S. R. 1992, 'A look at turnkey packages', *Informaa Quarterly*, vol. 8, no. 3, pp. 20–25.

Duggan, W. 1989, 'Technology—who's leading who', *Informaa Quarterly*, vol. 5, no. 4, pp. 9–10.

Hoo, M. D. 1990, 'The role of document management in office productivity', *Informaa Quarterly*, vol. 6, no. 3, pp. 13–15.

Horsfall, K. 1992, 'What makes a good records management package', *Informaa Quarterly*, vol. 8, no. 2, pp. 12–15.

Kreibig, D. 1989, 'Records management software: make or buy', *Records Management Quarterly*, vol. 23, no. 4, pp. 30–32.

Meggitt, A. 1994, 'Electronic document management', *Informaa Quarterly*, vol. 10, no. 2, pp. 16–19.

Meyer, F. E. 1989, 'Survey of records management software in Australia—1989', in International Records Management Council in association with the Records Management Association of Australia, 2nd International Congress, Perth, 11–14 December, *Papers Presented*, Promaco Conventions for the RMAA, pp. 179–278.

Poynton, T. 1992, 'Get active or get archived', *Informaa Quarterly* vol. 8, no. 3, pp. 26–32.

Robek, M. F., Brown, G.F. & Stephens, D. O. 1996, *Information and Records Management*, 4th edn, McGraw-Hill, New York, Chapter 9.

Rosenthal, M. A. 1993, 'Records management in Victorian government agencies', *Informaa Quarterly*, vol. 9, no. 2, pp. 12–14.

Williams, B. 1990, 'Case study: information retrieval: a practical approach', *Records Management Journal*, vol. 2, no. 1, pp. 4–14.

chapter ten

Electronic document management: tools and technologies

Overview

Electronic document management systems take various forms, depending on the particular implementation selected by an organisation. The core component is the document control system which is used primarily to index and retrieve documents, but in many cases to also perform other functions such as manage the disposal of the documents, control versions, create audit trails of document usage, and control access privileges. These document control systems are discussed in Chapter 9 under the broad heading of records management systems.

In the current stage of development of electronic document management, there are a range of other tools and technologies which may make up a particular electronic document management system or strategy. This chapter looks at some of these tools and technologies, namely, imaging, COLD, workflow systems, groupware, electronic publishing systems (including the Internet and intranets, and CALS), and EDI.

In reading this chapter, it should be borne in mind that the rate of technological development is so rapid that what is current today may be superseded tomorrow. The chapter is only intended to give a flavour of where electronic document management is situated in the late-1990s.

Why electronic document management?

For many organisations the development of strategies for managing their electronic documents has become a high priority.

Firstly, the volume of electronic documents in organisations is growing at a remarkable rate. Even though it is still estimated that between 70 and 80 per cent of documents are copied and kept as paper format, there is no doubt that the percentage will gradually reduce. Not only are organisations increasingly finding it more convenient and productive to use the electronic versions of documents as the working copies, but they are starting to question the enormous costs involved in printing, storing and working with documents in paper format, for example:

- The time involved in walking to a file room, locating a file, locating a document in a file
- Records management staffing
- Storage (equipment and space)
- Paper
- Time lost in retrieving files from secondary storage
- Time lost in photocopying.

Secondly, the type of information technology environment in which employees now operate, which is highly distributed and user centric, and in which office automation products such as word processing, and communication tools such as electronic mail, are readily available at the desktop, has led to a fundamental reduction in the level and quality of document management.

In the past, the universal pattern for document creation and distribution was for officers to draft correspondence, and the secretarial staff to type it and organise its distribution, including copies for the paper file. Now there is an increasing likelihood that officers will draft their documents on their PCs, spellcheck and format them, and send them via electronic mail or facsimile. In fact, improvements in electronic mail and facsimile card technology mean that even documents addressed to officers in other organisations may never be in paper format because they can readily be sent direct from PC to PC. In the same way, the formal written brief that has always been a customary part of the decision-making process may now be replaced by the manager collecting and collating the information directly from electronic sources such as databases or from colleagues via electronic mail.

Along with the significant changes to the way in which written communications are taking place, there is also an increasing emphasis on spoken communications using technology such as telephone voice mail systems[1] and telephone and video-conferencing.

A common pattern has developed for individuals and groups to establish their own electronic filing systems, which in many cases are poorly conceived, rapidly get out of control, but may well contain information of importance to the organisation beyond the individual or group which controls it.

The document management tools and technologies available to organisations today will not solve all of an organisation's document management problems. However, if their selection and implementation are based on a very clear understanding of the needs of the organisation, and combined with well developed and supported business rules and controls, they can be very effective in helping to ensure employees have access to the information they need.

> The question we should be asking is not whether imaging, or any other single technology, is the ideal metaphor for information management. Rather, we should determine how imaging and other document management technologies such as workflow, text retrieval, e-mail, word processing, database, and a myriad of others, including the existing legacy systems in paper and microform, come together to create a single point of access for all users throughout the organisation (Koulopoulos & Frappaolo 1995, pp. 17–18).

It is probable that some 80–90 per cent of the decision-making process in organisations now occurs via the telephone or electronic mail

Imaging

Imaging is a technology which continues to have a significant role to play in records management solutions. In the context of this chapter, imaging refers to the technology by which images of documents or pictures are made and stored on microfilm or computer media. Microfilm imaging systems have been widely used as an alternative to paper since the early part of the twentieth century. The more recently developed digital imaging technology, with storage on optical and magnetic media, also enables a substantial saving in physical storage space. Even if the paper copies have to be kept for legal reasons, they are unlikely to be referred to very often, if at all, and can be packed away in minimum space at a remote location. In addition, both microfilm and digital imaging systems eliminate some of the drawbacks of paper-based systems, including tedious manual filing, misfiling (it is estimated that 3 per cent of all paper documents are misfiled) and time wasted in physically going to a records area, retrieving a file and locating a record.

Digital imaging systems

Digital imaging systems have additional advantages over microfilm imaging systems and, in fact have the potential for a far greater impact on the way an organisation manages its information.

Firstly, they help to improve information flow around an organisation—once a document is scanned into a computer and saved, it can be sent electronically to different people for processing, simultaneously if appropriate. The alternative is the costly duplication and distribution of paper copies to the people who need the information, or the circulation of a single copy of a document for sequential actioning and the disadvantages of the delays that method of processing can entail. Imaging systems also eliminate the problems associated with conflicting needs for simultaneous access to the same paper files.

Combined with workflow systems, digital imaging becomes a particularly powerful tool.

Secondly, images can be retrieved much faster than can documents on a paper file, particularly if the file is stored in a location remote from the enquirer's workstation. In terms of client service and the ability to produce information quickly in response to a query, this represents a considerable benefit.

Thirdly, unlike the case of microfilmed documents, the documents in a digital imaging system can be digitally converted to text format using optical character recognition (OCR) software, then manipulated and searched. As with any electronic documents, information from converted documents can be extracted and fed into other systems for further viewing and manipulation.

Fourthly, at a time when organisations are using an increasing proportion of their internally created documents in their original electronic format (rather than always relying on printed copies as the source documents), digital imaging systems provide them with a way of managing all of their documents, both electronic and those received as paper, as a totally integrated information resource. That is, the systems enable organisations to create digital images of their paper documents and manage their access and storage along with other electronic documents. This makes it much easier to marry documents relating to a particular topic or transaction and to ensure they are all treated consistently (e.g. all destroyed at the same time according to a disposal schedule). It also makes it easier to control multiple versions of documents and to ensure the latest is consulted.

While imaging adds a powerful dimension to document management and the ability of an organisation to provide an integrated view of its information resources, any decision to implement an imaging system should still be guided by the principle that information should be managed in the format in which it was created unless conversion to another format adds value to the work being performed and reduces overall costs.

What is digital imaging?

Digital imaging is the ability to electronically capture, store, retrieve, display, process, distribute and manage information which is not already in digital form.

Digital imaging systems are computer systems designed to capture documents or pictures as images, to digitally store the images, and to retrieve, distribute, and display or print the images on demand.

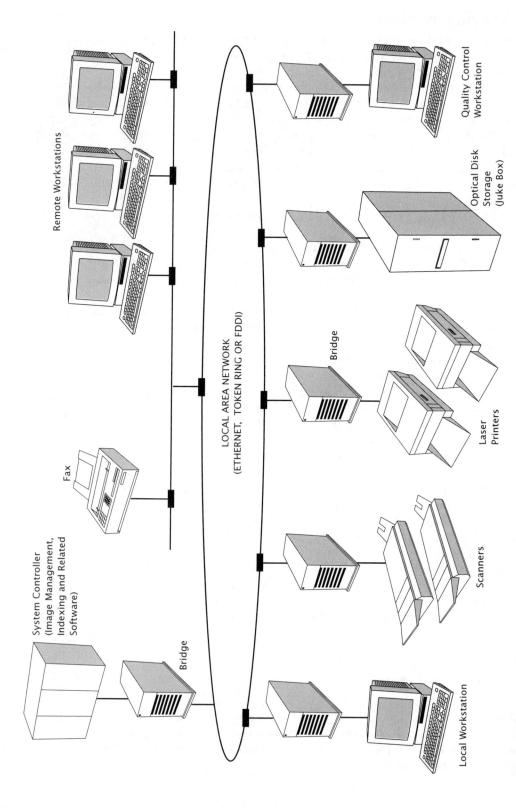

Figure 10.1 Imaging system devices on a network

Source: Based on a diagram from 'Integrating microfilm with digital technology', a seminar paper presented by Integrated Imaging Systems, December, 1990.
Note: Not all devices in a networked imaging system will necessarily be attached to the network. For example, to decrease the volume of work on the network, the scanning process may be done separately.

In document management applications, images are most commonly made from paper documents (e.g. invoices, insurance claims, medical records, incoming correspondence). They may also be made from microfilm, from facsimiles sent direct to the imaging system, from photographs, slides and video, or from computer-generated data transferred directly from another system. They may also be received as attachments to an electronic mail message.

Imaging systems generally have five main physical components—a systems controller (computer plus image management and related software), document scanner, storage device, printer, and storage media. The simplest imaging systems are stand-alone systems intended to be used by one operator working on a PC, possibly with an optical disk or CD (compact disk) drive attached. The larger systems (networked or mainframe) can have many devices (workstations, jukeboxes and drives, printers, scanners and storage controllers) attached.

Imaging systems include the following process components:

- Document capture
- Registration and indexing of document images
- Document image storage
- Document retrieval, display and printing.

Document capture

Document scanning

Scanners provide a shortcut method of entering information into a computer without having to type it. Pages or film are run through a paper or micrographic scanner and the information is digitised.

Documents have to be prepared for scanning—staples removed, corners flattened, etc. The physical quality of the document (including the type or handwriting) will be reflected in the quality of the image.

When evaluating scanners for a particular application, consider the following features/specifications:

Speed

Scanners vary from 300 to 10 000 pages per hour. In general, the price increases as the speed increases. With most scanners pages can be fed manually or automatically. There are also scanners which can handle double-sided documents automatically. In looking at a particular application, the speed of the scanner should be related to the capacity required. There is no point in purchasing a high speed scanner if the number of documents to be processed is twenty per hour.

Size of documents

It is important to ensure that the scanner will take all sizes of documents involved in the application. Most scanners will take up to A3 size documents, with some designed for larger engineering documents.

Resolution

This determines the level of detail that is transferred to the stored image. Scanning at a higher resolution means the detail is clearer but it also means each image takes up more storage space and takes longer to scan. Most systems scan at 200, 300 or 400 dots per inch (dpi). The clarity of the image required is the key issue in deciding which resolution is needed. Flexibility to change the resolution is important so that most documents can be scanned at low resolution, but some at high resolution if more clarity is needed for small print.

There are colour scanners available; colour images take up a lot more storage space than black and white images.

Optical character recognition (OCR)

Document capture may also involve the application of optical character recognition (OCR) to convert documents to an ASCII or word processing format. OCR can lead to substantial savings in data entry costs for organisations which process large volumes of information received in paper format.

Developers have been working on improving the reliability of OCR for years, but unfortunately it is still error prone. The most common type of problem is when the software cannot decide what a particular character is; the other problem is when it misreads a character (e.g. it turns an O into a C). The time taken to proof and correct documents needs to be taken into account when planning an application involving OCR. The more recently developed ICR (Intelligent Character Recognition), with its advanced technique for tackling recognition problems such as character ambiguity, ligatures and touching characters, achieves a better result (Mallen 1992, p. 9).

Until recent years, OCR was only capable of reading typed or printed copy. It is now being used to read handprinted (as opposed to handwritten) alphabetic and numeric characters which have been presented in a structured or constrained form. In this context it is called Hand Character Recognition (HCR). This development is starting to have a significant impact on the way in which information collected on forms is processed and stored; it also requires a reassessment of form design requirements.

A lot of research and development is being done on the recognition of handwriting but the differences in people's writing styles will continue to be a barrier.

Registration and indexing of document images

Commercially available imaging systems generally have a database for maintaining indexing information on the stored images. The best systems are where the indexing fields can be customised according to the particular application and where more than one application can be catered for at any one time.

In some applications the registration, indexing and retrieval of images will be controlled by a third party records management system.

Indexing of images manually is of course very time-consuming, whether done at the time of scanning or batched for later processing. The application of an OCR system, combined with text retrieval software, may be considered as an alternative to manual indexing. Or a combination of manual indexing (e.g. selection of key terms from the organisation's thesaurus) plus full text indexing using text retrieval software may be the most satisfactory solution. When documents need to be retrieved, text retrieval software is used to search for occurrences of particular words, phrases or other codes within a specified section of the document such as title, or within the full text.

Barcoding is another technique which can aid the indexing process. Each document is barcoded (usually with a meaningful number such as an invoice number) before scanning; the barcode is then used to link the index entry to the image.

Chapters 6 and 7 should be referred to for a more detailed discussion of indexing strategies and issues.

Document image storage

In an imaging system, storage space is a major consideration. Images take up far more disk space than do, for example, word processed documents. In fact, if they include graphics they can take about 500 times the space; even after compression, they can still take 50 times the space.

Images may be stored on magnetic or optical media. The choice of media is determined by the amount and frequency of reference to imaged documents, and the speed of access required. Documents which are accessed frequently may be stored on hard drives or even floppy disks. But for less used documents, magnetic tape, optical disk or CDs are far more economical.

The advantage of optical media is the enormous volume of data that can be stored on one disk or tape.

Optical disks are far more commonly used in imaging systems than optical tapes. Tape is cheaper but retrieval is much slower. When the technology has improved, tape will be useful for storing vast quantities of information which is seldom accessed.

Optical disks come in three main types—WORM, erasable, and CD.

1 **WORM (Write Once Read Many)**—binary information is burnt onto the disk by the use of a laser and cannot be deleted. Because the information cannot be altered, the legal profession tends to recommend WORM disks for document storage. (The index entry can of course be deleted, and the document is then no longer retrievable.)

2 **Erasable**—these are magneto-optical disks which can be rewritten. As the technology develops, the amount that can be stored on these types of optical disks keeps increasing.[2] This minimises the number of disk swaps required. In smaller imaging systems, optical disks are normally loaded manually into the drive. However, in the larger systems, jukeboxes are used to automatically load disks. They are operated by a robotic arm which selects and loads the disks as required. The life of the information on an optical disk is uncertain. Estimates from suppliers vary from 10 years to 100 years. The technology has not been around long enough for accurate information to be available.

3 **CD (compact disk)** is another optical medium which can be used for storing images. Its use has expanded very rapidly in recent years and the technology is evolving much faster than WORM and magneto-optical disks in terms of adherence to standards. At the current stage of development of CD technology, it is still only suitable for relatively small imaging applications.

CD technology was traditionally associated with publishing; in addition to audio applications, CD-ROMs were used mainly for the publication and distribution of bibliographic and full-text databases. They were also used extensively for distributing software. Document management applications were mainly limited to large government agencies and corporations where significant volumes of internal information had to be distributed to a number of locations.

Until fairly recently, CD-ROMs were expensive and rather cumbersome to produce; information to be recorded on CD-ROM had to be sent outside of the originating organisation to have a master made from which copies could be made.

However, the CD-Rs (CD-Recordables) now widely used are a great deal cheaper than the WORM or magneto-optical disks; combined with desktop CD recorders, and the widespread availability of CD drives as a standard PC component, they offer significant potential for the storage of images and other electronic documents and data.[3] It is interesting to note that the decreasing demand for floppy disks is partly attributed to the increased use of CD-R and other high capacity storage media.

New information can be added to a CD-R until it is full; however, like WORM disks, information on CD-Rs cannot be edited. Another factor about CD-Rs that needs to be taken into account in selecting a storage medium is that the speed of retrieval of information is much slower than WORM or magneto-optical disk or hard disk.

As with WORM and magneto-optical disks, the life of the information on a CD-R is uncertain.

At the time of writing, new CD-RW (CD-ReWritable) technology was due for release. Unlike the CD-ROMs and CD-Rs, CD-RWs can be re-recorded many times.

Document retrieval, display and printing

Once an image is stored, it can be retrieved via the indexing and retrieval system for displaying on a local or remote workstation or PC connected to the system. It can also be printed out on a high resolution laser printer, or it can be faxed direct to a remote location. Depending on the power of the printer, printing of images can be very slow; this needs to be taken into account in implementation planning.

Image display requires a certain screen size and resolution. If the imaging system is to be loaded onto an already existing computer mainframe or networked system, the existing workstation screens will not necessarily be suitable for displaying images. For example, VGA screens (commonly found on PCs), may be satisfactory for occasional viewing of images, but not for constant use. The VGA screen is the wrong shape to display a whole image (short and wide instead of tall and narrow). In addition, its definition is inadequate.

For users working frequently with images, a high resolution screen is essential.

It should also be noted that, as with disk space, images take a lot more memory than do, for example, word processed documents. So for this reason, not all PCs in an organisation may be suitable for viewing images unless their memory is upgraded.

A final point to note in relation to image display is that many imaging systems provide various image quality and enhancement features to improve display, for example, forms and border removal, auto-cropping, and deskewing.

Imaging applications

Imaging systems range from large complex centralised applications with 8000 or more documents relating to a particular type of transaction being processed per day, to medium decentralised or departmental applications with a variety of input documents, to small departmental or personal systems which involve little more than scanning.

Imaging systems are ideal for applications which involve transaction processing with different people doing different tasks, and for applications with high volume storage and high volume retrieval. Typical application areas are claims processing, medical records, and litigation documentation.

Transaction processing frequently involves a number of steps with different people being responsible for different sequential tasks. Work is often batch processed by one person before it is handed onto the next, so the timeframe for processing a transaction can be substantial. Using appropriate workflow software, imaging enables workflow to be redesigned so several processes can be carried out at once and documents can be sent between operators much faster.

Applications where incoming correspondence is scanned, stored as images or converted to text format, and sent to relevant employees for processing, are becoming increasingly common. These applications are designed to improve the speed with which correspondence is handled, to track action on correspondence, to help ensure consistent processing of matters, and to facilitate the future retrieval of documents.

As a side benefit, imaging applications may also enable organisations to deal with shortages of office space by freeing up areas normally taken by paper storage.

A strong argument often used by management against implementation of an imaging system is the need for original signatures for authorisations to proceed on a matter. However, digital signatures are becoming more widely accepted and the International Telecommunications Union has published a standard (X.209 standard) to manage these signatures in electronic documents. At the time of writing Standards Australia was investigating digital signature recognition in Australia.

Currently there is also software available which can read and match key characteristics of an original signature on different documents.

Figure 10.2   Combined microimager and scanner

Source: Reproduced with permission of Kodak Australasia Pty Ltd

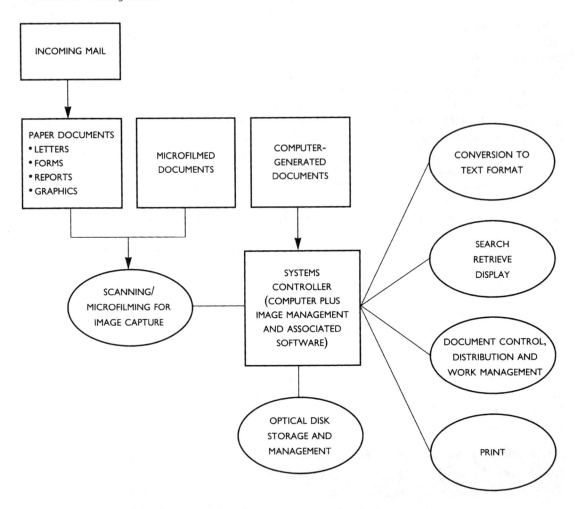

Figure 10.3 Document imaging system—physical and process components

It has been generally argued in the past that imaging systems are not cost-justifiable purely for storage applications. Paper or microfilm storage is still cheaper. This, along with concerns about the long-term stability of magnetic and optical storage media, and concerns about software and hardware obsolescence, has been the impetus for the development of hybrid systems. These systems allow documents to be stored as images for the initial high-activity period and then on microfilm for long-term storage. However, as media technology and capacities develop and grow, scanner speeds increase, and overall costs reduce, optical storage is being considered more seriously by organisations for long-term storage.[4]

Digital imaging system applications are not as widespread now as was generally predicted they would be. There are probably three main reasons for this. Firstly, the capital outlay on digital imaging systems can be very high, depending on what computer and communications equipment an organisation already has. Secondly, the technology associated with document imaging systems is developing so rapidly that organisations are hesitant to commit themselves to the current systems and equipment—they are playing a 'wait and see' game. And thirdly, organisations have been concerned over the legal status of digitised copies of records.

On the issue of costs, both capital and recurring costs are reducing all the time, particularly as media densities, scanner speeds and computer processing capabilities increase. On the legal issue, the new evidence legislation in Australia (at least at the Commonwealth level and in some states) ensures that digitised copies of records enjoy the same evidential weight as paper records.[5] So unless there is other legislation applying to particular categories of records which requires that they be kept in paper format, some organisations may decide to not keep the paper records. This option makes digital imaging systems a lot more attractive to organisations.

Examples of imaging applications in Australia

An example of a large application is the Australian Securities Commission's imaging system for all of the official registration documents for Australian companies. Prior to the introduction of the imaging system, all the documents went to the State Corporate Affairs Offices to be indexed and microfilmed. Processing time was high— it took up to eight weeks for a document to be available to the public. By October 1992, with the imaging system in operation, processing time was 24 hours and reducing. By late 1996 there were approximately 30 million images on the system, with about six to eight million images added each year. Enquirers interrogate the database and can fax copies of documents to themselves.

Other large applications in Australia include the following:

- The Victorian Land Titles Office has an Automated Land Titles system utilising optical disk technology
- The Australian Submarine Corporation Pty Ltd has an optical disk documentation management system to control the large volume of external and internal documents on its submarine project
- The GIO Life Insurance Head Office in Sydney has an imaging system to process its proposals
- Medicare has an imaging system to process its direct bill vouchers
- A number of hospitals have imaging systems for their medical records (e.g. Woden Valley Hospital, Australian Capital Territory)
- Imaging systems are also starting to appear in local government (e.g. City of Hobson's Bay, Victoria).

Microfilm imaging systems

It is often claimed that microfilm has 'had its day' and that optical disk storage of digital images will replace it as a non-paper storage medium. That may well be the case in the future, and possibly in the near future, but microfilm is still an option organisations may want to consider in certain circumstances. For example, they may consider it for high volume, low retrieval applications, or for applications where archival quality is critical or as an interim measure until they feel ready to invest in the necessary equipment for a digital imaging system. In addition, there is a large number of existing microfilm applications which may continue to be maintained for some time.

It is most important that a records manager implementing or taking over a microfilm storage application has a good understanding of the technology and equipment available so that he or she can make properly informed decisions. Information is readily available in the literature[6] and by contacting the major suppliers and talking to other organisations with microfilm applications.

Issues to be considered when evaluating and comparing microfilm and digital imaging technology for a particular application include:

- **Record usage**—how long are records active, what are the steps involved in processing the information and how many people are involved; how many people need to view the records and how often?
- **Media and system costs/capacities**—what will it cost to implement and maintain the system?
- **Duplication/backup costs**—what are the costs involved in providing for disaster or error recovery?
- **Legality of the records**—if stored as microfilm or digital images, will they be admissible in a court of law?
- **Longevity**—how long do the records need to be kept? (Microfilm is available in archival quality; the life of optical disk records is still uncertain and good quality control procedures are necessary to ensure refresher copies are made.)
- **Standards**—the product being considered must be compatible with other brands in the event of the organisation wanting to change or expand. If standards have not been applied to the technology, there must be at least gateways between the products.
- **Systems obsolescence**—this is not only dependent on the medium used, but also on the software/hardware which supports it. Microfilm will be readable in the future, as long as archival quality has been used. On the other hand, machine-based formats such as magnetic and optical media are dependent on the systems and hardware needed to access them being maintained.

COLD (Computer Output to Laser Disk)

COLD is a storage and retrieval technology which is used to process and index computer-generated reports. It enables desktop access to reports and incorporates search, view, processing, and print functions.

COLD is an alternative to COM (Computer Output on Microfilm); COM is microfilm produced directly from a computer by use of a COM recorder. It is likely that many existing COM applications will gradually be converted to COLD.

Typical applications for which COLD technology is useful include budget and other financial data, invoices, purchasing information, directories and inventories.

Workflow systems

Workflow systems are designed to help organisations automate business processes. They automate the flow of tasks and information around an organisation. They do this by a system of automatic routing of information relevant to the particular business process to the participants in that process. They can also be used to track the status of the process across the participants.

In designing a workflow for a business process, the administrator needs to define the tasks, the participants and their roles, and the workflows. In many workflow systems the task of actually setting up a workflow is relatively simple; it is the initial design stage based on a thorough understanding of the business process which is the most difficult.

Information within a workflow may be drawn from a range of sources, including a business system designed to manage the particular business process, paper documents, facsimiles, desktop applications, such as word processing and spreadsheet, forms, microfilm, computer reports, library resources, and voice. These information types may all be incorporated into a workflow. Imaging systems are often referred to along with workflow systems because they are the key tools for converting paper and film formats into images suitable for use in a workflow.

Benefits of workflow

One of the benefits of workflow is its ability to link information from disparate information systems around an organisation, whether these systems be individual, workgroup, business unit or corporate applications. These isolated information systems, which tend to proliferate in organisations over the years, are often an important source of information for business activities across the organisation, not just within the area where the particular systems reside. Although linking the information can pose problems due to variations in format and structure, workflow does provide the opportunity to make the links, while at the same time preserving the accessibility of the information for the originating individuals or workgroups.

Workflow systems are useful for transaction processing. They allow a workflow to be redesigned so that several processes can be carried out at once and transactions can be completed much faster than if they were handled manually in sequential steps. In addition, managers can monitor progress on tasks by checking their location and status on the workflow system (documents can't get stuck in employees' trays), and can ensure consistent application of business rules by building those business rules into the workflow.

Current workflow systems are successful for managing business processes which can be highly structured. Typical applications where workflow is being used successfully, usually in conjunction with imaging, include insurance claim processing, routing and tracking correspondence, routing forms in a quality management program, and accounts payable processing.

In general workflow systems are not suitable for situations where a lot of ad hoc changes to the workflows are likely to occur. The more changes that occur, the less cost-effective the process is likely to be. But the development of more intelligent and responsive workflow software will undoubtedly receive a lot of attention over the next few years.

With further development of the technology, workflow is likely to have a major role to play in the workplace of the future and could make a major contribution to improved recordkeeping. Used in conjunction with records management software, it can be very effective in linking together and controlling all of the information in a range of formats and from relevant core business systems needed for a particular business process, along with definitions of tasks and workflows and profiles of the participants. It can be used to create an audit trail to show that actions have been completed.

It is also a very powerful tool for assisting organisations to review and improve the management of their business processes. In designing a workflow, organisations must define the exact tasks, the information required, the participants, and the workflow. This review helps identify any bottlenecks and inefficiencies in the way the business process is currently being conducted and to introduce improvements.

Organisations establishing a quality management system under the ISO 9000 quality assurance standards commonly find they need to review workflows; they may implement workflow software to assist them in this process and to achieve ongoing improvements.

Groupware

Groupware is an umbrella term used for a software system which is based on the concept of people working together, sharing information and ideas.

It is particularly valuable when used to enable people in dispersed geographical locations to share information.

Lotus Notes is the best known groupware product.

Groupware runs on networks. It uses tools and strategies such as electronic mail, bulletin boards, conferencing, scheduling, and information replication,[7] as well as standard desktop products such as word processing. It can also be linked to the Internet or an intranet to provide enhanced publishing and distribution capabilities.

Groupware focuses on documents, including compound documents which may be a mix of text, graphics, images, video and audio, but it can also be used to draw down information from database systems for use within the group. In this way, like workflow systems, it is a powerful tool for linking together and drawing on disparate systems within an organisation.

Groupware is different from office automation. The latter focuses on helping people with individual tasks, such as producing a document or spreadsheet, whereas groupware is concerned with empowering groups to manage entire business processes.

Typical activities within the groupware environment include the following:

- Sharing of documents within a group for discussion purposes. This may include sending a document to the group seeking comments and ideas, or it may involve two or more people working together on the same document on their respective screens.
- Utilising workflow where processes must take place in sequential order.
- Tracking of progress on a particular matter.
- Scheduling of meetings.
- Accessing online reference materials, such as manuals, relevant to the group.

Koulopoulos & Frappaolo point out how the development of these software categories paralleled and were dependent on the development of hardware technology, that is, the PC and increasingly powerful versions of it, PC networking and client server architecture.

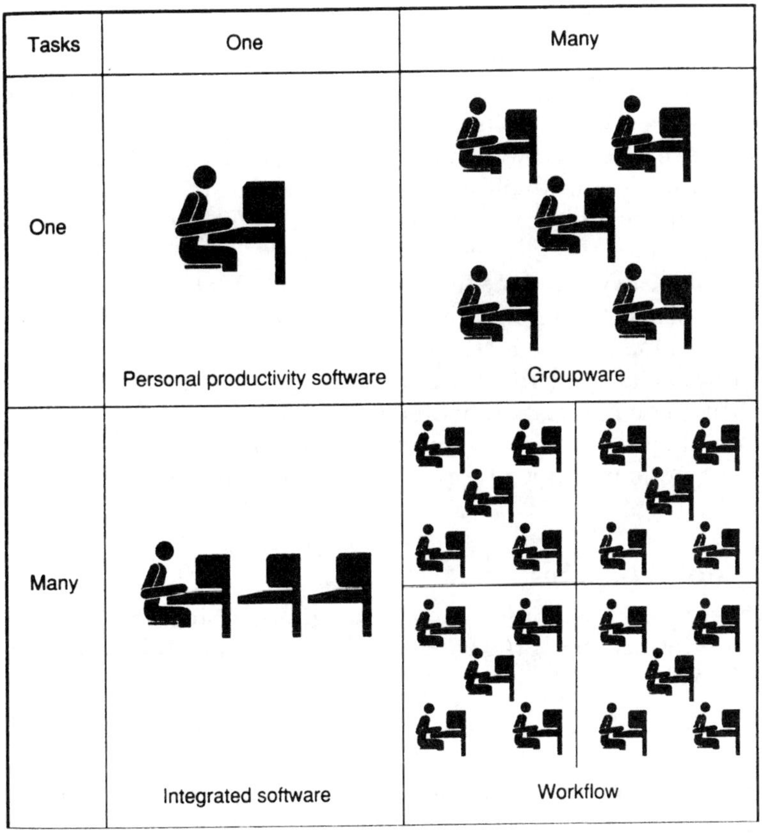

Tasks	One	Many
One	Personal productivity software	Groupware
Many	Integrated software	Workflow

Figure 10.4 Chart showing the range of software categories from personal productivity software and integrated multifunction software, to groupware and workflow software

Source: Reproduced from Koulopoulos & Frappaolo (1995) p. 55

Electronic document publishing

Internet and intranets as document publishing systems

The Internet features more and more frequently in the media and impinges on the business operations of organisations more extensively with every passing day.

Internet technology has enormous implications for the way information can be distributed in the workplace of the future, and in fact it is already having a substantial impact on many organisations. As with other technological developments which affect the way in which organisations manage their information, records managers need to consider what role they need to be playing in ensuring the technology is used to achieve the best outcome for the organisation.

What is the Internet?

The Internet is simply a collection of connected regional networks joining millions of 'host' computers in many countries of the world. It uses a set of common protocols for the exchange of information.

The Internet has been growing rapidly since the early 1980s but it is only in recent years that its use by individuals and corporations has really exploded. As at mid-1996 Internet usage had grown at approximately 100 per cent over the previous year and the number of registered users was about 13 million.

The costs of the development and use of the Internet has in the past been largely borne by the participating organisations (e.g. universities) but that is gradually changing as commercial use increases.

The Australian part of the Internet was originally developed as AARNet to promote better communication between researchers.

Every computer on the Internet and every person with e-mail (electronic mail) access has a unique Internet address. There are different rules covering these two types of addressing.

Internet tools and sites

There are a range of tools used for accessing, organising and interrogating vast amounts of information on the Internet. These include Telnet, Gopher and the World Wide Web.

- **Telnet** is used to log on to a range of databases, library catalogues and other special facilities
- **Gopher** is a menu-driven interface. It is used for searching across servers by making choices from a hierarchical system of menus.

World Wide Web (often referred to as WWW or the Web)

The Web is the most user-friendly and most widely used system on the Internet. It can be used to access any type of site on the Internet, not just WWW sites. It supports hypertext and hypermedia.

Hypertext is a system which enables the user to move from one point in a document to another in the same document or a different document simply by clicking with a mouse button on a highlighted name or topic. Hypertext allows the user to drill down and up and sideways within a group of documents. A hypertext system on the Web consists of four components—the Web pages, the links which are the paths connecting the various points in the Web pages, the buttons or highlighted words which the user activates to move from one point to another, and a browser which allows the user to navigate the system. There are various graphical Web browsers available. One of the most widely used is Nescape Navigator which allows access to text, pictures and sound.

Hypermedia is the same as hypertext but applies specifically to images and sound.

Web pages are designed using HTML (Hypertext Markup Language). HTML is, in turn, based on SGML (Standard Generalised Markup Language). SGML is the ISO

(International Organisation for Standardisation) standard for describing document structure.[8] It is designed to deal with the variations in documents and to bring some consistency to their structure for retrieval purposes. It is based on the hierarchical structure of documents and uses a system of descriptive tags for marking up text in electronic form. This allows documents to be used on any hardware, software or operating environment without loss of format. Under SGML each document type must have a Document Type Definition (DTD). DTDs represent the rules which govern the relationship between the structure and content of the document. HTML is the DTD for all WWW documents.

There are a number of Web page creation tools available, many of them via the Internet. However it is often still necessary to edit documents after using the tools to achieve the final result required.

Figure 10.5 A sample Web page, the home page for KPMG Australia

Note: The underlined words and headings are links to further information

Source: Reproduced with permission of KPMG, Australia

FTP (File Transfer Protocol)

FTP is used to send or receive files across the Internet. Huge numbers of files on the Internet are available for transfer, including software, documents, and graphics.

What is the Internet used for?

E-mail

Internet e-mail is used extensively by individuals and organisations to communicate with colleagues and customers.

Discussion lists, bulletin boards and newsgroups

These are used by people with a common interest to share and seek information and ideas.

Discussion lists are used to distribute e-mail messages to people with a common interest. They use a central server (listserv) which also acts as a central library of files which can be retrieved using e-mail commands. Users subscribe to the lists by sending their e-mail address to the listserv. There are a number of listservs of interest to the records management and archives profession (see Appendix D).

Information searching

There is a vast amount of information on the Internet which is of potential value to organisations. However it is also possible to spend a lot of time ploughing through information of little value. A good understanding of the various search engines used will minimise time wasted. Examples of Internet search engines include Altavista, Excite, Infoseek, Lycos and Yahoo.

Information found on the Internet includes directories (e.g. telephone), newspapers, government information, library catalogues, vendor information, information on organisations and their functions and services.

Downloading of information

A lot of information on the Internet can be downloaded, in some cases for free, in some cases at a cost. Such information includes documents, software and graphics.

Commercial transactions

The Internet is being used increasingly for electronic commerce. Initially it is mainly being used for downloading products with payment via credit card, but facilities such as home shopping and electronic banking are well on the way. The Internet is also used extensively for advertising.

What are intranets?

Intranets are internal communications networks, based on Internet standards. They use the technical protocols (TCP/1P) of the Internet to provide a platform for communication within organisations, no matter how large or physically dispersed they may be. Because Web browsers and servers are cross-platform, intranets have the great advantage of being accessible from different platforms and systems.

The term used for an extension to an organisation's intranet designed to make information available to the organisation's clients is called an extranet.

According to surveys, a very high proportion of medium to large businesses have or are planning an intranet.

Web applications using intranets generally fall into three categories:

- Communication on a one-to-many basis, such as distributing administrative policy and procedures, technical and product information, and news releases to staff.
- Two-way communication such as service desk operations.
- Many-to-many communications such as internal bulletin boards and databases.

Web publishing for internal communication requires the use of HTML authoring tools to create internal Web sites. Many organisations with intranets use a basic page design which employees can alter for particular applications.

Intranets provide some major benefits:

- They are an excellent alternative to distributing information on paper or even CD. They eliminate the requirement to distribute on a periodic basis multiple copies of documents such as manuals, reports and directories.
- The information can be readily updated as required.
- The hypertext format provides a user-friendly way for employees to access information, enabling them to search to the particular level they require. For example, an application which provides information about an organisation can be designed as both an induction tool for new employees as well as a source of more detailed information on the functions, activities and procedures of the organisation as required.
- They can be integrated with the organisation's business systems for access to corporate data.
- They are useful for distributing information to employees across different geographical locations and even to selected customers.
- They are relatively easy to implement and use and do not require a lot of training.

Security is a problem for organisations using the Internet rather than a private network for internal Web sites. Organisations need to weigh up the risks and develop guidelines on what sort of information can be distributed via the intranet.

It is sometimes predicted that intranets may replace a range of existing groupware-style products because they are cheaper and much easier to implement, but can still use a lot of the same tools such as bulletin boards, electronic mail and conferencing.

Impact of the Internet and intranets on records management

The use by organisations of the Internet and intranets presents new challenges and opportunities for records managers. As is the case with electronic document management in general, it is essential that the records manager works cooperatively with other relevant professionals (information technology, library, marketing, etc.) in the organisation to develop guidelines and rules for how information distributed on the Internet or an intranet is managed.

Internet e-mail usage

Internet e-mail guidelines must incorporate any special legal, ethical or confidentiality issues related to e-mail usage. Protocols and rules for how to present information are important, particularly in view of the tendency of employees to see e-mail as a personal informal tool rather than as a business communication system which identifies them as a member of their organisation.

As with internal e-mail messages, rules for transferring messages for retention as part of the documentation relating to a business activity must be developed.

Document presentation

Records managers can make a useful contribution to monitoring standards for document creation on the Internet and intranets and to ensure good recordkeeping practices are followed. They are well placed to advise on information layout issues, hypertext links, the type of contextual information about a document that needs to be captured, and procedures for document updating and for capturing a history of changes to a document.

Some of the electronic document management systems on the market have integrated products to enable the documents in their databases to be published on the Internet or an intranet. While this gives organisations added power in managing and distributing their recorded information, it also creates further challenges for the records manager in ensuring that recordkeeping standards are maintained throughout (e.g. that updated versions of documents are managed across the two locations).

EDI (Electronic Data Interchange)

EDI is the process by which business documentation is transmitted electronically through computer links. It is most commonly used for trading, therefore the records are usually of a transactional nature, such as purchase requests, delivery dockets and invoices. An example of a different sort of EDI application is the electronic lodgement of tax documents with the Australian Tax Office. EDI differs from electronic mail in that electronic mail requires someone to read and interpret the information, whereas in EDI the reading and interpreting is done automatically by the computer.

In the past, a barrier to the quicker spread of EDI was the lack of universally accepted standards for formatting documents. This happened because EDI was developed as industry specific technology. Now major vendors of EDI services use either the ANSI X.12 or the EDIFACT standard to ensure data from different partners can be exchanged.[9] It is estimated that EDI usage will grow by at least 50 per cent per annum until the year 2000.[10] It has already meant a substantial reduction in the volume of paper handled by those organisations employing it for business transactions. Besides saving paper work, EDI saves clerical effort and postage delays, and reduces the danger of errors in transcribing information. It can significantly reduce the time in which orders can be filled.

At the time of writing EDI software and systems using the Internet rather than special EDI networks were being developed. For example, the Federal Government's Commonwealth Electronic Commerce Service (CECS) called Transigo was due for release in March 1997. Transigo is to be used for advertising government tenders, lodging submissions, and processing orders, invoices and payments.

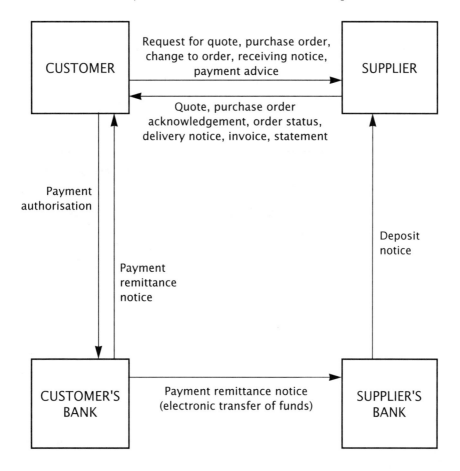

Figure 10.6 Transactions using EDI

Note: Based on a diagram 'Intercorporate Transactions using EDI' in Senn (1992) p.45

CALS (Continuous Acquisition and Lifecycle Support)

CALS stands for Continuous Acquisition and Lifecycle Support (formerly Computer Assisted Logistics Support). It was developed by the United States Department of Defence to accelerate the use of electronic text and graphics for preparing weapons systems manuals and specifications. It was a strategy for dealing with the phenomenal amount of paper involved in producing and distributing the manuals and the enormous problems in keeping them up-to-date.

The Commonwealth Government has endorsed CALS for use in Australia as part of its drive for open systems technology. The key goal of CALS is to ensure that information is independent of current and future technology (for example, that documents can be exchanged across mixed hardware environments, and that information created in applications that no longer exist can be accessed).

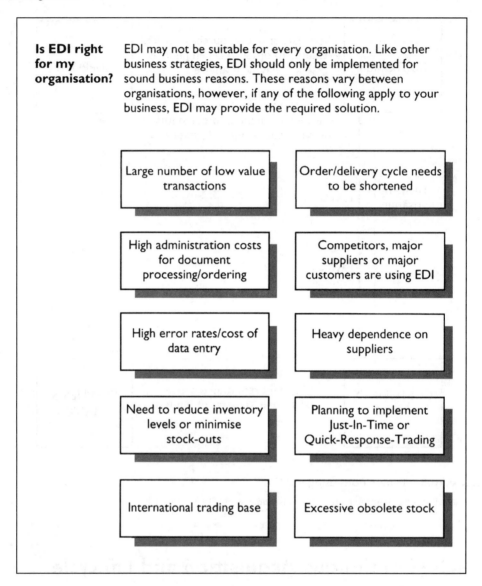

Figure 10.7 Reasons an organisation might implement EDI

Source: Reproduced from the EDI Action Kit, with permission of KPMG

While it has initially been introduced within the defence context, it is considered to have wide application in government and industry in general and has been adopted in areas such as telecommunications, aerospace, and the pharmaceutical industry.

CALS applies a range of international data exchange standards to facilitate the exchange of digital files within the Commonwealth Department of Defence and between Defence and industry. The standards cover things like imaging, document and report structure, and technical illustration. As an example, SGML (Standard Generalised Markup Language) is used for exchanging text. In addition Defence plans to use EDI (Electronic Data Interchange) networks using the international EDIFACT standard to send messages such as purchase orders and invoices between Defence and its trading partners.

The technical and support documentation for all new tenders for defence acquisition projects will have to be CALS compliant, unless it can be demonstrated that this would not be cost effective.

The CALS standards are now accepted internationally so there is increasing pressure on Australian industry to use CALS to aid their entry into export markets.

In organisations which have CALS compliant documentation, records managers have an important role to play in ensuring that the documentation meets record-keeping requirements and standards.

Exercises

1 Discuss the following statement: 'In the next decade, the postal officer will be obsolete in the office context.' For this exercise you will need to supplement your reading of this chapter with a study of the literature on current directions in office automation. Indexing tools such as *Business Periodicals Index* should guide you to some useful articles.

2 Locate details of four digital and/or microfilm imaging bureaus in your state. Attempt to include representative examples from the commercial, government and education sectors. Briefly describe the type of clientele each aims to reach and the services offered.

3 Search the Internet for references on document management principles and practices. List any references to work done in Australia on the topic.

Case study 10.1

In January 1992 the Airship Company decided to acquire an imaging and workflow system to manage the documentation and information flow for its domestic airship project. At that stage there were about 200 incoming paper documents per day from contractors, suppliers, government agencies and other sources. These documents averaged three pages each and an average of four photocopies of each document were made for distribution to the managers. Each document had to be processed, or at least viewed, by up to four departments before being filed away. In addition to the incoming documentation, there were about 100 computer-generated internal and outgoing documents related to the project created each day. It was envisaged that there would be a similar volume of daily documentation to be handled for the next five years.

Management wanted the following problems addressed:

- The excessive amount of paper being distributed and stored, and the highly labour-intensive nature of the current way of operating
- The significant processing delays caused by cumbersome paperflow
- The slow and unreliable retrieval of documentation when needed.

Your task

Outline the information that must be gathered and the decisions that must be taken in order to select a suitable imaging and workflow system for the company.

Questions

1 An increasing amount of important decision making in offices is taking place via verbal communication technologies (including one-to-one telephone links, telephone voicemail systems, and telephone and video conferencing). The dilemma for organisations is that in most cases these communications are not captured, except possibly in the form of a file note or minutes which rely on the memory of one of the participants. This is despite the fact that they may form important links in the chain of evidence relating to a business activity. How should the records manager tackle this problem, if at all? Should a record of telephone calls, messages, and conferences be captured, indexed and filed? Or converted to text format, and filed? Are there other ways of meeting recordkeeping requirements? What legal, ethical and technical issues might need to be taken into account?

2 A common pattern has developed in organisations for individuals and groups to establish their own electronic filing systems. Why has this happened? What problems has it caused for organisations? What approaches are organisations taking to deal with the problems?

3 A large legal firm has employed a records management consultant to investigate the feasibility of imaging its client files. It wants to know if it should opt for an electronic document management system to manage its current as well as completed files, or stay with paper for its current files and use microfilm for storing its completed files, or choose some other option, possibly combining microfilm with electronic technologies. What information would the consultant need to gather in order to arrive at a recommended solution?

4 In developing standards and procedures for managing an organisation's Internet Web page, what might be the respective roles of the Records Manager and the Librarian? What skills can each contribute to the process?

5 What issues might an organisation include in its guidelines for employees on the use of Internet e-mail?

Notes

1 In a voice mail system the spoken word is digitised. If a caller wishes to leave a message, he or she dials a number and dictates. The message is filed in memory and reconstituted back into voice when the recipient dials the mailbox.

2 At the time of writing optical disks ranged in capacity up to 25 gigabytes and it was predicted that they will become available in sizes up to 200 gigabytes.

3 At the time of writing the most commonly used CD-R stored 680 megabytes, but disks which could store up to 4.7 gigabytes were due to be released shortly.

4 An example is the Kodak Imagelink System. The microimager/scanner can either microfilm or scan or do both at the same time, and the Digital Workstation can automatically search for an image (microfilm or digital) and, if necessary, digitise it and send it around a network. See figure 10.2.

5 Amendments to the evidence legislation are discussed in more detail in Chapter 3.

6 For example, Linton (1990), Chapter 15, Robek, Brown & Stephens (1996), Chapter 10, and Smith & et al. (1995), Chapter 7.

7 With information replication, information is automatically copied from one server or workstation to another for shared use.

8   International Organisation for Standardisation 1986, *ISO 8879:1986, Information Processing—Text and Office Systems—Standard Generalised Markup Language*, Geneva.
9   Mackenzie (1992), pp. 26–27. This article also includes a listing of major EDI vendors and systems in Australia as at 1992.
10 *EDI Action Kit*, KPMG, Melbourne.

Additional information

There is a large body of literature on the topics covered by this chapter. In fact, technology issues now tend to dominate the records management literature. Some of the most useful papers in the Australian context are presented at seminars and conferences organised by the Records Management Association of Australia, the Australian Society of Archivists, IIM (Institute for Information Management), Australian Archives, and the universities; examples in the list of references are Hill (1994) and Hallams (1995). Unfortunately, these papers do not always receive very wide distribution beyond the participants and are not routinely acquired by many libraries.

A great deal has been written about electronic document management and digital imaging technology over the past few years. There is a lot of case study material, for example, Mithen (1994); informative papers also appear from time to time in the current information and business literature, for example, Lunin (1992) and Senn (1992). Tapper (1989), while several years old now, provides an excellent overview of the relative merits of microfilm, and magnetic and optical storage. Koulopoulos & Frappaolo (1995) is a thorough and detailed coverage of electronic document management theory and technologies. Wilson (1995) provides a useful framework for determining the potential benefits of electronic document management systems.

A book like this can do no more than provide background reading on technological developments of relevance to records management; the rate of change is very rapid and the only way for records managers to keep up-to-date with developments in such areas as digital imaging, CD and optical disk storage, workflow, and electronic information interchange is by monitoring the current literature and by keeping in touch with colleagues and system suppliers.

References

Chartres, N. 1991, 'Electronic data interchange', *Informaa Quarterly*, vol. 7, no. 3, pp. 36–40.

Chisholm, B. 1994, 'Working smarter through intelligent imaging', in Records Management Association of Australia, 11th National Convention, Adelaide, 11–14 September 1994, *Conference Papers*, RMAA, pp. 36–39.

'The Defence drive for CALS', 1991, *Directions in Government*, vol. 5, no. 6, pp. 25–26.

Douglas, J. 1993, 'Back to basics image processing', *Informaa Quarterly*, vol. 9, no. 1, pp. 19–22.

Hallams, P. 1995, 'The development of CALS within the Australian Department of Defence', in *Australian Archives Playing for Keeps Conference*, Canberra, 8–10 November 1994, The Authors and the Commonwealth of Australia, pp. 299–304.

Hill, C. 1994, 'Electronic trading: implications for the information manager', in Records Management Association of Australia, 11th National Convention, Adelaide, 11–14 September 1994, *Conference Papers*, RMAA, pp. 88–95.

Koulopoulos, T. M. & Frappaolo, C. 1995, *Electronic Document Management Systems*, McGraw-Hill, New York.

Linton, J. E. 1990, *Organising the Office Memory: The Theory and Practice of Records Management*, University of Technology, Sydney, Kuring–gai Campus, Centre for Information Studies Publications, Chapters 15 & 16.

Lunin, L. F. (ed.) 1992, 'Imaging systems: what, when, how', *Bulletin of the American Society for Information Science*, vol. 18, no. 5, pp. 9–17.

Mackenzie, G. 1991, 'Document imaging and electronic document interchange—an overview', *Informaa Quarterly*, vol. 7, no. 3, pp. 22–29.

Mallen, E. 1992, 'Intelligent character recognition: it's not just recognition anymore', *Bulletin of the American Society for Information Science*, vol. 18, no. 5, pp. 9–11.

Mathers, J. 1997, 'Using the Intranet', *Informaa Quarterly*, vol. 13, no. 1, pp. 8–14.

McDonald, P. W. 1991, 'Image system application in the banking and finance industry—a records management perspective', *Informaa Quarterly*, vol. 7, no. 1, pp. 33–38.

McKenna, F. 1992, 'Records Management and imaging—towards the paperless office', *Informaa Quarterly*, vol. 8, no. 3, pp. 16–19.

Mithen, B. J. 1994, 'Imaging: a case study—Australian Securities Commission Public Information Program', in Records Management Association of Australia, 11th National Convention, Adelaide, 11–14 September 1994, *Conference Papers*, RMAA, pp. 122–29.

Poynton, T. 1992, 'Get active, or get archived', *Informaa Quarterly*, vol. 8, no. 3, pp. 26–32.

Robek, M. F., Brown, G. F. & Stephens, D.O. 1996, *Information and Records Management*, 4th edn, Glencoe/McGraw-Hill, New York, Chapters 8, 10–12.

Ryan, D. & Murdock, A. 1996, 'The Internet and you', *Informaa Quarterly*, vol. 12, no. 3, pp. 6–12.

Senn, J. A. 1992, 'Electronic data interchange: the elements of implementation', *Information Systems Management*, vol. 9, no. 1, pp. 45–53.

Shepherd, E. 1994, 'Managing electronic records', *Records Management Journal*, vol. 4, no. 1, pp. 39–49.

Smith, P.A. et al. 1995, *Introduction to Records Management*, Macmillan Education Australia, Melbourne, Chapter 7.

Tapper, G. 1989, 'Alternatives to paper: micrographics and magnetic media', in P. Emmerson (ed.) *How to Manage Your Records: A Guide to Effective Practice*, ISCA Publishing, Cambridge, Chapter 6.

Wilson, J. 1995, 'A framework for identifying the business benefits of electronic document management', *Records Management Journal*, vol. 5, no. 2, pp. 93–99.

chapter eleven

Developing a vital records protection plan

Overview

Records protection should be an issue of concern to every records manager.

For all of an organisation's records, the records manager should do whatever is necessary to ensure adequate measures are taken against such elements as fire, floods, excessive humidity, pest infestations, theft, deliberate destruction and loss through carelessness. An additional step which the records manager should take to protect the information of the organisation is to develop a plan specifically designed to secure its vital records. This can be seen as a form of insurance premium for the organisation and could indeed, in extreme circumstances, end up being critical to the survival of that organisation.

Vital records are those records without which an organisation could not continue to operate. They are the records which contain information needed to re-establish the organisation in the event of a disaster which destroys all other records. They are the records which protect the assets and interests of the organisation as well as those of its clients and shareholders. It is estimated that about 10 per cent of the total records of an organisation can be classed as vital.

A program to ensure vital records are protected should be seen as an important component of a total records management program. Unfortunately, it is very easy for the records manager to keep putting the task of establishing such a program aside while more obviously pressing demands keep arising. Statistically, the chances of a major disaster happening to organisations in Australia from a phenomenon such as an earthquake are not high, but floods and fire are not as uncommon and it is not sensible to adopt the attitude of 'it would never happen to us'.

> Statistics show that more than 70 per cent of businesses whose paperwork and computer programs are lost in fires, go out of business within three years of the fires. Authorities estimate that there are more than 1500 businesses razed by fire in Australia each year (McDougall 1989, p. 18).

It is not sensible to adopt the attitude of 'it would never happen to us'

This chapter looks at the major elements of a vital records protection program—how to identify vital records, how to protect them, and what operating procedures need to be developed.

Identifying vital records

The process of identifying vital records, like assessing records for retention and disposal action, requires a sound overall understanding of the business objectives and functions of the organisation. In some cases records are obviously vital; in others the decision is not so clear-cut. It is expensive to set up special protection measures for records, therefore it is important to avoid the temptation to include everything that might be vital; it is equally important not to miss records that are indeed vital. The key to whether particular records will be included in the protection plan will be senior management's view of the level of importance of the particular functions to which the records relate, and whether the functions could be re-established without the records concerned.

The initial work of identifying vital records needs to be done in the broader context of analysing the recordkeeping requirements relating to the organisation's business functions and activities. In this process any existing vital records will be identified as well as any gaps. The strategies and tools for analysisng recordkeeping requirements are discussed in Chapter 4.

Insurance policies and schedules	Inventory control records
Minutes of board meetings	Legal documents
Internal policy documents	Loan agreements
Laboratory notebooks	Mortgages
Drawings and notes on products	Payroll registers
Pay rates	Personnel records
Annual reports	Workers' rehabilitation and
Bank balances	compensation scheme records
Certificates of incorporation	Research records
Copyrights	Securities
Corporate seals	Tax returns
Deeds	Technical reports
Contracts	Leases
Computer software programs	Customer and debtor lists
General ledgers	

Figure 11.1   Examples of potentially vital records

Class 1 Vital	Records without which an organisation could not continue to operate; records which give evidence of the legal status of the organisation, and which protect the assets and interests of the organisation, its clients and shareholders. Irreplaceable.	For example: ▪ Minutes of board meetings ▪ Accounts receivable ▪ Product specifications
Class 2 Important	Important to the continued operation of the organisation. Can be reproduced from original sources but only at considerable expense.	For example: ▪ Procedures manuals ▪ Accounts payable
Class 3 Useful	Loss would cause temporary inconvenience to the organisation. Replaceable.	For example: ▪ Most correspondence
Class 4 Non-essential	No value beyond the immediate purpose for which the records were created.	For example: ▪ Staff circulars about one-off events now completed ▪ Advertisements

Figure 11.2   Records classification

Source: Based on G. P. McKinnon, (ed.) 1977, *Fire Protection Handbook*, 14th edn, National Fire Protection Association, Boston, section 5, pp. 25–26

Vital records are most likely to be found in key functional areas such as finance, personnel, administration, sales, product design and manufacturing, and computing. It is important that all types of records are investigated, regardless of the media in which they are stored. Where electronic records are identified as vital, details of how to access them should also be documented.

Records remain vital for varying lengths of time—in general, a will remains vital until the estate is settled; a contract for the period of that contract; and an invoice only until it is paid.

Figure 11.1 lists some examples of potentially vital records; Figure 11.2 puts vital records into context with other types of records found in an organisation.

Methods of protection

Once the records manager has identified the vital records of the organisation, he or she needs to establish the nature of potential disasters for that organisation; then, given this information, the most cost-effective method of protecting the records.

There are guides to disaster classification in the literature; these provide useful background reading, e.g. Robeck, Brown & Stephens (1996), pp. 71–72. However, in order to assess potential disasters for a particular organisation, local geographical, environmental and political factors, and the nature of the work done by the organisation, must be taken into account. For example:

- What is the likelihood of fire or floods? What is the quality of the existing fire protection system for the building (if there is one)? How quickly is the fire brigade likely to respond? Are records stored in a warehouse which is prone to flooding in times of heavy rain?
- Is the organisation in an area prone to earthquakes?
- Is the work of the organisation of a sensitive nature which might attract bomb threats or theft?
- Is the organisation located in a building or geographical area prone to pest infestations?
- Is high humidity a feature of the local climate? If so, does the building have adequate temperature and humidity control?

Answers to these questions will provide the background information for deciding the level of protection that needs to be given to the vital records of the organisation. Other questions that will influence the level and type of protection chosen include:

- What is the volume of records to be protected, now and in the future?
- What is the retrieval rate likely to be and how quickly will the records be required?
- Are there special environmental conditions required for storage of the records (e.g. for computer media and microfilm)?

Protecting vital records can become an expensive process; it is important to weigh up the costs of the different levels of protection against the costs of potential loss of the records.

There are three common approaches to protecting vital records:

- Duplication and dispersal within the organisation's offices.
- Use of fireproof and secure storage cabinets or rooms within the organisation's offices
- Remote storage

Duplication and dispersal within the organisation's offices

The original and copies are dispersed to two or more locations around the organisation. The copies may be in paper or an alternative format such as microfilm, optical or magnetic media. This approach provides a fairly low level of protection but is relatively cheap and may be considered adequate by some organisations, particularly if there is more than one office building across which the copies can be spread.

Fireproof and secure storage cabinets or rooms within the organisation's offices

For an organisation with a small number of vital records that it wishes to protect, a lockable fireproof cabinet or a safe may be chosen for documents such as leases and contracts. Fireproof rooms are expensive to install but very effective if set up properly with fire resistance for a minimum of four hours, a fire detection system, temperature and humidity control, dust-free conditions, and a secure locking device or other controlled access system.

Figure 11.3   Vault for storage of computer media

Source: Reproduced with permission of Recall Total Information Management

Remote storage

Remote storage may be with a commercial storage company specialising in secure storage, in a bank vault if the quantity is not large, or in an offsite facility which is operated by the organisation and which has the necessary environmental fire protection and security features. Copies of the records may also be held in the office if frequent reference is required.

Commercial storage of records, including computer media, is an option chosen by an increasing number of organisations (see Figure 11.3). The relative merits of commercial and in-house records storage in general (not just vital records) is discussed in some detail in Chapter 12.

Operating procedures

Operating procedures need to be developed and written down to ensure that the vital records protection program is maintained properly. As with any area of operation, it is very easy for a situation to arise where a program set up by the efforts of a dedicated and hard-working individual is allowed to fall apart because of a lack of commitment by future staff. Well established procedures and guidelines approved by senior management will reduce the likelihood of this happening.

Procedures and guidelines should include:

- Who is responsible for maintaining the program. It may be entirely the respon-sibility of the records manager or responsibility may be spread across the business units which create and control the records. Allocation of responsibility and relative roles must be spelt out clearly, including who has access to the vital records storage area.
- A system for the vital records—where and how the records are registered, how the information about the records is accessed, and how the records are stored.
- The information that needs to be registered about each vital record, such as:
  — Category of record
  — A cross reference to the disposal schedule
  — Information on where copies are held
  — Reasons for protection
  — Method of protection, including type of copy (e.g. microfilm, computer media, acid free paper copy)
  — Supporting records (such as finding aids) needed to access or interpret the record
  — Retention period
  — Review procedures to check whether the record is still vital.
- Procedures to ensure new vital records are identified and included in the program.
- Procedures for transferring the records or copies to the secure storage area or facility.

VITAL RECORDS INVENTORY (BY DEPARTMENT)

ORIGINATING DEPARTMENT: CONTACT: TELEPHONE:

REF NO.	RECORD SERIES/TITLE	REMARKS (INCLUDING SPECIAL INSTRUCTIONS, SUPPORTING DOCUMENTS AND FREQUENCY)	LOCATION OF ORIGINAL	BACKUP COPY(IES)		RETENTION SCHEDULE REF.	EFFECTIVE DATE	STATUS REVIEWED
				Location	Format			

Figure 11.4 Sample vital records inventory form

Vital records protection planning is only one part of a contingency or disaster recovery planning. Contingency planning includes not just the protection of vital records but also of other data and documents, software, hardware, facilities, equipment, supplies and services. It is the development of a total plan to be implemented in the event of a disaster which prevents an organisation from functioning in total or in part. An area of contingency planning of critical concern to records managers is computer systems disaster recovery. It is becoming increasingly important as more and more of an organisation's information is created, processed and stored on computers and computer media.

Unfortunately, many organisations do not have well developed and regularly reviewed contingency or disaster recovery plans. Records managers can encourage the development of such a plan and start the process by developing a vital records protection program. They can also play an important role in assisting the computer manager in two tasks:

• Ensuring that proper backup procedures for computer files are in place throughout the organisation and not just for those files under the direct control of the computer staff, and
• Organising suitable storage arrangements for the backup copies of computer files.

For those readers interested in seeking more information on contingency or disaster recovery planning, there are references included at the end of this chapter.

Exercises

1 Review the literature on records protection for the following information:
   • Technical (as opposed to administrative) details on measures that can be taken to protect records (paper, microfilm and electronic) against damage by fire, water, inappropriate temperature and humidity levels, pests, and dust.
   • Measures that can be taken to reconstruct records damaged by fire, water, inappropriate temperature and humidity levels, pests, and dust.

   Summarise your findings.

2 Choose any organisation (20+ staff) known to you and arrange an interview with the staff member responsible for records management procedures or with the administration manager. The topic of the interview is to be the protection of the organisation's vital records. (Check that he or she is prepared to be interviewed on the topic; some may consider it inappropriate to speak on matters relating to security of the organisation's information.)

   Start the interview by explaining what you mean by vital records and give some examples. Ask questions on the following topics:

   • Does the organisation have records it has identified as vital?
   • Has it taken action to protect those records and if so, what?
   • If it has not taken action to protect them, what methods of protection would it see as appropriate for the records?
   • What procedures has it in place to protect its computer data in general (i.e. not just vital electronic records)? Does it make backup copies of all/some of its computer files? How does it store them?

Questions

1 Taking local government as an example, what are likely to be the main categories of vital records? Think about both those categories of records which may apply to many types of organisations (as listed in Figure 11.1) as well as records relating to functions special to local government.
2 How should the records manager set about establishing which records need to be covered by a vital records protection plan?
3 What factors will determine the selection of storage media for vital records (acid free paper, microfilm, etc.)?
4 What implications has the increasing trend to store records in electronic format have for a vital records protection plan?
5 What does the phrase **disaster recovery planning** refer to? How does it relate to vital records protection planning?

Additional information

There are two aspects in particular related to vital records protection (and, in fact, records protection in general) about which readers may need to seek further information. The first one is the measures that can be taken to protect the records; two useful references are Robek, Brown & Stephens (1996, Chapter 4) and McKinnon (1981 section 10, Chapter 10). The literature of archives management is also a valuable source of information on the topic. The second aspect is contingency or disaster recovery planning; a selection of articles include the following: Balon & Gardner (1987), Bulgawicz & Nolan (1988), Jones (1995), Pember (1996), Romei, Fernberg & Malik (1995). Chapter 11 in Penn, Pennix & Coulson (1994) is a useful overview of disaster recovery and planning; and Khoo (1991) is a valuable paper on computer systems disaster recovery planning. There are many other useful references on the topic in both the computer and the facilities management literature.

The Australian Standard AS 4390.6–1996 (Standards Australia 1996) deals with both aspects of vital records protection. It includes a definition of vital records, information on how to protect records, and an appendix setting out the contents of a model disaster response plan.

References

Balon, B. J. & Gardner, H. 1987, 'Disaster contingency planning: the basic elements', *Records Management Quarterly*, vol. 21, no. 1, pp. 14–16.

Bulgawicz, S. L. & Nolan, C. E. 1988, *Disaster Prevention and Recovery: A Planned Approach*, ARMA International, Prairie Village, Kansas.

Doig, J. 1996, *Disaster Recovery for Archives, Libraries and Records Management Systems in Australia and New Zealand*, Centre for Information Studies, Wagga Wagga, NSW.

Fortson, J. 1992, *Disaster Planning and Recovery: How-to-do-it Manual for Librarians and Archivists*, Neal-Schuman Publishers, New York.

Jones, K. 1995, 'Contingency planning in LAN/WAN environments', *International Journal of Network Management*, vol. 5, no. 2, pp. 77–81.

Kenny, A. 1989, 'Establishing a vital records program', *Records Management Journal*, vol. 1, no. 2, pp. 54–60.

Khoo, B. 1991, 'Records and facilities protection: are we prepared in the event of a disaster?', in Records Management Association of Australia, 8th National Convention, Darwin, 15–18 September, *Proceedings*, RMAA, pp. 55–84.

Linton, J. E. 1990, *Organising the Office Memory: The Theory and Practice of Records Management*, University of Technology, Sydney, Kuring-gai Campus, Centre for Information Studies Publications, Chapter 10.

McDougall, J. 1989, 'Planning ahead for your company security', *Informaa Quarterly*, vol. 5, no. 3, pp. 17–19.

McKinnon, G. P. (ed.) 1981, *Fire Protection Handbook*, 15th edn, National Fire Protection Association, Boston, section 10, Chapter 10.

Pember, M. E. 1996, 'Information disaster recovery: an integral component of corporate risk management', *Records Management Quarterly*, vol. 30, no. 2, pp. 31–37.

Penn, I. A., Pennix, G.B. & Coulson, J. 1994, *Records Management Handbook*, 2nd edn, Gower Publishing Co., Aldershot, Hants, Chapters 10 & 11.

Ricks, B. R. & Gow, K. F. 1988, *Information Resource Management: A Records Systems Approach*, 2nd edn, South-Western Publishing Co., Cincinnati, OH, Chapter 20.

Robek, M. F., Brown, G. F. & Stephens, D.O. 1996, *Information and Records Management*, 4th edn, Glencoe/McGraw-Hill, New York, Chapter 4.

Romei, L. K., Fernberg, P. M. & Malik, M.S. 1995, 'Disaster recovery: are you ready?', *Managing Office Technology*, vol. 40, no.1, pp. 26–28, 30, 32.

Standards Australia 1996, *Australian Standard AS 4390–1996, Records Management, Part 6: Storage*, Homebush, NSW.

chapter *twelve*

Storage of inactive records

Overview

Substantial savings through a well-managed program for the storage of inactive or non-current records can be readily demonstrated. Because such records are seldom accessed, they can be stored away from the main office area in less costly space. It is also acceptable to store them more densely than active records. Reviewing and implementing storage arrangements for inactive records needs to be tackled in the early stages of establishing a records management program; this is particularly important if existing filing systems in the office need to be cleared out of large volumes of inactive records.

Inactive records are those records which are seldom accessed but which must be retained for occasional reference, or to meet statutory retention requirements, or for their long-term value for legal or other reasons. There is a category of records in between active and inactive records which are referred to as **semi-active**; examples of such records are 'previous year' records which are needed for reference when the current year's work is being done. Local work patterns will dictate whether these records are best kept with the active records, in intermediate storage, or with the inactive records. It is useful to document the decisions on such matters in the disposal schedule of an organisation so that transfer of records at the appropriate time becomes automatic.

If the inactive records of a particular organisation include records which are identified as having long-term value, these may be separated out for special in-house treatment or may be transferred, after their operational value has ceased, to an archival authority.

There are three critical steps in ensuring that the inactive records of an organisation are stored in the most suitable way both from the users' and management's point of view.

Figure 12.1   How inactive records should not be stored

1 The development of a disposal schedule

Such a schedule is used to ensure that records are retained for the appropriate period of time; it can also be used to provide a process for the transfer of records from expensive office space to secondary storage. Records disposal scheduling is discussed in Chapter 4.

2 Making decisions on storage media

Decisions need to be made on whether records will be kept in paper format, on microfilm, or in magnetic or optical format. Despite the advances in microfilm and computer storage technology, the majority of organisations still keep the bulk of their records in paper form; as a general rule it is still the cheapest form of storage.

3 Making decisions on storage facilities

This third step is the topic of this chapter. It looks at how to select the most appropriate type of storage facility for the records of an organisation, how to cost and plan an in-house facility, and it also looks briefly at the main methods used for secure records destruction.

The Australian Standard AS 4390.6–1996 is devoted to storage. It looks at how to select storage facilities and systems, and emphasises the need to look at the characteristics of different types of records in assessing storage requirements. This chapter expands on some of the aspects of storage facilities presented in the Standard.

Choosing a storage facility

Major options

1 To use space in the existing office building which is unsuitable for office accommodation but which meets the physical and environmental requirements for records storage. This sort of space may be suitable for organisations with a relatively small volume of inactive records to store; it may also be used for intermediate storage of semi-active records which are not accessed often but need to be onsite for quick reference.

2 To set up a storage facility in warehouse space in an area where rents and land values are lower than for the main office building. Such storage facilities are often referred to as records centres. They vary from centres with very large volumes of records which are staffed on a full-time basis and provide full storage, reference and retrieval services by trained personnel, to facilities where each business unit of the organisation is allocated a section and looks after its own records.

3 To use the services of a commercial records storage company. There are quite a number of such companies operating in Australia. At the one extreme they simply store boxes lodged with them and retrieve boxes on request; at the other extreme they offer a wide range of records management services including storage, retrieval of individual records, files or boxes, file and box tracking, listing and packing of records, sale of boxes, production of client-specified reports, and secure destruction of records. Some of the government archival agencies offer secondary storage facilities on a commercial basis in addition to their archival storage.

Information to be gathered

• What is the volume of records to be stored and what is the likely level of growth, if any? Predicting growth can be very difficult—some organisations expand and contract at an alarming rate with mergers, takeovers and changes in their market fortunes.

• What type of records are to be stored? Paper, microfilm, computer media, slides, photographs, plans?

• What environmental conditions (e.g. temperature and humidity levels) are needed for the different types of records?

• How often are the records needed? What is the estimated retrieval rate?

• How quickly do records need to be retrieved in both routine and urgent situations?

• How often do users need to browse through a range of records looking for information or can they normally specify an exact file or magnetic tape or other such item?

• What level of security is required on the records? Are there different levels of confidentiality on the records?

- What level of service is required? Is a simple storage and retrieval service adequate or does the organisation need other services as well, such as retrieval of individual records or specific information from records?
- How long do records need to be kept? What proportion are of long-term value?

Commercial storage versus in-house storage

In-house storage in this context refers to storage in a facility operated by the organisation owning the records, regardless of whether the storage area is within the organisation's office building or in separate warehouse premises.

An organisation may decide to use a commercial records storage company for very simple reasons; the most likely ones are that it has only a fairly small volume of records to be stored but no suitable storage area, or it has run out of space in its own facility and has no room for growth. Another reason may be that the organisation simply does not want the administrative hassles of running a storage facility; it would prefer to pay someone else to do the job, regardless of whether it costs more or not. On the other hand, an organisation may decide it has to develop its own facility because there is no commercial records storage service close enough geographically for it to use.

However, if both options are to be considered, then it is essential that the records manager carries out a thorough comparison of the relative benefits and costs of each in the light of the organisation's requirements. If a decision is made to use a commercial service, then quotations from a number of companies should be sought and carefully compared.

Criteria for assessing commercial records storage services

Protection of records—protection against unauthorised access

What sort of security system does the building have? Electronically activated doors? Electrical burglar alarm system? Closed circuit television? Guards? Are there adequate backup procedures in place in case the main system malfunctions?

Who is allowed access? What sort of checks are made on the staff?

What measures are taken to protect against unauthorised access to the delivery vehicles? Are they fitted with radio and alarm systems?

Protection from environmental hazards

The records storage company should be prepared to provide details of its fire protection measures, including how they meet the requirements for protecting different types of records (such as computer media) and how often the equipment is checked. If there is any doubt about the adequacy of their measures, advice can be sought from the local fire authority.

Note that halon gas extinguishing equipment has been commonly installed to protect computer media; it is now considered environmentally unacceptable and alternatives must be found.

There are differing views on the desirability of installing sprinkler systems in records storage warehouses. Some people argue that they are necessary—water damaged records can usually be restored; fire damaged ones seldom can. Others argue that they are a hazard in themselves because of the water damage that can occur if they go off accidentally. Good early smoke detection systems minimise the need for a sprinkler system to operate.

What measures are taken to ensure against flooding, excessive temperature and humidity levels, pests such as silverfish and mice, and dust? If the company accepts non-paper records such as computer media and microfilm, does it provide the necessary temperature and humidity controls? (See Figure 11.3 in the previous chapter for an illustration of a computer media vault.)

Protection against pests such as silverfish and mice is important

Figure 12.2 represents Australian Archives' recommended standards for environmental conditions for long-term storage of various types of records. These standards have been developed for use by the Australian Government but clearly have general applicability.

Australian Archives

Guidelines for the Storage of Permanent and Long-Term Temporary Value Commonwealth Records (30 Years and Over)

FORMAT	ENVIRONMENTAL CONDITIONS			SAFETY AND PROTECTION				PROTECTIVE PACKAGING
	Temp/Rh	Air	Lighting	Fire	Security	Housing	Containers	
Paper: files, cards, volumes, computer printout and other papers	20°C ± 2°C 50%RH ± 5%	well-ventilated and filtered to exclude: dust and other particles; acidic and oxidising gases	UV filtered fluorescent lighting timer controlled switches	heat/smoke detection fire alarms sprinkler system extinguishers	24-hour physical or electronic surveillance alarm systems controlled access	powder coated or baked enamel metal shelves	archival quality acid-free boxes	archival quality acid-free file covers, folders or envelopes
Paper: maps, plans, charts	20°C ± 2°C 50%RH ± 5%	well-ventilated and filtered to exclude: dust and other particles; acidic and oxidising gases	UV filtered fluorescent lighting timer controlled switches	heat/smoke detection fire alarms sprinkler system extinguishers	24-hour physical or electronic surveillance alarm systems controlled access	powder coated or baked enamel metal shelves or plan cabinets flat storage	archival quality acid-free folders or containers	archival quality acid-free enclosures or interleaving
Photographic media (black and white): sheet film, cine film, x-rays, microforms, glass plate photos	<18°C ± 2°C 35% RH ± 5% records stored at <10°C must be acclimatised before and after cold storage	well-ventilated and filtered to exclude: dust and other particles; acidic and oxidising gases degrading cellulose acetate or nitrate film must be isolated from other records	UV filtered fluorescent lighting timer controlled switches	VESDA (very early smoke detection apparatus) fire alarms extinguishers gas flooding or sprinkler system	24-hour physical or electronic surveillance alarm systems controlled access	powder coated or baked enamel metal shelves glass plates require stationary shelving and vertical storage	archival quality acid-free containers or boxes glass plates require additional shock protection	archival quality acid-free sleeves, envelopes, enclosures or canisters
Photographic media (colour): sheet film, cine film	<5°C 35% RH ± 5% records must be acclimatised before and after cold storage	well-ventilated and filtered to exclude: dust and other particles; acidic and oxidising gases	UV filtered fluorescent lighting timer controlled switches	VESDA (very early smoke detection apparatus) fire alarms extinguishers gas flooding or sprinkler system	24-hour physical or electronic surveillance alarm systems controlled access	powder coated or baked enamel metal shelves	archival quality acid-free folders or containers	archival quality acid-free sleeves, envelopes, enclosures or canisters frozen material must be in sealed vacuum packages
Magnetic Media: computer tapes and disks, video tapes, audio tapes, magneto-optical disks	18°C ± 2°C 35% RH ± 5%	well-ventilated and filtered to exclude: dust and other particles; acidic and oxidising gases	UV filtered fluorescent lighting timer controlled switches	VESDA (very early smoke detection apparatus) fire alarms extinguishers gas flooding or sprinkler system	24-hour physical or electronic surveillance alarm systems controlled access	non-magnetisable shelving	non-magnetisable, archival quality sealed containers, cassette cases or sleeves	non-magnetisable, archival quality sealed containers, cassette cases or sleeves
Optical Media: compact and mini disks, laser disks	18°C ± 2°C 35% RH ± 5%	well-ventilated and filtered to exclude: dust and other particles; acidic and oxidising gases	UV filtered fluorescent lighting timer controlled switches	VESDA (very early smoke detection apparatus) fire alarms extinguishers gas flooding or sprinkler system	24-hour physical or electronic surveillance alarm systems controlled access	powder coated or baked enamel metal shelves	archival quality acid-free containers or boxes	archival quality acid-free envelopes or enclosures
Miscellaneous: gramophone discs, models, objects, mixed media items	20°C ± 2°C 50% RH ± 5%	well-ventilated and filtered to exclude: dust and other particles; acidic and oxidising gases	UV filtered fluorescent lighting timer controlled switches	heat/smoke detection fire alarms sprinkler system extinguishers	24-hour physical or electronic surveillance alarm systems controlled access	powder coated or baked enamel metal shelves stationary shelving gramophone discs require vertical storage	archival quality acid-free containers or boxes	archival quality acid-free enclosures or wrapping

Figure 12.2 Guidelines for the storage of permanent and long-term temporary value Commonwealth records (30 years and over)

Source: Reproduced with permission of Australian Archives

Protection against inadvertent loss

What procedures are in place to minimise the chance of misfiling records or boxes? A number of the larger companies in Australia have introduced a checking method whereby both shelf locations and boxes have barcodes and the two are matched on a computerised system whenever a box is shelved. A similar type of barcoding system is used to ensure files are refiled in the correct boxes.

Plans for growth

What plans has the company made for handling growth in the demand for records storage? What happens when the existing warehouse is full?

Retrieval service

What is the guaranteed turn-around time for routine deliveries of requested items? How quickly can urgent items be delivered? Is the retrieval service on a twenty-four hour basis (that is, can items be requested at any time of the day or night)? What backup arrangements exist if the regular vehicles are not available? Does the company offer retrieval of boxes and individual files, or just boxes? Do the services and schedules offered meet the needs of the organisation?

Secure destruction

Does the company offer a secure destruction service for records stored both onsite and offsite? What methods does it use? How does it ensure security? (The different methods for destroying records are discussed later in this chapter.)

Media stored

Does the company accept the types of records the organisation wants to store?

Quality of relationship with clients and reputation of the company

How knowledgeable are the staff regarding the records management principles behind the sort of service they are providing? Are they cooperative and flexible in meeting special needs? Does the company have a good reputation for reliable service (low error rate and ability to meet time-lines) and attention to security? (This may require a bit of smart investigation. If the company is taking appropriate security measures it will not reveal the names of its clients; but clients would normally be the main source of information on quality of service.)

Other services

What other services does the company provide which might be useful to the organisation? For example:

- Retrieval and faxing of individual records in urgent situations
- Facilities for clients to use records onsite—room, photocopier, facsimile and telephone facilities
- Client-specified reports

- Reporting on boxes due for destruction
- Sale of boxes and stationery
- Packing of records
- Cataloguing of records—manually or onto computer
- Micrographic or imaging services—conversion of paper records to microfilm or digital images.

These types of services can be particularly appealing to an organisation that would prefer to pay for records management services rather than provide staff to do them in-house.

Contracts and charging

What type of contract does the company require? Are there any traps?

What protection is there against inadequate service? What happens if the organisation wants to pull out all of its boxes?

What are the liability clauses? Ideally there should be full protection against loss of the information in the records, not just the physical records themselves; realistically most records storage companies will not accept liability for information lost because of the potentially enormous premiums involved and the difficulty of estimating the value of information.

It is wise to seek legal assistance in reading the contract and negotiating suitable amendments.

How are the charges worked out? How are increases calculated? And can the organisation negotiate stable prices for a reasonable period of time? Can special charges be negotiated for the initial transfer of records to the company?

Charges are usually based on costs for storage per box per week, lodgement of new boxes, transport, permanent withdrawal of boxes and destruction. There will be additional charges for other services such as listing of records, urgent retrievals and supply of new boxes. The records manager should estimate the organisation's likely use under each charge category in order to arrive at an estimated annual total cost for storing records at each of the companies from which quotations have been received. Retrieval and growth rates will have a major bearing on overall costs; these factors need to be estimated as accurately as possible.

Estimating costs of operating an in-house facility

Even if it is apparent that commercial storage can offer substantial administrative and user benefits to an organisation, the final decision is likely to be based on security and access concerns and/or a comparison of costs. Security and access concerns are often perceived rather than real. Users feel the records will be more secure if kept under the direct control of the organisation, and they are concerned that they will not be able to get hold of the records as quickly as they need them. If the difference in cost between using a commercial records storage service and operating an in-house facility is fairly small, then the decision will probably be based on security and access issues; if the difference is substantial, the cheaper option will probably be chosen.

To calculate the cost of operating an in-house facility or records centre, the records manager needs to be clear on a number of issues:

- **Access requirements**—how often records are required and how quickly. This will determine possible locations for the facility; it will also affect staffing and retrieval costs.
- **The volume of records to be stored** and the estimated growth rate over a five-year period. (Five years provides a reasonable basis for planning.) This will determine the amount of space required.
- **The level of service to be provided**—simple maintenance of the facility for business units to store and retrieve their own records or a more extensive service including retrievals, photocopying, production of reports, monitoring of box and file movements. This will determine the type of facilities and equipment needed, and staffing costs.
- **Types of records to be stored**. This will affect the type of facilities, equipment and environmental controls required.

Capital and recurrent cost factors to be taken into account in calculating the total cost of operating an in-house facility include:

- Rental or purchase
- Rates and taxes
- Depreciation
- Insurance
- Phone/facsimile machine
- Computer and barcode equipment
- Power
- Salaries and wages
- Vehicle lease/purchase/maintenance
- Boxes
- Destruction of records
- Storage and retrieval equipment (racking, ladders, etc.)
- Building and equipment maintenance
- Fire protection
- Security systems/services
- Environmental controls
- Staff amenities.

Cost savings that can be achieved from operating a storage facility as opposed to leaving records in the office can be presented in terms of the following two factors:

1 Comparative storage costs of office space and storage facility. Robek Brown & Stephens (1996, p. 463) highlight potential space savings in these terms:

> … when records are housed in a typical modern office in standard four-drawer file cabinets, they require 1 square foot of floor space for each cubic foot of records. In comparison, when they are stored on shelves in a records center that ratio can be increased to 5 cubic feet of records to each square foot of floor space.

When these differences in floor space requirements are seen in terms of rental costs alone, the size of the savings becomes quickly apparent. (It is worth noting that rent on space in a city office building in Australia can be as much as twenty times the rent on warehouse space in the suburbs.)

2 Cost savings that result from the setting up of controls to ensure the regular flow of records from office to the storage facility.

Selection criteria for warehouse space

If the records manager is faced with the task of locating a warehouse site from which to operate a storage facility or records centre, there are a number of selection criteria to be taken into account.

- Suitability of the security system already in place.
- Environmental controls (e.g. air conditioning if high humidity is a feature of the area).
- Adequacy of the fire protection measures. Not only should there be adequate fire protection equipment and systems, but, in addition, if the building is shared with other tenants, there should be suitable separation measures to minimise the chance of fire spreading from another part of the building. The time it will take for the fire brigade to respond to a call should also be checked.
- Provision for parking plus a loading bay for trucks.
- Proximity of main road for ease of access.
- Electricity and telephone services.
- Not prone to flooding.
- Suitable areas for office, staff amenities, receiving and processing area, work areas for users.
- If racking is already in place, it should meet fire and safety regulations in terms of length, height, and clearance from sprinkler heads; local regulations should be checked for these details. Floor strength should be appropriate; the advice of an engineer should be sought on this matter. Aisles should be wide enough for easy access and for the use of ladders or other retrieval equipment.
- If racking is not already installed, the layout (location of walls, pillars, etc.) and ceiling height must be suitable for such an installation.
- Good fluorescent lighting. Whether racking is already installed or not, good lighting down every aisle (or future aisle) and in the work areas is essential.

In-house storage facilities: equipment and operating procedures

Shelving

In inactive records storage the access rate is likely to be fairly low. Thus the main priority in choosing shelving is maximising the use of available space; ease of access becomes a second priority.

Racking

The most common type of shelving used is open racking. This consists of shelving bays, usually double-sided or back-to-back to maximise the use of floor space. Boxes can be stacked up to three high on each shelf. The standard height for a small to medium-sized operation is equivalent to eight boxes (e.g. one box high on eight shelves, or two boxes high on four shelves, or three boxes high on two shelves and two boxes high on a third shelf). It is certainly possible to build racking higher than this, but it is only cost justifiable for large operations because of the expensive retrieval equipment required, such as hydraulic lifts or catwalks (see Figure 12.3).

Figure 12.4 shows two standard sizes of storage boxes. Figures 12.5 and 12.6 use these storage boxes to illustrate floor space requirements and linear capacity of different-sized shelving bays. Figure 12.7 shows some basic fire protection requirements for shelving layout.

Figure 12.3 Example of racking on a large scale

Source: Reproduced with permission of Recall Total Information Management

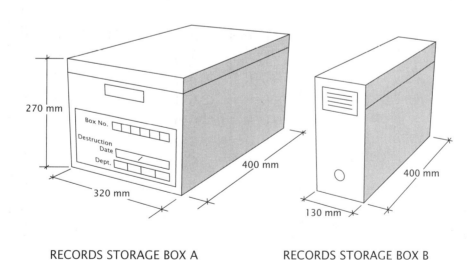

RECORDS STORAGE BOX A   RECORDS STORAGE BOX B

Figure 12.4 Standard storage boxes

Source: Reproduced with permission of Rack and File Commercial Pty Ltd, Melbourne

1 Modular steel shelving (Adjustable)

900 wide shelving
(floor space 1.5m²)
Box A = 2 per shelf x 7 levels x 4 bays = 56
Box B = 6 per shelf x 7 levels x 4 bays = 168

1200 wide shelving
(floor space 1.5m²)
Box A = 3 per shelf x 7 levels x 3 bays = 63
Box B = 9 per shelf x 7 levels x 3 bays = 189

2 Longspan (or universal channel) shelving

1800 wide shelving
(floor space 1.5m²)
Box A = 5 per shelf x 7 levels x 2 bays = 70
Box B = 13 per shelf x 7 levels x 2 bays = 182

3600 mm

	No. of files (1 file = 10 mm)	No. of files per m²
Box A = ... = 56	1792	1195
Box B = ... = 168	2184	1456
Box A = ... = 63	2016	1344
Box B = ... = 189	2457	1638
Box A = ... = 70	2240	1493
Box B = ... = 182	2366	1577

Figure 12.5   Storage box A versus box B (see Figure 12.3): storage boxes on different sized shelving bays illustrating floor space requirements and linear capacity

Source: Reproduced with permission of Rack and File Commercial Pty Ltd, Melbourne

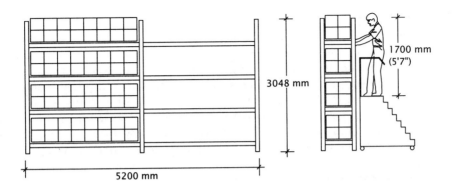

Shelf dimension:	2600 long x 838 wide – 4 5m^2
Boxes stored:	2 high x 2 deep x 8 across x 4 levels
Total boxes stored:	256
No. of files (1 file = 10 mm):	8192
No. of files per m^2	1860

Figure 12.6 Storage boxes on long-span racking

Source: Reproduced with permission of Rack and File Commercial Pty Ltd, Melbourne

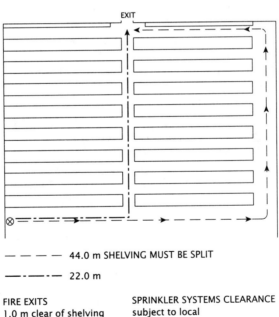

— — — — 44.0 m SHELVING MUST BE SPLIT

—·—·— 22.0 m

FIRE EXITS	SPRINKLER SYSTEMS CLEARANCE
1.0 m clear of shelving	subject to local
40.0 m maximum distance	building authorities
from furthest point	range: 300–1000 mm

Figure 12.7 Shelving layout showing fire protection features

Source: Reproduced with permission of Rack and File Commercial Pty Ltd, Melbourne

Mobile shelving

Mobile shelving is a good option for storing smaller quantities of inactive records. It is not uncommon for a situation to arise where the records manager has converted an active filing system of an organisation from mobile shelving equipment to open static shelving and, in the process, has freed up a quantity of mobile shelving which can then be used for secondary storage. A word of warning—if a mobile storage unit is to be used for storing records in boxes, it is essential to ensure that there is a good match between the linear space required by the boxes on each shelf and the length of each shelf. It is very wasteful of space if a shelf will fit three and a half boxes! This may seem obvious but there is plenty of evidence of organisations not taking this into account.

Ladders

These, of course, must meet safety standards. They should be easy to transport up and down the aisles. They should also have a platform at the top for placing a box and sorting through records.

Other retrieval equipment such as hydraulic lifts and fork-lifts are only needed for very large operations. Fork-lifts can be hired if needed for moving boxes on pallets.

Containers

The standard box or carton for storing records measures 400 mm long x 320 mm wide x 270 mm high. Boxes should be strong and easy to assemble, with hand-holes at each end and a space for labelling. They should be tested to make sure there is no tendency for the bottom to collapse when the box is full. There are a number of brands on the market in Australia; they are generally cheaper if purchased in bulk direct from the suppliers.

Other-sized containers may be needed to protect different types of records or for different applications; for example, tubes for plans and drawings, 'transfer' boxes for transferring the contents of lever arch files.

Finally, there are the storage boxes which clip together into stacks up to about twelve high. These boxes open from the front to enable records to be retrieved. Their big advantage is that they eliminate the need for shelving, although they do not necessarily work out cheaper than shelf storage; their disadvantage is that it is harder to separate out boxes ready for destruction.

Shelf arrangements

The chief requirement is to choose as simple a system as possible. The most common method used is to number the actual shelf spaces (e.g. bay 15, space 20 or row 4, space 98) and then to assign each box to the first available space. The space location becomes the box number. The advantage of this type of random shelving is that there should never be any need to move banks of boxes to fit in new ones; the disadvantage is that boxes cannot be located together in logical groups (for example, by client, subject or destruction due date).

A very successful variation is to place a barcode on each shelf space and on each box, and to record the match on a database whenever a box is shelved. This system means that boxes can be shelved and reshelved in a totally random manner. Speed and accuracy are the major advantages here; the first space found can be used for a box, and boxes cannot be misplaced on the shelves. The system requires a portable barcode reader plus the necessary hardware and software to download the data to the main database.

Packing records and transferring them to storage

The transfer of records to storage should take place on a periodic basis according to a schedule maintained by the records manager. The actual identification of records to be transferred should be based on the disposal schedule.

Clear instructions need to be developed for packing records into storage boxes. This is particularly true if business units pack their own records. Examples of instructions might be:

- Transfer any records in hard binders to soft covers.
- Pack records by destruction or review date; print destruction or review date on the label on the outside of the box. (This speeds up the process of culling records in storage.)
- Prepare list of box contents; place copy in box and distribute other copies according to requirements (Figure 12.8). (If box contents are listed manually, then it is also necessary to maintain an index to enable access to the records in storage by file title or file number.)
- Annotate each file with box number.
- Pack files spine up with an identifying number (e.g. a barcode number) clearly visible.
- Do not fill boxes to a weight over 16 kg, however, make sure there is no space wasted within this limit.

Recording of box and file storage locations and movements

A record of the movement of files and boxes in and out of storage needs to be maintained. This includes new boxes received and their assigned shelf locations, the contents of the boxes as listed at the time of packing and any later amendments, boxes permanently withdrawn or destroyed, and files and boxes borrowed out of storage. By far the most satisfactory method is to maintain a computerised system on which all of this information can be recorded and appropriate reports can be produced. If possible, the system should incorporate barcoding to control the location of the boxes on the shelves and the movement of files and boxes. There are a number of software packages available which are specifically designed for this type of application; alternatively, the organisation may have an automated records management system which includes the control of inactive records as one of its functions (See Chapter 9).

Secure destruction of records

Depending on the volume of records to be destroyed, an organisation may do its own destruction, contract an outside company to arrange it, or opt for a combination of the two.

RECORDS TRANSFER FORM

ORIGINATOR: TELEPHONE:

DEPARTMENT: DATE:

MEDIA TYPE: REVIEW FOR
DESTRUCTION ON:

BOX NO

(assigned by Records Centre)

BOX CONTENTS

Complete in duplicate: original - place in box
          duplicate - keep for your record

Record of movement

	ref.	title	date	responsible officer	out	to	in
1							
2							
3							
4							
5							
6							
7							
8							
9							
10							
11							
12							
13							
14							
15							
16							
17							
18							
19							
20							

RECORDS CENTRE USE

RECEIVED BY: DATE:

DESTRUCTION DATE:

Figure 12.8 Sample form for box transfer information and contents listing

The most common method of secure in-house destruction is shredding; most other methods are either not environmentally acceptable or are too expensive for in-house use. Shredders are ideal for instant destruction of confidential material and they provide secure enough destruction to meet the needs of most organisations. Shredders range from desktop to very large models.

Some of the major recycling companies and records storage companies offer secure destruction services. An increasing number of other companies are also in the business—their processes need to be checked out very carefully to ensure the destruction meets the organisation's security requirements. A particular company being considered should be prepared to organise an inspection of the facilities used. Pricing needs to be looked at carefully—the recycling companies may offer free collection of recyclable paper; the relative benefits of their services need to be weighed up against what is being offered by the companies that charge to arrange secure destruction.

It is generally accepted now that paper should be recycled; this has become a key criterion for selecting a company to arrange destruction of paper records. Paper is usually shredded then pulped. Non-paper records such as microfilm and computer media are more of a problem. Incineration is becoming less and less environmentally acceptable and in fact is not permitted in some areas. Alternatives for microfilm are shredding or granulation. (Granulation chops the item to confetti size.) Fortunately, computer media generally do not have to be destroyed because they are re-used; however, on occasions when destruction is necessary (as may be the case with optical and CD media), granulation is effective.

Standard destruction services offered include:

- Location of security bins or bags in the offices of an organisation—these can be delivered and collected for secure destruction of the contents either on request or on a scheduled basis.
- Collection of bulk records for secure destruction (for example, if an organisation is clearing out a warehouse).
- Destruction of records from commercial records storage.
- Certificates of destruction—these should be supplied as proof of destruction. They should give the date of destruction and list enough information to identify records destroyed by container (for example, box or bin numbers). The records manager needs to link these certificates with more detailed listings where the destruction has been of actual records as opposed to general waste.

Exercises

1   A records storage company offers the following rates to an organisation which has 10 000 boxes of paper records it wishes to transfer from warehouse accommodation to commercial storage:

Storage per box per week	$0.07
Lodgement fee per box	$1.00
Retrieval of file or box	$2.00
Refile of file or box	$2.00
Transport of file or box (one way)	$5.00
Permanent withdrawal of box, including secure destruction	$6.00
Supply of boxes (1–500)	$3.00
(501–1000)	$2.00

- These rates are to remain stable for two years from the time the contract is signed; from then on, increases will be tied to increases in the CPI.
- The organisation estimates it will add 600 new boxes to storage each year and have 400 destroyed. It currently retrieves approximately twenty files or boxes per week from its warehouse and predicts this amount will not change greatly.
- Calculate the total annual cost for each of the next five years for the organisation to store its records with this company.

2 Search through the office and records management journals for advertisements and other promotional literature on products and services available in Australia relevant to the storage of inactive records. Make a list of the products, their suppliers, any pricing information given, their functions and potential value to the records manager.

Case study 12.1

As records manager at the Australian Society for the Promotion of Paper Products you have convinced management of the need for a properly organised and staffed records centre.

Currently, there are about 3500 linear metres of records stored in various mobile storage units, storerooms and other nooks and crannies around the main office building. You estimate that about 200 linear metres will be added each year and 120 destroyed. You have discussed with the computer manager the desirability of storing the computer back-up tapes at the records centre and have decided that these should continue to be stored with a commercial records storage company where the appropriate environmental controls are ensured.

You will have one full-time staff member to run the facility. This person's role will be to receive new boxes for storage, maintain a computerised listing of box locations, remove boxes ready for destruction and arrange for their collection, retrieve files or boxes as requested and refile them on return, carry out periodic stock-takes and generally maintain the facility in good condition.

Your task

1 Calculate the amount of floor space that will be needed to store the organisation's records for the next five years plus provide adequate office and processing space.
2 Assume that you have located suitable premises; the floor area is square in shape with roller-door access from the street, a 4 m^2 office in one corner and three pillars down the centre of the area. Design a layout for the racking, processing area and other staff amenities. Indicate dimensions for all elements of the layout.

Questions

1 A records manager wishes to transfer the inactive records of an organisation from the basement of its office building to a commercial records storage company one hour's drive away. The users of the records resist the proposal on the grounds of decreased level of security and access. What arguments and information should the records manager present to convince the users of the appropriateness of the change?
2 Out of all the possible criteria for assessing commercial records storage services, which four are likely to be the most important for organisations?

3   How would the records manager set about comparing costs of storing inactive paper records as paper, microfilm, or digital images? What cost factors would have to be taken into account?

4   What are the likely trends in the storage of records? For example, will the records storage companies of today be still offering the same services in twenty years' time? Will they have a different focus in terms of media stored and type of services offered? Will many organisations still be operating their own offsite storage facilities?

5   An organisation is told that a pile of its documents have been found in the gutter near the premises of the company which handles the destruction of its records. What measures can the organisation take to ensure its records are destroyed securely in the future?

Additional information

There is not a great deal of literature specifically on inactive records storage facilities, whether these be commercially or in-house operated. All of the references listed below are good; Robek, Brown & Stephens (1996, Chapters 17–18) is particularly useful for technical guidance on planning a storage facility including methods for calculating space requirements. The Australian Standard AS 4390.6–1996 provides valuable information on storage requirements and facilities. Other standards covering specific aspects of storage are also relevant. Examples are:

- AS 1670–1995 Automatic fire detection and alarm systems—system design, installation and commissioning.
- AS 3636–1989/90 (duplicates BS 4783–1988, parts 1–5) Data storage and transfer media—storage, transportation and maintenance of magnetic media for use in data processing and information storage.
- AS 3674–1989 Storage of microfilm.
- AS 4084–1993, and supplement 1 Steel storage racking.
- BS 1153–1992 Processing and storage of silver gelatin-type microfilm.
- BS 5454–1989 Recommendations for storage and exhibition of archival documents.
- ANSI/NFPA 232–1995 Standard for the protection of records (National Fire Codes, vol. 6).
- ANSI/NFPA 232AM–1991 Manual for fire protection for archives and records centers (National Fire Codes, vol. 10).

One of the most valuable ways for the records manager to gather information is to approach those companies offering services and equipment related to records storage and seek their proposals on how best to meet the needs of the organisation. Both discussions with these companies plus a careful study of their proposals can lead to a much better understanding of the issues and options involved.

References

Hardcastle, S. 1989, 'Providing storage facilities', in *How to Manage Your Records: A Guide to Effective Practice*, P. Emmerson (ed.), ICSA Publishing, Cambridge, Chapter 5.

McDonald, P. W. 1993, 'Outsourcing evaluation: a case study—choosing a secondary storage provider', *Informaa Quarterly*, vol. 9, no. 2, pp. 16–21.

Penn, I. A., Pennix, G. B. & Coulson, J. 1994, *Records Management Handbook*, 2nd edn, Gower Publishing Co., Aldershot, Hants, Chapters 16 & 17.

Ricks, B. R. & Gow, K. F. 1988, *Information Resource Management: A Records Systems Approach*, 2nd edn, South-Western Publishing Co., Cincinnati, OH, Chapter 4, pp. 66–74.

Robek, M. F., Brown, G. F. & Stephens, D.O. 1996, *Information and Records Management*, 4th edn, Glencoe/McGraw-Hill, New York, Chapters 17–18.

Standards Australia. 1996, *Australian Standard AS 4390–1996, Records management, Part 6: Storage*, Homebush, NSW.

appendix A

Filing rules

Although manual card indexes are gradually disappearing from records management programs, there are still other areas where consistent application of filing rules is essential (e.g. alphabetical arrangements of files on shelves).

The following filing rules were published by the Records Management Association of Australia. In the original version there were twenty rules (rules 1–19 are represented here). They were included in H. E. Haxton (1988) *Records Management Primer*, revised edition, Records Management Association of Australia, Queensland Branch, section 1, pp. 16–18.

These rules apply to English and European names only; alternate rules apply for Asian and Middle Eastern names.

1 Names of individuals
Transpose names. Consider the last name first, first name second, and middle name or initial last.

2 Alphabetical order
Each word in a name is an indexing unit. Arrange names in alphabetical order by comparing similar units in each name. Consider second units only when the first unit in both names are the same.

3 Single last name or initial
Any last name, when used alone, precedes the same last name with a first name or initial. Any last name with only a first initial precedes a last name with a complete first name. This rule is sometimes stated 'Nothing comes before something'.

4 Surname prefixes

A last name prefix is not a separate unit but is considered part of the last name. These prefixes include D', Da, de, De, Di, Du, Fritz, La, Le, M', Mac, Mc, Van, Van der, Von, Von der, and others.

The correct rule for 'Mc' and 'Mac' is to index them exactly as they are spelt. However if you wish to adopt the same approach as the telephone book, (i.e. treat Mc & Mac as if spelt Mac), then be consistent. This is particularly useful when you are not sure if the name is McDonald or MacDonald.

5 Names of organisations

Names of organisations are indexed and filed exactly as they are written when they do not contain the complete name of an individual (see Rule 6).

6 Organisation names containing complete names of individuals

When the organisation name includes the complete name of an individual, the units are transposed for indexing in the same way as the names of individuals (see Rule 1).

7 Article 'the'

When the article 'the' occurs at the beginning of a name, it is placed at the end in parenthesis. When it occurs in the middle of a name, it is placed in parenthesis but not moved. In both cases it is not an indexing unit and is disregarded in filing.

8 Hyphenated names

Hyphenated organisation names are considered as separate indexing units. Hyphenated last names of individuals are considered as one indexing unit. This applies also to hyphenated names of individuals whose complete name forms part of a organisation name.

9 Abbreviations

Abbreviations are considered as though the name were written in full. Single letters (other than abbreviations) are considered as separate filing units.

10 Conjunctions, prepositions and organisation endings

Conjunctions and prepositions are disregarded. Organisation endings, such as Ltd, Inc, Co, Bros, etc. are treated as though they were written in full and considered as separate indexing units.

11 One or two words

Names that can be spelt either as one or two words, such as points of the compass, are indexed and filed as one word.

12 Compound geographic names

These are considered as separate units, except where the first part of the name is not an English word, such as the 'Sans' in 'Sans Souci'.

13 Possessives

When a word ends in apostrophe 's', the 's' is not considered in indexing and filing. Sometimes stated as 'Consider everything up to the apostrophe'.

14 Australian and foreign government departments

There is no specific rule, however the generally accepted principle is to consider the names first by governing authority, that is, federal, state, local; then the name of the department, bureau, division, commission or board. Treating the words 'Department of', 'Bureau of', etc. in parenthesis is also acceptable. Careful cross referencing should be made as names change when governing parties change.

15 Other political subdivisions

Names pertaining to other political subdivisions such as shires and county councils are filed under the name of the state, city or town, and then subdivided by the title of the department, bureau, commission or board as applicable.

16 Numbers

Any number in a name is considered as though it were written in words and is indexed and filed as one unit, for example, forty four.

17 Titles and degrees

Titles or degrees of individuals, whether preceding or following the name, are not considered. They are placed in parenthesis. Designations of seniority such as 'Jnr' and 'Snr' are placed in parenthesis and considered only when the names are otherwise identical.

Exception A. When the name of an individual consists of a title and one name only, such as Queen Elizabeth, it is not transposed and the title is considered as a filing unit.

Exception B. When a title or foreign article is the initial word of a firm or association name, it is considered for indexing and filing, for example, 'Queen's Arms Hotel'.

18 Addresses

When the same name appears with different addresses, the address is then considered for indexing in the following order—(a) suburb (b) street (c) state. (If two identical names are in the same street, the names are then arranged in ascending order of street number.) For example:

- Smith, Tom—Armidale
- Smith, Tom—Brighton, 10 Main Street
- Smith, Tom—Brighton, 20 Main Street

19 Banks and branch offices

Organisation names are considered first, then the suburb or town, then the street address is considered only if there are two branches in the same suburb, town or street.

Records Management Association of Australia (RMAA)

History

The RMAA was founded in 1969 and incorporated in 1975 as a registered company. It is a non-profit organisation with branches throughout Australia. Its members are managers, administrators and others employed or interested in records management in business and government.

Mission

To develop records management as a vital business activity.

Vision

By 1997 to be recognised as the professional body for, and the national authority on, records management.

Role and activities

The Association provides a forum for the exchange of ideas and knowledge to:

- Develop workable standards and practices for managing records
- Assist those individuals and organisations engaged in records management

It maintains a wide range of activities including courses, conferences and workshops. It provides various publications including a regular journal, *Informaa Quarterly*, to keep members abreast of the activities of the Association and within the profession at large. It also distributes materials from conferences and workshops.

It plays a watch-dog role over the development of records management courses. It has played a significant role in three major projects in recent years:

- The preparation of the Australian Standard AS 4390–1996, published by Standards Australia
- The development of the TAFE (Technical and Further Education) national core curriculum in records management
- The development of competency standards for records management and archives personnel in Australia.

Membership

The Association has approximately 2000 members. There are three types of membership:

- **Ordinary**—for records management students and others working or interested in the industry. Ordinary members may not vote or sit on Branch Council.
- **Professional**—for full-time professionals in the field. Professional members may seek the status of Associate, progressing to Member or Fellow, depending on their contribution to the profession.
- **Corporate**—organisations may join as corporate members and send three nominees to participate in Association activities.

Records management and archives courses in Australia

This list of courses should not be taken as definitive; it represents the best available information as at late 1996. It was compiled by the Federal Education Committee of the Records Management Association of Australia and is reproduced in full (with a few modifications) from the *Informaa Quarterly*, vol. 12, no. 4, 1996, pp. 32–34.

Courses in records management as offered across Australia

Organisation	Course information	Location
ACT		
University of Canberra	**BA in Information Management** 3 years f/t, can be undertaken p/t Faculty of Communication (06) 201 5064	Belconnen
Canberra Institute of Technology	**Dip. in Business (Records Mngt)** 2 years f/t or equivalent p/t	Canberra
	Certificate IV in Business (Records Mngt) 1 year f/t or equivalent p/t Rita O'Brien (06) 207 3263	
New South Wales		
TAFE:		
Northern Sydney Institute	**Diploma of Information Technology (Records & Information Management)**	Nth. Sydney Campus
Western Sydney Institute	Same as above	Mount Druitt
Western Sydney Institute	**Certificate in Information Technology (Records Administration)**	Mount Druitt
	Certificate 111 in Information Technology	Most metro. locations
Western Sydney Institute	**Statement of Attainment in Records Management Skills**	Mount Druitt Wagga Wagga
Hunter Institute of Technology	(Students can do a records elective in the **Certificate 111 in IT**, and may then proceed into the Certificate IV and progress into the Diploma)	Newcastle

It should be noted that for semester 1, 1997, application for the Diploma is through UAC (University Admission Centre). Applications closed on 27 September, 1996, but late applications may be submitted. Please refer also to the 1997 TAFE NSW Handbook, (pp. 230–231) for individual course descriptions.

Charles Sturt Uni Riverina	**BA (Lib. & Info Studies)** Distance Ed. 3 years f/t , 6 p/t Roy Sanders (069) 332 417	Wagga Wagga
University of NSW	**Grad Dip. Info. Mgt.–Archives/Records** 1 year f/t, 2 p/t	Sydney
University of NSW	**Master of Info.–Archives/Records** 4 years p/t, 3 f/t Ann Pederson/Ray Locke (02) 9385 3438	Sydney
University of Technology	**Bach. Applied Science** 3 years f/t, 6 p/t (02) 9330 1222	Sydney

Queensland

Southbank Institute of TAFE	**Advanced Certificate in Records Management** 2 years p/t (07) 324 46025	Kangaroo Point Campus

Tasmania

Hobart TAFE	**Certificate in Records Management** Charmaine Baker (002) 337 342	Hobart

South Australia

Adelaide Institute of TAFE	**Certificate in RM**	Light Square
SA Institutes of TAFE	**Advance Cert. in Office Procedure** Assoc. Dip. of Business (Office Admin.) George Smith (08) 8269 0100	Elizabeth Gillies Plains Panorama
Uni of South Australia	**Bachelor of Arts in Library & Info. Mgt** **Grad Dip Info Studies (Library & Info. Mgt.)** **Grad Dip Corporate Info & RM** Prof. Michael Brittain (08) 8302 4410 or 8302 2376	Magill Magill Magill

Victoria

Monash University	**B. Information Management** 3 years f/t David Foott (03) 9905 2955	Clayton
	Grad Dip Info Mgt (Recordkeeping) 1 year f/t or 2–3 years p/t; on campus/external Frank Upward (03) 9905 2949	Clayton
	M Info Mgt (Recordkeeping) 2 years f/t or 4 years p/t; on campus/external Frank Upward (03) 9905 2949	Clayton
RMIT	**Grad Dip Info Mgt (Archives & Records)** 1 year f/t or 2 years p/t Bruce Smith (03) 9660 5818	Melbourne
	Grad Dip Info Mgt (Info Services) 1 unit in RM Bruce Smith (03) 9660 5818	Melbourne
	B. Business in Info & Library Management 1 unit in RM Bruce Smith (03) 9660 5818	Melbourne
	M. Bus (Info Technology) 1–3 units Bruce Smith (03) 9660 5818	Melbourne
Swinburne Uni of Technology	**Certificate in Records Certificate 2** 1 year f/t or 2–3 years p/t Joan Brain (03) 9214 6776	Prahran

	Certificate in Records Management 4	Prahran
	1 year f/t or 2–3 years p/t	
	Joan Brain (03) 9214 6776	

Victoria Uni of Technology	**B. Business Management**	St Albans
	1 unit in RM	
	Janet Souter (03) 9365 2394	
	Grad. Dip. In Administrative Mgt.	St Albans
	1 unit in Information Management	
	Penny Bassett (03) 9365 2285	

Western Australia

Curtin Uni of Technology	**Bachelor of Applied Science (Records Management)**	Perth
	3 years f/t or p/t equivalent;	
	available on-campus or external mode	
	HECS	
	Honours	Perth
	1 year f/t or p/t equivalent;	
	available on-campus or external mode	
	HECS	
	Graduate Diploma in Records Management and Archives	Perth
	1 year f/t or p/t equivalent;	
	available on-campus or external mode	
	HECS and full fee option	
	Masters of Applied Science (Information Management)	Perth
	2 years f/t or p/t equivalent;	
	available on-campus or external mode	
	HECS and full fee option	
	Doctor of Philosophy	Perth
	3 years f/t or p/t equivalent	
	available on-campus or external mode	
	HECS and full fee option	

Edith Cowan Uni	**Bachelor of Science (Communication and Information Technology)**	Claremont
	3 years f/t or p/t equivalent	
	(includes a minor in records management: 6 units)	
	Available on-campus mode	
	HECS	
	University Certificate in Public Sector Records Management	Claremont
	1 year p/t (4 units)	
	available external mode	
	Full fee paying option	
	Graduate Diploma of Science (Archives and Records)	Claremont
	1 year f/t or p/t equivalent (8 units),	
	available external mode	
	Full fee paying option	
	Master of Science (Information Science)	Claremont
	(Research or Coursework mode)	
	2 years f/t or p/t equivalent;	
	available on-campus or external mode	
	HECS	

| TAFE | Full details not yet available, but will conform to National ACTRAC Modules as resources permit. A structured framework showing course progress and prerequisites is being developed. The **Diploma of Records Management** will be available full-time from 1997. | |

Useful Internet sites and listservs for records management students

Internet sites

This list includes a selection of the more useful sites at the time of writing. New sites are constantly being added to the Internet.

Archives of Australia web site

http://www.aa.gov.au/

Includes links to the Australian Archives home page as well as other Australian archival institutions (state archives, etc.) and professional associations.

Australian Archives home page

http://www.aa.gov.au/AA_WWW/AA_Home_Page.html

Includes information about Australian Archives including its services, publications and events. Includes a link to the *Archives Act 1983* and to 'Accessing our holdings'.

Australian Archives 'Accessing our holdings'

http://www.aa.gov.au/AA_WWW/AA_Access/AA_Access.html

Links to the Australian Archives database.

Archives Authority of New South Wales

http://www.records.nsw.gov.au

Valuable for its inclusion of publications and newsletters, recordkeeping policies and standards, holdings and finding aids, general records disposal schedules, and destruction guides.

Has links to Australian sites, including other state archival authorities, and overseas sites, including National Archives and Records Administration (NARA) in the US.

Australian Council of Archives

http://www.aa.gov.au/AA_WWW/ProAssn/ACA/ACA.HTM

Includes information on the objectives, programs, membership of the ACA. Also a copy of the document 'Corporate Memory in the Electronic Age: Statement of a Common Position on Electronic Recordkeeping'.

Public Record Office Victoria

http://www.vicnet.net.au/~provic/Welcome.html

Includes information on its services, holdings and finding aids, events, and publications; also full copies of newsletters.

NSW State Rail Authority

http://www.ozemail.com.au/~bc514684/

A demonstration site of the Authority's intranet. Includes manuals, policies and procedures, Freedom of Information documentation, business groups within the Authority and links to their home pages, organisational structure. A useful model.

Records Management Association of Australia

http://www.taunet.net.au/rmaa/

Includes information on the Association—its aims, contacts, services and membership.

Australian Society of Archivists

http://www.aa.gov.au/AA_WWW/ProAssn/ASA/

Under construction at the time of writing. Includes information on the Society, membership, publications and the Society's listserv; also some position papers.

Monash University Records and Archives Service

http://www.monash.edu.au/magpie/

Includes information on access, holdings and location.

National Archives and Records Administration (US)

http://www.nara.gov/

Includes guide to NARA's organisation, services, holdings and events.

NARA Office of Records Administration

http://www.nara.gov/nara/rm/nihome1.html

Provides guidance and assistance to US federal agencies on managing records. Includes sections on Guidance (records schedules, records management services, e-mail requirements, Federal requirements on records management); Publications; Training.

ARMA International (Association of Records Managers and Administrators)

http://www.arma.org/hq/
Information about the group and the benefits of membership. Includes links to other sites.

University of Pittsburgh School of Information Sciences

http://www.lis.pitt.edu/~nhprc/
Devoted to the Functional Requirements for Evidence in Recordkeeping Project. Covers papers on the four major areas—literary warrant, functional requirements, production rules, metadata specifications. Includes a Bibliography on Electronic Records.

Further information on useful sites may be found in Davidson, J. & McRostie, D. 1996, 'Webbed feet: navigating the Web', *Archives and Manuscripts*, vol. 24, no. 2, pp. 330–51.

Listservs

Listservs are a useful way of keeping up with developments in the records management community. While most of the listservs given below have an archival orientation, they also include information of interest to records managers.

Listservs operate rather like mailing lists—a subscriber's name is added to the group; the subscriber then receives a copy of all messages sent to the group, and can also send messages. The process of subscribing involves sending a message to the address in the following format—leave subject line blank, enter into body of message 'subscribe nameofgroup yourfirst namelast name'.

RECMGMT

listserv@SUVM.SYR.EDU
Covers a whole range of records management issues, including electronic records and software packages. American emphasis.

AUS-ARCHIVISTS

majordomo@asap.unimelb.edu.au
A listserv started by the Australian Society of Archivists for discussion of archival issues in Australia.

ERECS-L

LISTSERV@UACSC2.ALBANY.EDU
Specialises in issues concerned with electronic records.

ARCHIVES
LISTSERV@MiamiU.MUOhio.Edu
A heavily used listserv covering a wide range of topics.

Forms management

Forms dominate our lives. They account for a significant proportion of corporate records.

In many organisations forms proliferate uncontrolled. If a need arises to collect information, either on a one-off or an ongoing basis, the likely result will be a new form. It is also possible that the form will be designed, produced and distributed by the staff concerned, without any centralised coordination or controls over standards. Unfortunately there are large numbers of forms which simply add to the burden of paperwork in our society without achieving any worthwhile benefits.

Forms, if well designed and used appropriately, are powerful tools for the collection, processing and dissemination of information. They enhance the workflow within an organisation, they speed up information handling processes, they reduce costs. However for an organisation to ensure it uses forms in the most beneficial way for its operations, it needs to establish a centrally coordinated forms management program. A forms management program establishes controls over all of the processes of requesting, designing, producing, storing, distributing, reviewing and disposing of forms.

Goals of a forms management program

The goals of a forms management program are:

- To ensure only those forms that are needed are developed.
- To review, update and consolidate existing forms and to eliminate any that are not necessary
- To design forms that are effective in gathering and processing information
- To ensure that forms are designed appropriately for the target group (e.g. that the captions on the forms and the instructions for use are clear and in an appropriate language)
- To establish uniform standards for design and physical specifications
- To ensure forms are reproduced and disseminated in the most economical way possible without compromising quality
- To ensure stocks of paper forms are maintained where needed.

Responsibility for forms management

Ideally the forms management program should sit within the organisation's records management program. The records manager, or other staff member designated as forms manager, should coordinate the forms management program, drawing on forms analysis and design expertise as appropriate. Few organisations in Australia have full-time forms designers. More commonly, a staff member will have forms design responsibilities along with other system or graphic design functions. His or her role will be to assist staff to develop effective forms and to design the final format.

Program components

Because forms may be generated from so many different points within an organisation, it is essential to obtain maximum ongoing staff cooperation and participation in the program. Strategies to achieve this include making sure that procedures are well documented and available to all staff, appointing a liaison person in each business unit, and providing training in forms design and use.

A forms management program includes the following components:

- An inventory of all forms currently used by the organisation
- A standard numbering system
- A descriptive catalogue for staff use, including a copy of the latest version of each form
- A process to review and approve forms
- Forms design guidelines
- Procedures for the production of forms
- Storage and distribution procedures.

An inventory of all forms currently used by the organisation

Information is documented on:

- The purpose and frequency of each form
- Any existing form control numbers
- The format of each form and the method of completion (such as pen on paper or via a keyboard)
- The method of processing the data collected (such as by manual compilation of results, or by keying data into a computer system for processing, or by transferring data by a mark sensing device or scanner into a computer system for processing)
- Information on production and stocking
- Titles of related forms.

A standard numbering system

The numbering system should be as simple as possible. A commonly used system consists of originating business unit code followed by number of the form for the business unit followed by month and year of latest revision (for example, ADM/060/0297); an even simpler solution is to use a straight running number plus month and year of revision—this avoids any problems caused by changes in business unit functions. The allocation of form numbers should be controlled centrally.

A descriptive catalogue for staff use

The catalogue provides information on the purpose, use, distribution and availability of each form. The descriptive information is accompanied by a copy of the latest version of the forms.

A process to review and approve forms

This applies to existing and proposed forms.

Staff at a number of levels need to participate in the review process—the managers of the business units which originate, receive and also process the forms, the records manager or other staff responsible for coordinating the forms management program, and the forms design specialist.

The review process involves assessing each form in terms of a number of factors:

- How well it will enable the required information to be gathered
- Whether it is really necessary or whether the information could be gathered via an amended existing form
- Whether all proposed copies are necessary
- Whether the instructions are clear
- How well the layout of the form meets the data entry and retrieval requirements (e.g. if the information is to be keyed into a computer system, it should appear on the form in an order and style that will enable the data entry operator to achieve maximum speed)
- Whether the proposed method of production is the most economical
- In the situation where a form is distributed already completed (e.g. a bank statement), whether the information is presented clearly and all codes and symbols are explained.

The analysis and review of existing forms is likely to result in changes, deletions and consolidations.

Forms design guidelines

The forms design guidelines should help the forms designer to properly analyse what information needs to be collected before deciding on the content and layout of the form. They should provide guidance on how to design forms which will keep the error rate, the printing and paper or system costs, and the amount of labour involved in completing the form, to a minimum. They should cover how to break down the information required into categories, how to decide on the order of the information, what style and language to use, and how to present the instructions. Depending on the facilities available in the organisation, they may also cover the use of computer graphics or forms design software, or they may lay down requirements for drafting forms in a format ready for a graphic or forms designer to work with.

Procedures for the production and stocking of forms

Paper forms

Various options for the production of forms need to be considered and decisions made on issues related to physical format, printing and collating. A reasonable strategy is to produce the majority of forms inhouse using graphics or forms design software, a laser printer and the organisation's reproduction equipment, but to send forms out to a professional forms designer if they are to be completed by clients or other members of the public. It may also be decided to use an outside printer if multipart forms are required.

Minimum and maximum stock levels should be established plus a procedure for purging obsolete forms. An inventory of supplies should be maintained to ensure stocks are replaced when the supply reaches the minimum level.

If forms are sent outside for printing, it is particularly important to have an effective monitoring system to ensure stocks do not run out. With the trend to produce forms inhouse on a laser printer, it is easier to replenish stocks when needed and also to avoid the situation where copies are wasted because a particular form is no longer needed or has been amended.

Electronic forms

Electronic forms can be very easily and quickly amended and distributed. Some workflow systems and forms design systems include forms routing and tracking. This means that the distribution of forms can be automated and the location of forms can be tracked at any time. Electronic forms can be integrated with business systems which require information for processing, for example, online timesheets can be integrated with a client billing system.

glossary

This glossary provides definitions of selected terms from the text.[1] Explanations of other terms not included here may be located in the text via the index.

Accountability: AS 4390.1–1996: The principle that individuals, organisations and the community are required to account to others for their actions. Organisations and their employees must be able to account to appropriate regulatory authorities, to shareholders or members, and to the public to meet statutory obligations, audit requirements, relevant standards and codes of practice, and community expectations.

Accurate: AS 4390.3–1996: Records must accurately reflect the transactions that they document.

Action officers: The personnel in the organisation who take action on, or deal with the correspondence received by an organisation. Correspondence is directed to them for action. The term is most commonly used in the government environment.

Active records: Those records which are retrieved and consulted frequently, or which contain information of immediate relevance to the current activities of the organisation.

Ad hoc disposal authorisation: Authorisation which is given on an 'as needed' basis by a government archival agency for the destruction or transfer of public records which are not covered by a disposal schedule.

Adequate: AS 4390.3–1996: Records should be adequate for the purposes for which they are kept. Thus, a major initiative will be extensively documented, while a routine administrative action can be documented with an identifiable minimum of information. There should be adequate evidence of the conduct of business activity to be able to account for that conduct.

Administrative: Relating to the management and direction of the organisation, such as policy, finance and budget, and human resources.

Agency specific disposal schedule/authority: A disposal schedule (*see* Disposal schedule) covering the disposal of records which are unique to a particular public office (*see* Public office). *See also* General disposal schedule/authority (GDA).

Appraisal: AS 4390.1–1996: The process of evaluating business activities to determine which records need to be captured and how long the records need to be kept, to meet business needs, the requirements of organisational accountability and community expectations.

Archive: AS 4390.1–1996: The whole body of records of continuing value of an organisation or individual. Sometimes called 'corporate memory'. (AS 4390.1–1996). The term is also used to mean a place where inactive records of continuing value are kept and preserved for legal, historical or research purposes. Archives may be set up by government or private organisations.

Archives: AS 4390.1–1996: Those records that are appraised as having continuing value.

Array: *see* Mutually exclusive terms in array.

ASCII: American Standard Code for Information Interchange. A software-independent and widely used set of binary codes or bytes, each code representing a letter or symbol, which facilitates inter-computer communications. Documents stored on computer in ASCII are searchable in free text mode.

Audit: The official examination and verification of accounts and records, especially of financial accounts, under statutory requirements. *See also* File census or file audit.

Audit (File): *see* File census or file audit.

Audit trail: The deliberate and systematic generation of recorded evidence of business activities for present and future accountability.

Authentic: AS 4390.3–1993: It must be possible to prove that records are what they purport to be and that their purported creators have indeed created them.

Authority list: *see* Controlled vocabulary, *and* Thesaurus.

Automatic abstracting: A system by which an abstract of a document is produced automatically, without human effort, based on the document's keywords and phrases.

Automatic indexing: Indexing without any human input, whereby the computer selects terms to represent the document using statistical algorithms and powerful software.

Backup copies: Additional copies made of data resulting from transactions or work undertaken on computers. These copies may then be stored in locations alternative to the usual location to provide protection in case of loss of the original, computer system damage, or unforeseen damage to facilities.

Barcoding: In the records management context, barcoding usually refers to that part of an automated document/file tracking system which replaces the manual keying of user/location codes or names and file/document identification numbers. User codes and file numbers are represented by labels (barcodes or bar codes) containing a series of thick and thin vertical lines or bars which represent numeric or alphanumeric data. The labels are scanned using a light pen, wand or scanner attached to a barcode reader. By passing the scanner over both barcodes, the document or file is recorded against the particular user or location. This information is then downloaded into the records management system and the file movement records are updated.

Benefits: *see* Tangible benefits *and* Intangible benefits.

Bit-mapped images: Images stored in digital form as a pattern of pixels on a grid. Documents stored in this form are not in ASCII (*see* ASCII), and are therefore not searchable in free text mode.

Boolean searching: The facility to link separate concepts of a query using 'and', 'or' and 'not' operators when searching a computerised database.

Bring-up system: *see* Resubmit system.

Broad indexing: *see* Specific versus broad indexing.

Browser: A program which allows the user to navigate and search through the information (text and often pictures and sound) provided on particular servers on the Internet.

Business activity: AS 4390.1–1996: Umbrella term covering all the functions, processes, activities and transactions of an organisation and its employees. Includes public administration as well as commercial business.

Business classification: *see* Classification.

Call-up system: *see* Resubmit system.

CALS: (formerly standing for Computer-Assisted Logistics Support, but currently standing for Continuous Acquisition and Life-cycle Support). Consists of a range of internationally accepted standards (for imaging, document and report structure, and technical illustration) which have been developed to facilitate the exchange of digital files independently of current and future technology, i.e. across mixed hardware environments and in applications which are no longer in use.

Capture: AS 4390.1–1996: A deliberate action which results in the registration of a record into a recordkeeping system. For certain business activities, this action may be designed into electronic systems so that the capture of records is concurrent with the creation of records.

CAR: *see* Computer assisted retrieval (CAR).

Case files: Files in which a specific name is the subject of a file (usually the names of people, organisations, places, actions, events, etc.). The names are often represented as numbers. Examples are client records, personnel records, insurance records, contracts and lawsuit files. *See also* Self indexing.

CD-ROM: (Compact disc read only memory). A 4.75 in. optical digital disk commonly used for storing and distributing sound, image and ASCII textual databases and software. CD-ROMs are manufactured in quantity from a master copy, or produced singly on a peripheral device called a CD recorder. Once a disk is completed, users can neither write to the disk nor remove information. *See also* Digital imaging systems.

CD-R (CD-Recordable): A CD-ROM (*see* CD-ROM) to which new information can be added until it is full, but information on it cannot be edited.

CD-RW (CD-ReWritable): A CD-ROM (*see* CD-ROM) to be released soon on the market which can be re-recorded many times.

Census (File): *see* File census or file audit.

Centralised versus decentralised: The terms 'centralised' and 'decentralised' are often used in relation to the physical location and the control (tracking and indexing) of records. Records may be located in a central filing area (centralised), or with/near the staff who use them most (decentralised). Similarly, control may be exercised by the records management unit of the organisation, or by the staff in the individual departments. Often location is decentralised, while control is centralised.

Charge-out system: *see* Tracking system.

Classification: AS 4390.1–1996: The process of devising and applying schemes based on the business activities which generate records, whereby they are categorised in systematic and consistent ways to facilitate their capture, retrieval, maintenance and disposal. Classification includes determining document or file naming conventions, user permissions and security restrictions on records. Comment: This textbook distinguishes between business classification which focuses on the business activities which generate records of evidential value and knowledge-base classification which focuses on documents which are maintained for their intellectual content. In broad terms classification is defined as the process by which the records of an organisation are categorised or grouped into retrieval units, whether by function, subject, or other criteria.

Classified order: An arrangement of records into classes or groupings according to some logical or systematic order. The classified arrangement is a hierarchy of groups and sub-groups, e.g. as represented by the metaphor of a branching tree. Commonly in computerised systems the appearance of a menu of alternative categories signifies reliance on a classified order from general to specific. In hardcopy systems numeric, alphabetic, or alpha-numeric codes are used to express the logic of the classified order for filing purposes.

Client: Used in the sense of client/server computing. A client is a program or computer on a network which accesses files from a server program or computer on the network. *See also* Server.

COLD (Computer Output to Laser Disk): A storage and retrieval technology by which laser disk images are produced directly from a computer. It is commonly used to process and index computer-generated reports.

COM: *see* Computer output on microfilm (COM).

Communication: *see* Information.

Complete: AS 4390.3–1996: A record must contain not only the content, but also the structural and contextual information necessary to document a transaction.

Compliant: AS 4390.3–1996: Records must comply with the recordkeeping requirements arising from the regulatory and accountability environment in which the organisation operates.

Comprehensive: AS 4390.3–1996: Records must document the complete range of the organisation's business.

Compound document: A document which includes information in more than one format, for example, text, graphics and image.

Computer assisted retrieval (CAR): Refers to the automated retrieval of microfilm images using a system which combines an external index to the images with a method for locating the images on a film.

Computer output on microfilm (COM): Microfilm produced directly from a computer by the use of a recorder (called a COM recorder). The transfer of data to microfilm is usually by tape or disk, but systems for online transfer are available.

Contingency planning: The development of a recovery plan that can be implemented by an organisation in the event of a disaster which prevents the organisation from functioning in total or in part. It is concerned with the protection of computer systems, vital records, facilities, equipment, supplies and services.

Controlled vocabulary: An alphabetical list containing terms or headings which are authorised or controlled so that only one heading or form of heading is allowed to represent a particular concept or name. The controlled vocabulary is sometimes supplemented with a set of rules for formulating headings. It contrasts with natural language. A controlled vocabulary is also referred to as a thesaurus.

Corporate: Refers to both public and private sector organisations. The accountabilities of a corporate body are spelled out by law. The term 'corporate' often simply means 'of an organisation' as in the phrase, 'a corporate plan'.

Correspondence management: Correspondence management is concerned with establishing control over the written communications of an organisation. It applies to both communications within the organisation and with outside persons and organisations.

Correspondence records: Recorded communications to and from personnel in the organisation, for example, letters, memoranda and reports, often on policy and administrative matters.

Cost–benefit analysis/study: A study in which the costs of alternative new systems and their likely benefits are compared with those of the current system.

Cost effectiveness: A measure of goal attainment or quality in relation to costs.

Cost efficiency: A measure of the amount of resources expended in relation to the outcomes or quality achieved. The lower the expenditure to achieve a given output, the greater the efficiency.

Costs: *see* Development costs *and* Operational costs.

Current records: *see* Active records.

Decentralised: *see* Centralised versus decentralised.

Descriptors: Terms assigned by an indexer to represent the subject(s) of a document/file. The term is used slightly differently in different indexing approaches.

Development costs: Costs associated with the setting up of a new system, such as consultants' fees and equipment.

Diary system: *see* Resubmit system.

Digital imaging systems: Computer systems which are designed to capture documents or pictures not already in digital form, to digitally store the images, and to retrieve, distribute, and display or print the images on demand. They are often called optical disk systems because optical disks are generally used to store scanned images. *See also* Optical disk.

Digital signatures: A signature in an imaging system which can be read by special software. The software can match key characteristics of a signature on different documents.

Disaster classification: In the records management context, this refers to the process of deciding the level of protection that needs to be given to the vital records (*see* Vital records) of an organisation.

Disposal: AS 4390.1–1996: A range of processes associated with implementing appraisal decisions. These include the retention, deletion or destruction of records in or from recordkeeping systems. They may also include the migration or transmission of records between recordkeeping systems, and the transfer of custody or ownership of records.

Disposal authority: AS 4390.1–1996: A formal instrument that defines the retention periods and consequent disposal actions authorised for classes of records which are described in it.

Disposal classes: AS 4390.1–1996: Classes of records performing or recording similar activities and therefore having the same retention period and disposal action.

Disposal schedule: A list of the record series of an organisation with directions for how the records are to be disposed of (*see* Disposal) after their creation and initial use. The schedule is a written statement of how long each series (or group of series) is to be retained (e.g. a period of years or indefinitely), and may also include instructions on when records are to be transferred to secondary storage or archives, or destroyed.

Document scanning: Scanners provide a shortcut method of entering information into a computer without having to type it. Pages or film are run through a paper or micrographic scanner and the information is digitised.

Document Type Definition: *see* DTD.

Documents: AS 4390.1–1996: Structured units of recorded information, published or unpublished, in hard copy or electronic form, and managed as discrete units in information systems. Comment: A document becomes a 'record' when it provides evidence of a business transaction. The information technology community tends to use the term 'document' in the sense of electronic document.

DTD (Document Type Definition): Under SGML (*see* SGML) the set of rules which each document type must have to govern the structure and content of the document. HTML is the DTD for all World Wide Web documents.

EDI (Electronic Data Interchange): The process by which business documentation is transmitted, read and interpreted electronically through computer links. It is most commonly used for trading.

Electronic Mail: *see* E-mail (Electronic mail).

Electronic records: Although the term electronic records can refer to analogue materials (e.g. commercial videotapes), in this text it refers generally to records held in digital form on magnetic or optical computer storage media.

E-mail (Electronic mail): Software which enables a user to send messages from a computer via communication networks to selected other computers, locally or internationally. Each e-mail user has a unique system address.

Environmental controls: These are measures taken to ensure against flooding, excessive humidity levels, pests such as silverfish and mice, and dust, etc.

Equipment: *see* Filing equipment.

Erasable magneto-optical disk: Unlike conventional optical disks, the erasable magneto-optical disk is a disk on which data can be stored, moved, changed, and erased. *See also* Optical disk.

Evidence: AS 4390.1–1996: Information that tends to prove a fact. Not limited to the legal sense of the term. Evidential value. Proof or evidence of the origins of an organisation/person and of how business is/was conducted.

Extranet: An extension to an organisation's intranet (*see* Intranet) designed to make information available to the organisation's clients.

Facet: A group of terms which share a common characteristic.

Facet analysis: A method for constructing a thesaurus and classification scheme which depends on grouping terms into facets. *See also* Facet.

Facsimile machine: A machines which transmits facsimile copies (faxes) of printed out or written data via telephone lines.

Fax: *see* Facsimile machine.

Fax card: A card installed in a user's PC which enables the user to send and receive faxes directly from/to her/his computer.

Feasibility study: *see* Records management needs analysis.

File: A group of related documents, usually located within a file cover and held together by a file fastener. A file may have a number of separate parts, stored within the same file cover, or in separate covers. Also refers to a set of data held on computer.

File audit: *see* File census or file audit.

File census or file audit: A stocktake of all the organisational files stored in a designated area. A file census or audit is usually carried out to gather data to update the file tracking system.

File integrity: *see* Integrity of records.

File movement system: *see* Tracking system.

File server: *see* Server.

File tracking system: *see* Tracking system.

FTP (File Transfer Protocol): A client-server protocol for sending or receiving files (consisting for example, of documents, software, graphics) across the Internet.

Filing equipment: Refers to the hardware (such as shelving units and cupboards) in which records are housed. *See also* Filing supplies.

Filing sequence: The physical arrangement or ordering of files. It is always necessary to give each file some kind of unique identification number or address to enable it to be stored for retrieval.

Filing software: *see* Filing supplies.

Filing supplies: Refers to the software (such as file covers, binders, guides, colour labels, file clips and index cards) used to contain, protect and label records. *See also* Filing equipment.

Filing system: In this text a filing system is an information storage and retrieval system. The term incorporates all aspects of the system, namely its physical location, classification and indexing methods used, filing sequence, filing procedures, supplies and equipment, file tracking, and the technologies used in the system's implementation.

Fiscal: Relating to financial matters in general.

Flowchart: A diagram showing the stages of an operational process.

Forms management: Forms management is concerned with establishing controls over all the processes of requesting, designing, producing, storing, distributing, reviewing and disposing of forms.

Free text searching: Searching by every word (other than stop words) in the full text of a document, a record description, a field, or a combination of fields within a record description. Sometimes used in the literature to refer to natural language.

Full text searching: A system in which all the words in the whole document (other than a stoplist) are searchable.

Function: AS 4390.1–1996: The largest unit of business activity in an organisation or jurisdiction.

Fuzzy logic: In text retrieval refers to a search engine making the search specifications more vague than that input by the searcher. For example in some relevance ranked searching approaches, for an AND search, the computer will undertake both an OR search as well as an AND search, but the AND search result will receive a higher ranking.

GDA (General Disposal Authority): *see* General disposal schedule/authority (GDA).

General disposal schedule/authority (GDA): A disposal schedule (*see* Disposal schedule) covering the disposal of records common to a number of public offices (*see* Public office), for example, central government accounting, building and services, stores and transport, and school records, and also common categories of municipal records. *See also* Agency specific disposal schedule/authority.

Gopher: A menu-driven information retrieval system used for searching the Internet across servers (*see* File server) by making choices from a hierarchical system of menus.

Groupware: A software system on a network which is based on the concept of people working together, sharing information and ideas. Koulopoulos & Frappaolo (1995, p. 287) define the term as 'Software that automates and manages a single task among multiple workers'.

GUI: Graphical user interface.

Hand Character Recognition: *see* HCR.

Hardcopy: Refers to documents and records in paper format and in any other formats which are not electronic, for example, microfilm, videocassettes and sound cassettes in analogue form.

Hardware: The physical components (i.e. processors, disks, terminals, printers, etc.) of a computer system. Sometimes also used to refer to the shelving units and cupboards, etc. in which records are housed.

HCR (Hand Character Recognition): A form of OCR (*see* OCR) now being used to read handprinted (as opposed to handwritten) alphabetic and numeric characters which have been presented in a structured or constrained form.

HTML (Hypertext Markup Language): A standard language used for marking up World Wide Web (*see* World Wide Web) pages with format styles and links within the same and different documents.

Hypermedia: The same as Hypertext (*see* Hypertext) but applying specifically to images and sound.

Hypertext: In the context of this book, hypertext is a system which enables a user on the Internet to move from one point in a document to another in the same document or a different document by clicking with a mouse button on a highlighted name or topic.

Hypertext Markup Language: *see* HTML

ICR (Intelligent Character Recognition): A further development from OCR (*see* OCR) which offers a more advanced technique for tackling character recognition problems.

Imaging systems: *see* Digital imaging systems. Apart from digital imaging, the term can also refer to photographic imaging systems e.g. photocopiers, or systems for the photographic reproduction of documents in microform.

Inactive records: Those records which are seldom accessed, but which must be retained for occasional reference, or for legal or archival reasons. *See also* Active records *and* Semi-active records.

Indexing: AS 4390.1–1996: The process of establishing and applying terms or codes to records, to be used to retrieve them and to search for and analyse information in records across classifications. Comment: Index terms may be derived from a record by the computer or assigned by a human indexer to enhance retrievability. Human indexing may consist of labelling of concepts using pre-established categories (e.g. from a thesaurus, classification scheme or metadata repository) or it may augment record content with additional semantic elements (e.g. adding the spelled out form of an acronym) so that search engines have an optimal chance of retrieving a required document in whatever category or database it is situated. *See also* Classification *and* Metadata.

Information: The content of communication. (Communication is defined as the processes by which meaning is conveyed among people or between people and information storage systems.)

Information management: A professional field concerned with optimising the uses of information, using both social and technical approaches.

Information systems: AS 4390.1–1996: Organised collections of hardware, software, supplies, policies, procedures and people, which store, process and provide access to information.

Intangible benefits: Benefits which are not easily quantifiable in dollar terms.

Integrated management of records: The management of records via one system rather than many.

Integrity of records: The completeness and authenticity of records. File integrity is maintained if the file is complete, and its documents are in their correct order.

Intelligent Character Recognition: *see* ICR (Intelligent Character Recognition).

Internet: A collection of connected regional networks joining millions of 'host' computers in many countries of the world. It uses a set of common protocols for the exchange of information.

Intranet: Internal communications networks based on Internet standards. They use the technical protocols (TCP/IP) of the Internet to provide a platform for communication within organisations, no matter how large or physically dispersed they may be.

Inventory: *see* Records inventory.

Inviolate: AS 4390.3–1996. Records must be securely maintained to prevent unauthorised access, alteration or removal.

Knowledge-base classification: *see* Classification

LAN (Local area network): A computer network within a given local area, for example, linking computers, terminals, printers and other devices within a single office building.

Legacy systems: Previous generation/version information technology architectures and their contents whose dysfunctionalities need to be overcome in deploying new generation/version information technology.

Legal value: Broadly, deriving authority from the law. *See also* Statutory retention requirements.

Life cycle of records: The 'life' of a record is viewed as consisting of five phases: creation, distribution, use, maintenance and disposal.

Listserv: A central server (*see* Server). A program for distributing e-mail messages to people on discussion lists and acting as a central library of files which can be retrieved using e-mail commands.

Meaningful: AS 4390.3–1996: The contextual linkages of records must carry information necessary to correctly understand the transactions that created and used them. It should be possible to identify a record within the context of broader business activities and functions.

Menu driven: A system in which sets of options are presented to the user at the terminal so that the user can very simply choose the application, function or task required.

Metadata: Metadata is a description or profile of a document or other information object. The description may contain data about the context, form or content of the document. In an electronic environment metadata are attached to, or form an integral part of, each record. Such metadata may denote a classificatory category to which the record belongs, or may identify or describe the record according to other attributes.

Microfiche: A fine-grain, high resolution, transparent sheet of film usually 6 in. x 4 in. used to record images reduced in size from the original. Usually arranged in a grid pattern. *See also* Micrographic(s).

Microfilm: Documents reduced by photographing onto film stock which then becomes the medium for storage and viewing. It is suitable for low reference, sequentially ordered documents, or high reference, randomly arranged documents controlled by a computer-based retrieval system. *See also* Micrographic(s).

Micrographic(s): Micrographics refers to the technology and processes concerned with the storage of optically reduced images of records on some type of coating on a transparent base of plastic called a film. It refers not just to the filming but also the supporting hardware. The microfilm medium has standardised on three formats: 16 mm and 35 mm roll film in cartridges or on reels and 750 mm film cut to make microfiche.

Modem: A device used to link a terminal to a remote computer system or online database via telephone lines.

Multiple numbering system: A category-based approach to the physical arrangement of files in which the file numbers are divided into primary, secondary and tertiary elements, so that related files are grouped together, and the file numbers are translatable into their subject categories.

Mutually exclusive terms in array: Terms grouped so that they share the same relationship with a broader term, but no two terms from the group would logically be combined in a compound topic.

NAP: *see* Normal administrative practice.

Natural language: Refers to situations in which no controlled vocabulary is used. Indexing and or retrieval may be based on words from the texts of documents or elsewhere (e.g. from titles), but not from a controlled/authorised list of terms.

Normal administrative practice (NAP): This concept allows for the destruction on a routine basis, without authorisation, of records which have no continuing value to the organisation.

Notation: A numbering or coding system.

OCR (Optical Character Recognition): Scanning and conversion software and processes by which printed, typed and now handprinted text can be input to a computer and converted to ASCII (*see* ASCII) or similar digital format using pattern matching.

Operational costs: Costs which are ongoing, such as salaries, ongoing supplies, space and rental.

Optical Character Recognition: *see* OCR (Optical Character Recognition).

Optical disk: Storage technology using laser beam to store large amounts of data at relatively low cost. Binary information is burnt onto the disk and cannot be deleted. *See also* WORM (Write Once Read Many) and under Erasable magneto-optical disk.

PICS (Platform for Internet Content Selection): Developed by the Massachusetts Institute of Technology's World Wide Web Consortium (W3C), PICS is a set of technical standards to enable Web site authors to attach labels, descriptions (or metadata) to their sites to make it possible for filtering software to block access to that site. Future applications may use the labelling system for information searching purposes. See http://www.w3.org/PICS/

Post-coordinate indexing: Terms in a multi-aspect (compound/complex) topic are entered singly as individual indexing units, and are combined at the searching stage, using Boolean operators (*see* Boolean searching). *See also* Pre-coordinate indexing.

Pre-coordinate indexing: Terms in a compound or complex topic are combined at the indexing stage into a single subject heading. *See also* Post-coordinate indexing.

Project records: Records related to a specific project, such as correspondence, notes, product development documentation.

Provenance: Based on original ownership and the office(s) or person(s) who created and used the records.

Proximity operators: A method of searching an online retrieval system which makes it possible to stipulate that in the retrieved text nominated terms must be adjacent to each other, or must occur in the same sentence or paragraph, or within a certain number of terms from each other.

Public office: Pertaining to federal, state and local government agencies and instruments. The term includes central government departments, statutory authorities, local government bodies, state schools, colleges and universities, public hospitals, police stations, courts and prisons.

Public records: Records providing evidence of the business activities of persons or agencies exercising public office (*see* Public office).

Quality records: AS 4390.1–1996: Records used to demonstrate conformance to specified requirements and effective operation of quality systems under the AS/NZS ISO 9000 series.

Readers (Retrieval terminals): A generic name for the viewing device for micrographic material stored on various types of film.

Record: *see* Records.

Record life cycle: *see* Life cycle of records.

Record series: 'A group of identical or related records that are normally used and filed as a unit and which permits evaluation as a unit for disposal scheduling purposes' (Robek, Brown & Stephens 1996, p. 585). A series may consist of one or many records.

Recordkeeping: AS 4390.1–1996: Making and maintaining complete, accurate and reliable evidence of business transactions in the form of recorded information.

Recordkeeping systems: AS 4390.1–1996: Information systems which capture, maintain and provide access to records over time.

Records: AS 4390.1–1996: Recorded information, in any form, including data in computer systems, created or received and maintained by an organisation or person in the transaction of business or the conduct of affairs and kept as evidence of such activity. Comment: A telephone conversation would not be viewed here as a 'record' unless a sound recording or transcript were made of it, and kept as evidence of a business activity. The terms 'record' and 'document' are not synonymous. Only those documents which provide evidence of business activities are regarded as records. Other documents may provide valuable background information for business activities.

Records appraisal: *see* Appraisal.

Records disposal: *see* Disposal.

Records continuum: AS 4390.1–1996: The whole extent of a record's existence. Refers to a consistent and coherent regime of management processes from the time of the creation of records (and before creation, in the design of record-keeping systems), through to the preservation and use of records as archives.

Records inventory: A complete and detailed summary of records, and their housings, which are held by an organisation or part of an organisation. It may include all (or some) categories of records regardless of whether they are held in central filing systems or in individual offices, in paper, microfilm or machine-readable format.

Records life cycle: *see* Life cycle of records.

Records management: AS 4390.1–1996: The discipline and organisational function of managing records to meet operational business needs, accountability requirements and community expectations

Records management feasibility study: *see* Records management needs analysis.

Records management program: A plan of action for achieving control of the records of an organisation. An integrated records management program takes into account the information needs of the organisation as a whole, and recognises the interdependence between the different information management functions in the organisation.

Records management needs analysis: An analysis of records management solutions for an organisation in the light of requirements, and the value, costs and practicability of the solutions. The needs analysis usually includes a cost benefit analysis (*see* Cost–benefit analysis). (A needs analysis is also known as a feasibility study.)

Records retention and disposal schedule: *see* Disposal schedule.

Records series: *See* Record series.

Registration: AS 4390.1–1996: The act of giving a record a unique identity in a record-keeping system.

Registry: The organisational unit or section where mail is registered, distributed and filed. The term is most commonly used in the government context.

Response time: The time which an online system takes to respond to a user's command.

Resubmit system: A manual or automated system which records the requests of users for files to be returned to them on a pre-determined date for follow-up action. Details of the files to be resubmitted are entered into the system, and a printout or display of files due for resubmittal is run each day. In a manual system, a daily diary is checked for this purpose. (Also called bring-up system, call-up system or diary system.)

Retention and disposal schedule: *see* Disposal schedule.

Retention periods: The specific time periods for which records are kept prior to their destruction. *See also* Sentencing of records.

Retrieval terminals: *see* Readers (Retrieval terminals).

Scanners: *see* Document scanning.

SDI (Selective Dissemination of Information): A system by which a user is supplied with information on subjects of her/his interest on an ongoing basis.

Secondary storage: Storing of semi-active and inactive records, generally in facilities which are cheaper than those used for active records.

Selective Dissemination of Information: *see* SDI (Selective Dissemination of Information).

Self indexing: A form of indexing in which the file titling appears to be self-evident, for example, client records, personnel records. *See also* Case files.

Semi-active records: A category of records in between active and inactive records. (*see* Active records *and* Inactive records.) 'Previous year' records which are needed for reference when the current year's work is being done are an example of semi-active records.

Sentencing of records: Deciding where, and how long records should be kept. *See also* Disposal schedule.

Sequential numbering system: The physical arrangement of files which is based on giving each new file the next number in a running number sequence.

Series: *see* Record series.

Server (or File server): A computer program or computer in a network which makes files available for access on request from other programs or computers in the network called 'clients'.

SGML (Standard Generalized Markup Language): A standard language (ISO 8879: 1986) for marking up text in electronic form so that the format of the text can be preserved when it is moved to another computer platform or application.

Software: The program or programs (sequence(s) of instructions) needed to enable the computer system to carry out its processes. Sometimes also used in records management to refer to the file covers, binders, guides, colour labels, file clips and index cards used to contain, protect and label records.

Specific versus broad indexing: With specific indexing the term, or set of terms assigned by an indexer for a particular document matches as closely as possible the generic level of the concept(s) being represented in that document. For example, a document about 'humpback whales' is indexed under 'humpback whales', not 'whales'. Often contrasted with broad indexing where the index terms are broader in scope than the concepts in the document.

Stand-alone computer system: A computer system that is self-sufficient for its functions and not connected to a computer network.

Standard Generalized Markup Language: *see* SGML.

Statutory retention requirements: Legislation requiring the retention of specific categories of documents relating to various business or administrative activities, such as personnel, tax and audit.

Stoplist (or stop word list): In a computerised file retrieval system a stoplist is a set of common words, such as 'and', 'but', 'although', and 'the' which the computer ignores in searching.

Storage: AS 4390.1–1996: The function of storing records for future retrieval and use.

Supplies: *see* Filing supplies.

System vocabulary: Refers to the terms assigned to records by which the records will be retrieved. This vocabulary may be controlled, natural or a combination, and generally reflects term usage within the organisation. *See also* Controlled vocabulary *and* Natural language.

Systematic approach: Based on a considered order, method, or plan.

Systems study: *see* Records management needs analysis.

Tangible benefits: Benefits which can be quantified in dollar terms.

TCP/IP (Transmission Control Protocol/Internet Protocol): The communication protocol on which the Internet is founded. Other Internet protocols, for example FTP and Gopher, are placed on top of it.

Telnet: An Internet protocol (or a program) used for logging on to a range of databases, library catalogues and other special facilities.

Terminal digit filing: A variation on the sequential numbering system in which numbers are read from right to left in small groups, beginning with the terminal or end group. This approach to filing order achieves a spread of files across the sequence, instead of having all the most recent files at the end of the sequence.

Thesaurus: An alphabetical list of allowed and non-allowed terms, usually with cross references to link the non-allowed and allowed terms, and to suggest suitable related allowed terms. Also referred to as a Controlled vocabulary. In records management a thesaurus is a classification tool used in file titling.

Tracking: AS 4390.1–1996: Capturing and maintaining information about the movement and uses of records.

Tracking system: The automated or manual system which maintains information on where a hardcopy document/file is at any one time, whether it is with a particular user, on the shelves, or in secondary storage. (Also referred to as a File movement or Charge-out system.)

Transaction: AS 4390.1–1996: The smallest unit of business activity. Uses of records are themselves transactions.

Transactional records: Records giving evidence of a transaction, usually created in everyday business, such as forms, invoices and cheques.

Truncation: A method of searching an online retrieval system which omits the last few letters of a word or phrase.

Uncontrolled vocabulary: *see* Natural language.

User pays: In the records management context, 'user pays' usually refers to the situation in which the departments in an organisation are required to budget and pay for records management services provided by the records management unit in their organisation.

User permissions: AS 4390.1–1996: Privileges allocated to employees determining the extent of access to records and authority to author/originate, add alter and dispose of records in a recordkeeping system.

VGA (Video graphics array): A high resolution monitor with very good screen definition.

Vital records: Those records without which an organisation could not continue to operate, i.e. those containing information needed to reestablish the organisation in the event of a disaster which destroys all other records. Vital records are those which protect the assets and interests of the organisation as well as those of its clients and shareholders.

The Web: *see* World Wide Web.

Web browser: *see* Browser.

Wildcard searching: Using a character like * for more than one letter and an @ for a single letter within or at the beginning/end of a word when one is searching an automated system and one is not sure of its exact spelling, or one needs to locate all words with the same root.

Workflow systems: These are systems which automate the flow of business around an organisation. They involve a system of automatic routing of information relevant to a particular business process to the participants in that process and tracking the status of the process across participants.

World Wide Web (WWW or the Web): The most widely used browser system (*see* Browser) on the Internet. It can be used to access any type of site on the Internet (not just WWW sites), and supports both hypertext (*see* Hypertext) and hypermedia (*see* Hypermedia).

WORM (Write Once Read Many): An optical disk computer storage device which can only be written on once, and then becomes a 'read only' medium.

WWW: *see* World Wide Web.

Note

1 The full citation for AS 4390.1–.6–1996 referred to in the Glossary is Standards Australia, *Australian Standard AS 4390–1996, Records Management*, Homebush, NSW, 1996. Part 1: General; Part 2: Responsibilities; Part 3: Strategies; Part 4: Control; Part 5: Appraisal and Disposal; Part 6: Storage.

index

Notes:
- Definitions are also provided in the Glossary.
- Definitions drawn from the Australian Standard AS 4390–1996 are indicated in the index by the sub-heading 'AS 4390–1996 definition'.
- The letter *n* after a page number indicates a note.
- Page numbers in italics refer to illustrations.

AARNet 230
abstracts 125
access requirements
    in automated records management
        systems 201–02
    to inactive records 259
    to physical records 108, 109
    see also privacy; security of information
access to computers 108
accountability
    in records management 47, 63
        AS 4390–1996 definition 46
        see also recordkeeping, requirements
    reflected in business classification
        schemes 115
Accounting and Audit Standards 57
accounting records 6, 56–57, 117
    in business information systems 105
    retention periods 50
accurate records
    AS 4390–1996 definition 107
    attribute of documents 107
acronyms 157
active records, transfer to secondary
    storage 173
activities-based classification schemes *see*
    business classification schemes
activity logs, needs analysis methodology 36
ad hoc disposal authorisation 85
adequate records 98
    AS 4390–1996 definition 98
administrative records 6
alphabetical name arrangement 171, 271
AltaVista 132, 232
annotations to documents 108
ANSI X.12 standard 234

ANSI/NISO Z39.19–1993 154, 164
appraisal of records 89
    AS 4390–1996 definition 63
    review of practice 65
    see also business classification schemes;
        disposal schedules; records
        inventories; retention of records
archival agencies
    role in authorising disposal 82–86
    role in authorising disposal of records
        79–80
    see also names of specific agencies e.g.
        Queensland State Archives
archival value, of records 77, 251
Archive Authority of NSW, Records
    Management Office, *Keyword AAA*
    Thesaurus 122, 146
archives, AS 4390–1996 definition 7
Archives Act, 1983 (Commonwealth) 55
archives administration, as recordkeeping
    profession 4, 12–13
Archives Authority of NSW
    disposal schedule for local government
        82
    General Records Disposal Schedule 85, 122
Archives Authority of NSW, Records
    Management Office 119
array of terms, thesaurus construction
    150–51
AS 4390–1996 xv, 2, 4–5, 26, 56, 110
    and automated records management
        systems 199
    and business classification schemes 34,
        65–66, 112, 114, 145
        attributes 114–15
    on levels of retrieval 128

model implementation plan 45
on protection of vital records 249
on recordkeeping requirements 47
on records attributes 93
    see also entries under specific
      attributes *e.g.* compliant
on records in business information
  systems 106
on registration 117–18
AS/NZ ISO 9000 5
audit trails, electronic documents 108
audits of records 14
Australian Archives 110
  environmental standards 256
  general disposal authority 84, 85
  and preservation of electronic records 85
  on records in business information
    systems 106
Australian Privacy Charter 54, 57
  case study 58–59
Australian Records Retention Manual 49,
  60, 80
Australian Securities Commission 14
  digital imaging system 225
Australian Standard 4390–1996 *see* AS
  4390–1996
Australian Submarine Corporation, digital
  imaging system 225
Australian Taxation Office 14
  booklets on records retention 50
  on records attributes 93
authentic records
  AS 4390–1996 definition 107–08
  attribute of documents 108–09
authorisations *see* digital signatures
authority list *see* controlled vocabulary;
  thesaurus
automated document and file tracking
  systems 186–88
automated document management systems
  see automated records management
  systems
automated filing systems 183
automated records management systems
  146, 194–210
  additional information 212
  development 196–97
  functional requirements 200–05
  implementation 209–10
  and Internet publishing 234
  manuals 207, 210
  reporting and statistics 207
  requirements *199*

reviews 210
selection 197–99
support and training 207–09
technical requirements 206–07
training 210
see also electronic documents,
  management
automated retrieval systems
  file titling 121
  indexing 119, 125
automatic indexing 131

background documents 7
barcode labels 188
barcode reading equipment 186, 188
barcoding 186–88, 204
  in digital imaging systems 220
benefits *see* intangible benefits; tangible
  benefits
Boolean searching 126, 130
broad headings, in indexing 122, 126–27
broader term (BT), thesaurus 154, 157
budgeting 30
bulletin boards 232
business activities, AS 4390–1996 definition
  11
business classification schemes 34, 65–69,
  107, 114–15, 145
  AS 4390–1996 on attributes 114
  compared with knowledge classification
    schemes 115
business information systems, retention of
  records 106

call-up systems 189
CALS 235–37
capital gains tax, retention of records 49
CARMS II, records management system 195
case files 6, 168
categories of terms, thesaurus construction
  148–53
CD-Recordables 221
CD-ReWritable technology 222
CD-ROMS 238*n3*
  digital imaging systems 221–22
CD-Rs 221, 238*n3*
CD-RW technology 222
CDs, digital imaging systems 219, 221, 233
CECS 234
centralisation vs decentralisation 167–68
charge-out systems *see* document and file
  tracking
citation order *see* combination order

classification 113
 AS 4390–1996 definition 114
 AS 4390–1996 on 112
 knowledge-base, construction of scheme
   and thesaurus 145–63
 related to indexing 119
 for retrieval 112–18
classification schemes, use in information
   retrieval 147
clerical staff, records management 15
coding systems 159–60
coding systems see also notation; numbering
   systems
COLD storage and retrieval technology 226
colour coding
 file covers 184
 files 173, 174, 178
COM (Computer Output on Microfilm)
   226
combination order, classification schemes
   159
commercial storage see records storage
   companies
Commonwealth Electronic Commerce
   Service 234
compact disks, digital imaging systems
   219, 221, 233
competency standards 24
complete records, AS 4390–1996 definition
   98
compliant records 93–97
 AS 4390–1996 definition 93
compound documents, defined 128
comprehensive records 107
 AS 4390–1996 definition 107
Computer Assisted Logistics Support
   235–37
Computer Output on Microfilm 226
Computer Output to Laser Disk 226
computer records see electronic records
computer-based indexing see automated
   retrieval systems, indexing
consistency, in indexing 127
contextual information 122
 automatic capture 201
 retention 98–99
Continuous Acquisition and Lifecycle
   Support 235–37
controlled vocabulary 121
 indexing 124–25
 see also thesaurus
corporate names, indexing and filing
   125–26, 273–74

corporations legislation 50
correspondence 6, 14, 168, 204
 filing 178
 handling in digital imaging systems 223
 processing of mail 171–72
correspondence management systems see
   document-based management systems
cost–benefit analysis 44n3
 needs analysis 38
cost control 30
costings, needs analysis study 32
costs
 automated records management systems
   209
 of commercial storage 258
 data gathering 34
 digital imaging systems 224–25, 225
 of in-house storage 258–59
 of misfiling 173
 of space 175

database shells 195
decentralisation see centralisation vs
   decentralisation
descriptors 114
 in business classification schemes 123
destruction of records see secure
   destruction
development costs 38
diary systems 189
digital imaging systems 217–22
 defined 217
 applications 222–25
 Australian applications 225
 case study 237
 network 218
digital signatures 108
 in imaging systems 223
disaster planning see protection of records
discussion lists, Internet 232
dispersal of records, as a precaution against
   loss 245
disposal authority see disposal schedules
disposal of public records, legislative
   provisions 55
disposal of records 89
 AS 4390–1996 definition 63
 in automated records management
   systems 197, 204–05
 case study 86–87
 review of practice 65
 without authorisation 85
 see also business classification schemes

disposal schedules 79–86
  inactive records 252
disposal without authorisation 85
DOCS Open records management system
  195, *202, 203*
document and file tracking
  in automated records management
    systems 203–04
  inactive records 265, 266
  see also barcoding
document and file tracking systems 186–89
document-based management systems 118
document capture, in digital imaging
  systems 219–20
document clustering 130
document creation
  on the Internet 234
  standards *see* document style
document maintenance rules 103
document management, distinguished
  from records management 195–96
document management systems *see*
  automated records management systems
document profiles 99
document retrieval, in digital imaging
  systems 222
document scanning, digital imaging
  systems 219, *223*
document style 99–100
  on the Internet 234
  see also templates
document tracking *see* document and file
  tracking
document type definitions 231
documents 117
  AS 4390–1996 definition 7
  definition in policy documentation 7, 29
  registration 118
  see also electronic documents; records
DTD *see* document type definitions
duplication of records, as a precaution
  against loss 245

EDI 234–35, 237
EDIFACT standard 234, 237
education, records management, 23–24,
  277–79
electronic commerce 232
Electronic Data Interchange 234–35, 237
  adoption 236
electronic document management systems
  see automated records management
  systems

electronic document publishing 229–34
electronic documents
  audit trails 108
  growth in number 214–15
  management 214–37
  tracking 204
  see also electronic records
electronic mail *see* e-mail
electronic publishing *see* electronic
  document publishing
electronic records 2, 6–7, 64, 92, 110
  admissibility in court 2, 51–53
  attributes 94–95
  authorisations 108
  automated records management systems
    198, 202
  disposal 10, 85
  links with paper records 173
  and metadata 123
  records inventories 72–73
  records management systems 195, 196,
    214–37
    additional information 239
  see also electronic documents; e-mail
electronic records management systems *see*
  automated records management systems
e-mail 2, 11, 215
  case study 109
  compared with EDI 234
  on the Internet 232
  retention of records 105–06
environmental hazards, security against in
  commercial storage 254–56
equipment 30
  for filing 174–83
    selection 175
    types 175–83
  for in house storage 260–65
erasable optical disks 221
Evidence Act, 1995 (Commonwealth) 7, 52
Evidence Act, 1995 (New South Wales) 52
Evidence Act, 1958 (Victoria) 51
Evidence Amendment Act, 1990 (South
  Australia) 52
evidence legislation 51–53
evidential value of records 5, 7, 10, 47–48,
  77, 145
  and business classification schemes 114,
    115
  see also vital records
examination records, retention 85
explicit knowledge 13
extranets 13

facet analysis 146–47, 148–53, 163*n1*
facilities, for records management 30
facsimile card technology 215
FAQs 132
file audits 186
file-based management systems 118
file censuses 186
file clips *185*
file covers 184
file movement *see* document and file
    tracking
file titling 119–23
    and avoidance of misfiling 173
    exercises 133–35
    structures 121
file tracking *see* document and file tracking
File Transfer Protocol 232
Filemaster, records management system
    195
files
    defined 117
    creation 117, 171
    registration 118
filing, responsibility for 173
filing cabinets 175–76
    linear capacity 177
filing equipment 174–83
    evaluation 183
    selection 175
      case study 190–92
    types 175–83
filing order, classification codes 160
filing rules, 271–72
filing sequence 168–71
filing supplies 174, 183–84
filing systems 118
financial institutions legislation 50
fire protection, in commercial storage
    254–55
fireproof storage 245
first dimension, records continuum 11
flowcharts 36, 37, 44*n2*
form letters 102
forms, use of 99
forms management, 284–87
fourth dimension, records continuum 12
free text scanning 129
free text searching 129
freedom of information 2
    legislation 53, 55
Frequently Asked Questions 132
Fringe Benefits Tax, retention of records 49
FTP 232

full and accurate records, attributes
    93–109, 110*n2*
full text indexing 220
functional analysis 107
    in developing a business classification
      scheme 66–69
functional classification *see* business
    classification schemes
functional requirements, automated
    records management systems 200–05
fuzzy logic, in searching 131

general disposal schedules 82–85
Gopher 230
groupware 2, 128, 228, 233
    defined 13
guide letters and paragraphs 103
guidelines, records disposal 86

halon gas fire protection systems 254
Hand Character Recognition 220
hardware *see* equipment
HCR 220
health legislation 51
help screens 207
hierarchical file titling 122–23
historical significance *see* archival value
HTML 230–31
    in intranets 233
hypermedia 230
hypertext 128, 230
    search systems 130
Hypertext Markup Language 230–31
    in intranets 233

ICR 107, 220
identifiers
    in records management systems 200
    registration 118
    thesaurus 125
Image System Compliance Criteria (South
    Australia) 52
imaging *see* digital imaging
in-house storage
    facilities 260–65
    inactive records
      costs 258–59
      selection of warehouse space 260
inactive records
    defined 251
    incorrect storage *252*
    packing 265
    records of file movements 265

storage 251–67
    additional information 269
    transfer to storage 265
Income Tax Assessment Act, 1936
    (Commonwealth) 93
index, to classification scheme 163
index languages see indexing, vocabularies
indexing
    AS 4390–1996 definition 118–19
    AS 4390–1996 on 112
    case study 140–41
    document images 220
    process 123–27
    related to classification 119
    for retrieval 112
    technologies 129
    vocabularies 124–27
indexing features, automated records
    management systems 202
Information Exchange Steering
    Committee 110
information gathering, needs analysis study
    34–36
information management, and records
    management 13
Information Privacy Principles 53
information searching see searching
information technology 127–28
    see also digital imaging systems, Internet;
        intranets; optical character
        recognition; and headings beginning
        with the word 'automated'; or with
        the word 'electronic'
informational documents 7
intangible benefits 38
Intelligent Character Recognition 107, 220
International Telecommunications Union
    223
Internet 2, 13, 127
    commercial transactions 232
    defined 230
    as a document publishing system
        229–32, 233–4
    downloading of information 232
    impact on records management 233–34
    search engines 132–33
    useful sites, 280–83
    uses 232–33
intranets 2, 13, 13–14, 127, 128
    defined 232
    as document publishing systems 232–33
    impact on records management 233–34

inviolate records, attribute of
    documents 108
ISO 9000 see quality assurance standards

job completion forms 103–04

Keyword AAA Thesaurus, Records
    Management Office, NSW 122, 146

keywords
business classification schemes 114
in business classification schemes 123
business classification schemes, see also
    Keyword AAA Thesaurus
knowledge-base classification
    schemes
        compared with business classification
            schemes 115
        construction 158–63
        use in records management 158
    and thesaurus construction 146–57
knowledge management, and records
    management 13
Kodak Imagelink System 238$n4$

ladders 264
LAN see local area networks
lay-out, facet analysis 151–53
legacy documents 206
legal needs, recordkeeping requirements
    48
legislation see statutory requirements; also
    names of specific acts, e.g. *Evidence Act,
    1995* (Commonwealth)
levels of retrieval 128
Libraries and Archives Act, 1988
    (Queensland) 55
life cycle of records 9–10
Linton's Keyword System 121
local area networks 2, 127
longevity of information
    microfilm 226
    optical disks 221, 222, 226
Lotus Notes 128, 228
management support 15
    for needs analysis 31, 38
    for records management policy 29
manual document and file tracking systems
    185–86
manuals see procedure manuals; user guides
meaningful records 98–105
    AS 4390–1996 definition 98

metadata 12, 98–99
  in automated records management
    systems 196, 197, 201
  and electronic records 123
  and the Internet 133
  in records continuum 12
  repositories 119
methodology
  needs analysis study 33, 34–38
  records inventories 73
Mezzanine, records management system
  195
microfilm imaging systems 216, 225–26
  digital imaging systems compared with
    217
microfilm records, admissibility in court
  51, 226
microimager 223
middle digit filing 170
misfiling 28, 173
mission see organisational mission and
  objectives
multi-skilling 2
multiple numbering systems 158, 169
mutually exclusive terms, in arrays 150

N-grams, searching 129
names see corporate names; personal names
naming rules, for electronic documents 103
NAP 85
narrower term (NT), thesaurus 154, 157
National Curriculum, records management
  education 23, 25n3
National Records and Archives
  Competency Standards 24, 26n4
natural language indexing 121
natural language vocabulary, indexing
  124–25
needs analysis 28–29, 31–38
  case study 39–43
  management support 31, 38
  report 38
newsgroups 232
non-text formats, retrieval 129
normal administrative practice 85
notation, classification schemes 159–60
NT (narrower term), thesaurus 154, 157
numbering systems 159–60
  see also coding systems; multiple
    numbering systems; self-numbering
    systems; sequential numbering
    systems

objectives
  of needs analysis study 31, 32
  organisational, relationship to
    functional analysis 66
  of a records survey 72
OCR 106, 217, 220
operating procedures, records protection
  246–48
operational costs 38
operational needs, recordkeeping
  requirements 47
optical character recognition 107, 217, 220
optical disks 219, 221–22
  storage capacity 238n2
orders in array, classification schemes 158
organisational mission and objectives
  relationship to functional analysis 66
  and thesaurus construction 147
organisational names see corporate names
organisational structure, place of records
  management 20–22, 30
Original Document Rule 51, 52
outsourcing of records management
  services 23
paper records 2, 7, 92, 166–89, 219
  digital imaging systems compared with
    217
  files 117
  links with electronic records 173
  sizes 91, 219
para-professional staff, records
  management 15
pattern recognition 129
payroll tax, records retention 50
personal names, indexing and filing
  125–26, 271–72
personnel
  for needs analysis study 32
  records management 15, 30
    see also records managers
personnel records 6, 117
pest control, in commercial storage 255
phrase headings, in a thesaurus 155
physical inventories 73
PICS system 128
Platform for Internet Content Selection
  128
post-coordinate indexing 126
practice manuals see procedure manuals
pre-coordinate indexing 126
precision measure 129, 131
Privacy Act, 1988 (Commonwealth) 53

privacy legislation 53–54
Privacy and Protection of Data Bill, 1994 (New South Wales) 54
procedure manuals
    automated records management systems 207, 210
    document style 99
    quality assurance 94–97
    record attributes 98
    and records attributes 93
    records protection 246–48
professional education *see* education
professional staff, records management 15
profiling 99
project records 6, 168
proper names
    alphabetical filing 171
    indexing 127
    indexing and filing 125–26
    in a thesaurus 125
proprietary information 7
protection of records 241–48
    additional information 249
    against inadvertent loss 257
    methods 244–46
proximity operators, in searching 130–31
Public Record Office, Victoria
    disposal schedule *83*, 85
    General Disposal Schedule for Examination Records 85
    local government disposal schedule 82
public records, retention 55
Public Records Act, 1973 (Victoria) 55
public records offices *see* archival agencies; names of specific agencies *e.g.* Queensland State Archives
pull-out reference tables *178*

quality assurance standards 60*n6*
    recordkeeping requirements 55–56, 61
    records compliancy 94–97
quality endorsed companies 56
quality management 2
Queensland State Archives, local government disposal schedule 82
questionnaires, records inventories 73

racking, in-house storage of inactive records 260–63
ranking *see* relevance ranking
recall measure 128–29
RecFind, records management system 195

record keeping *see* recordkeeping
record series 69, 70, 72, 77, *116*, 117, 167–68
    defined 71, 142*n1*
    disposal *see* disposal schedules
recordkeeping
    AS 4390–1996 definition 9
    control over 12
    definition in policy documentation 29
    requirements 46–57, 69
        see also business classification schemes
    strategies 92–109
        change agents 92
    systems 9
        goals 91–92
recordkeeping profession 4
recordkeeping requirements 47
recordkeeping strategies 91–92
records
    AS 4390–1996 definition 7
    appraisal *see* appraisal of records
    attributes 5, 93–109, 110*n2*
    categories 5–6
    classification (by importance) 243
    control 1
    definition in policy documentation 29
    differentiated from archives 7
    disposal 10
    disposal *see* disposal of records
    life cycle 9–10, 12
    physical forms 5, 91
    retention *see* retention of records
records appraisal *see* appraisal of records
records centres 253
records continuum 4, 10–12
    AS 4390-1996 definition 10
records inventories 71–76
    defined 71
records management
    AS 4390–1996 definition 8
    change factors 28–29
    compared with archives administration 12–13
    definition in policy documentation 29
    as a discipline 12–13
    distinguished from document management 195–96
    education 23–24, 277–79
    function *see* records management, role
    and information management 13
    its importance 1, 8–9
    and knowledge management 13

needs analysis 28–29
personnel 15, 30
place in organisational structure 20–22,
    30
policy 29
program
    AS 4390–1996 model
        implementation plan 45
    components 3, 29
    implementation 38, 45
as recordkeeping profession 4, 12–13
role 2–4, 8–9, 14–15
systems 29–30
Records Management Association of
    Australia 4, 23, 275–76
records management needs analysis *see*
    needs analysis
Records Management Office, NSW,
    Archive Authority *see* Archive Authority
    of NSW, Records Management Office
records managers
    job advertisements and specifications
        15–20
    case study 24–25
    qualifications 23
    role and responsibilities 12, 14–15,
        15–20, 65
records retention *see* retention of records
records retention schedules *see* disposal
    schedules
records storage *see* storage of records
records storage companies 253
    assessment 254–58
records surveys 71–73
recycling companies, destruction of
    records by 267
registration 117–18
    in automated records management
        systems 200–01, 205
    document images 220
related term (RT), thesaurus 154, 157
relevance judgements 129
relevance ranking
    search engines 132
    search methods 131–32
remote storage 246
reports, from automated records
    management systems 207
resolution, in digital imaging systems
    219–20, 222
resubmit systems 189
retention periods *see* disposal of records

retention of records
    authorisation form 78–9
    periods 77–79
    statutory requirements 47, 48–55, 69,
        78, 93
    see also disposal of records
retrieval
    in imaging systems 222
    levels of 128
    of records in commercial storage 257
retrieval concepts, identification 124
retrieval systems
    evaluation 128–29
    see also classification; indexing
rotary shelving units 182
RT (related term), thesaurus 154, 157

sales tax, records retention 50
scanners, in digital imaging systems 219,
    223
schedule order, knowledge-base
    classification schemes 158–59
scheduling, records disposal *see* disposal
    schedules
scope, of needs analysis 31
scope notes 151, 154
search engines, Internet 131, 132–33
searching
    on the Internet 232
    see also search engines
searching features, automated records
    management systems 202
searching technologies 129–33
second dimension, records continuum 12
secondary storage *see* inactive records,
    storage
secure destruction 265, 267
    of records in commercial storage 257
secure storage 109, 245
security of information 108–09, 175
    in automated records management
        systems 201, 203, 207
    on the Internet 233
    see also privacy
see also references 151
see references 126, 154
self-numbering systems 170
semi-active records 251, 253
sequential numbering systems 170
SGML 230–31, 236
shelf arrangements, inactive records
    264–65

shelving, in-house storage of inactive
    records 260
shelving units
    mobile 180–81, 264
    static 176, 180
        linear capacity 177
    static and mobile compared 181
shredding 267
signatures *see* digital signatures
software support *see* support services
specific headings, in indexing 126–27
speed of scanners, in digital imaging
    systems 219
sprinkler systems, fire protection 254–55
Standard Generalised Markup Language
    230–31, 236
standards, records disposal 63, 86
State Archives of Western Australia, local
    government disposal schedule 82
statistics, production by automated records
    management systems 207
statutes of limitation 49
statutory requirements, retention of
    records 47, 48–55, 69, 78, 93
stemming *see* truncation
stoplists 129, 131
storage boxes *261*, 262–63, 264
storage capacity, digital imaging systems
    221
storage media
    imaging systems 221–22
        costs 224
        see also microfilm; optical disks
    inactive records 252, 257
storage of records
    commercial storage vs in-house storage
        254
    inactive records 251–69
    for security 245–46
    selection of facilities 252–67
structural information, retention 98
style *see* document style
sub-categories of terms, thesaurus
    construction 148–51
subject classification *see* knowledge-base
    classification
substantiation records, retention periods 50
suffix arrays, searching 129
supplies, for filing 183–84
support services, automated records
    management systems 207–09

system down strategies 210
systems architecture, automated records
    management systems 198

tacit knowledge 13
tangible benefits 38
Tax File Number Guidelines 53
taxation records
    retention periods 49–50, 93
    series 117
technical requirements, automated records
    management systems 206–07
Telnet 230
templates, document style 101–02
term summing 131–32
terminal digit filing 170
terms of reference, needs analysis 31
text retrieval software 220
thesaurus 119
    defined 145
    in automated records management
        systems 201
    construction 125, 147–58
        collection of terms 148
        scope of thesaurus 148
    exercise 136–40
    relationship to classification 145
    use in digital imaging systems 220
    use in indexing 121
    use in information retrieval 147
    use in large organisations 146
    see also Keyword AAA Thesaurus
thing–type relationships 150–51
third dimension, records continuum 12
timeframe, needs analysis study 32, 33
titling
    electronic records 123
    files 119–23
tracking *see* document and file tracking
trade practices legislation 51
training
    in use of automated records
        management systems 210
    in use of records management systems
        207
transaction processing 223, 227
transactional files 168
Transigo 234
TRIM records management system 195,
    205
truncation, in searching 130, 131

USE references 154
used for (UF), thesaurus 154, 157
user guides
    classification schemes 163
    thesaurus 157
user needs, and thesaurus construction 147

vault storage *245*, 246
vital records 48
    defined 241
    identifying 242–44
    protection planning 241–48
        additional information 249

voice mail 215, 238*n1*

walk thru inventories 73
warehouse space, storage of inactive
    records 260

web sites
    Internet 230–31, *231*
    intranets 233
Web, The *see* World Wide Web
weighted term summing 131–32
wildcard searching 130
workflow, arrangement 173
workflow software 128
workflow systems 217, 226–68
World Wide Web 128, 230–31
    sample page *231*
WORM (optical disks) 221
Write Once Read Many (WORM), optical
    disks 221
WWW *see* World Wide Web

X.209 standard 223

Yahoo 132, 232